CHILDREN
OF BONDAGE

MEMBERS OF
THE AMERICAN YOUTH COMMISSION

Appointed by the American Council on Education

CHILDREN OF BONDAGE

The Personality Development
of Negro Youth in the Urban
South

BY ALLISON DAVIS AND JOHN DOLLARD

Prepared for
The American Youth Commission

AMERICAN COUNCIL ON EDUCATION
Washington, D.C., 1940

All names of persons and institutions used in the case histories in this book are pseudonyms. In no instance does a name refer to any person or institution now existing, or having existed in the past.

The life histories have been obtained from living persons, however; in some cases certain unimportant details which might be identifying have been slightly altered to protect the individuals involved. In each case, written permission to publish the materials has been granted to the publishers by the parents of the individual.

FOREWORD

THIS volume is the report of one of several studies which were conducted concurrently but in different sections of the United States. All of these investigations were the outgrowth of the American Youth Commission's desire to see wherein Negro youth faced distinctive problems in their development as individual personalities. The volumes in this series are:

Children of Bondage: The Personality Development of Negro Youth in the Urban South, by Allison Davis and John Dollard

Negro Youth at the Crossways: Their Personality Development in the Middle States, by E. Franklin Frazier

Growing Up in the Black Belt: Negro Youth in the Rural South, by Charles S. Johnson

Color and Human Nature: Negro Personality Development in a Northern City, by W. Lloyd Warner, Buford H. Junker, and Walter A. Adams

Each of these studies is based upon conditions as found in the particular area and uses methods of research especially adapted to those conditions. All, however, are pointed at the central problem: "What are the effects upon the personality development of Negro youth of their membership in a minority racial group?" The studies supplement each other in the insights which they contribute to an understanding of this problem.

In addition to these volumes based upon original field research, a summary of the knowledge previously available concerning Negro youth in the United States has been prepared for the Commission and published under the title In a Minor Key: Negro Youth in Story and Fact, by Ira DeA. Reid.

These studies of Negro youth were begun under the Commission's former director, Homer P. Rainey, now president of the University of Texas. In the initial planning of them, Dr. Rainey was assisted by Robert L. Sutherland, professor of sociology in Bucknell University, who later served as associate director of the Commission in charge of studies of Negro youth. A summary of the findings of the entire project, together with a program of recommendations for educational and social planning, is being prepared by Dr. Sutherland for publication under the tentative title, *Color, Class, and Personality*.

For assistance in organizing and carrying on the investigations on which these reports are based, the Commission is indebted to many individuals and organizations. These include the authors of the various reports, the other members of the staff, and those individuals and institutions whose assistance is acknowledged by the respective authors. In addition, mention should be made of the services of a special advisory committee which was called together early in 1938 to assist in organizing the project. Will W. Alexander, executive director of the Commission on Interracial Cooperation and a member of the American Youth Commission, served as chairman of this committee. The other members of the committee, in addition to several of the scholars who later joined the staff, were Ambrose Caliver, senior specialist in Negro education, United States Office of Education; George A. Lundberg, of the faculty of Bennington College; Fred McCuistion, southern field agent, General Education Board; Charles Thompson, dean, college of liberal arts, Howard University; Robert C. Weaver, director of racial relations, United States Housing Authority; and Caroline Zachry, director of research, Progressive Education Association.

The American Youth Commission was established in 1935 by the American Council on Education from which it received a mandate to:

1. consider all the needs of youth and appraise the facilities and resources for serving those needs;

2. plan experiments and programs which will be most helpful in solving the problems of youth;

3. popularize and promote desirable plans of action through publications, conferences, and demonstrations.

As in the case of other staff reports prepared for the Commission, the authors of the present volume are responsible for the statements which are made; they are not necessarily endorsed by the Commission or by its Director. The Director does take responsibility for the organization of all research projects, the selection of staff, and the approval of staff reports as meriting publication. The Commission is responsible for the determination of the general areas in which research is conducted under its auspices, and from time to time it adopts and publishes statements which represent specifically the conclusions and recommendations of the Commission.

FLOYD W. REEVES
Director

PREFACE

INTEREST in the processes through which human personalities develop is widespread. Unusual indeed is the individual who does not wish to learn more about the reasons why some persons aggressively dominate their environment, while others become timid, clinging-vine personalities; why some strive ambitiously to achieve higher standards, while others are satisfied with decreasingly low levels of accomplishment; and why some react violently against members of alien groups and others are tolerant of people of another color or condition of birth. These are problems not only of special interest to the educator, the social worker, the psychologist, and the sociologist, but also of general interest to everyone who is concerned with acquiring an understanding of human nature.

By looking steadily and long at the life experiences of eight selected Negro adolescents and of many others whose cases are on file but not here fully reported, the authors of the present volume have followed their original assignment of revealing what it means to be born a Negro. In so doing they have also contributed significantly to our knowledge of the socializing process itself. They have come closer to the intimate lives of youth than the environmentalists usually do; and they have avoided divorcing personality traits from the cultural milieu in which they develop as the individualists sometimes do. Their purpose has been rather to analyze the ways in which the growing personality reacts to those rewards and punishments, those incentives and taboos, which form the dynamic, social world experienced by the child in his travels toward adulthood. Common to both Negro and white children are the variable demands by means of which family, clique, and class sanctions define success and failure for the individual. Unique with the Negro child are the caste-like taboos which limit the ceilings of his economic and social ascent, force him to find compensatory satisfactions, and set the bounds within which the different levels of his own society will be fixed.

In giving special attention to the southern urban Negro, and in going deep into the personalities of a limited number of youth, this volume by Allison Davis and John Dollard reports case studies in an unusual manner, explores processes in personality development from a combined psychological and cultural point of view, and analyzes in detail the life experiences of individuals born into a special status in one important section of American society.

This volume results from a process of collaboration between authors who differ in race, professional training, and place of residence, but who worked together in the field research in New Orleans and later in the analysis of the data and the preparation of the manuscript in New Haven with such a keen appreciation of each other's contribution and point of view that the product was tempered by far more intellectual criticism and tested by more varied criteria than could have been possible had the work been done by either scholar working alone.

Allison Davis, who was in charge of the southern urban division of the Negro youth study, was graduated *summa cum laude* from Williams College in 1924. He has received master's degrees from Harvard University in both English and anthropology. A fellowship from the Julius Rosenwald Fund enabled him to continue his study at the London School of Economics under the direction of Bronislaw Malinowski and Launcelot Hogben, and a similar award is enabling him to complete his doctoral work at the University of Chicago at the present time. He was professor of anthropology and head of the division of social studies at Dillard University in New Orleans, 1935-40. Under the direction of W. Lloyd Warner and in collaboration with Dr. and Mrs. Burleigh Gardner, Mr. Davis made a socio-anthropological study of a number of Mississippi communities in 1933-35. The volume resulting from this study will be published by the University of Chicago Press under the title, *Deep South.*

John Dollard, who collaborated in the supervision of the field research staff and in the writing of the present volume, received his Ph.D. degree from the University of Chicago. He was assistant to the president of the University of Chicago, 1926-29, held a Social Science Research Council fellowship for study in Germany in 1931-32, was assistant professor of anthropology at Yale University, 1932-33, was later appointed research assistant, and is now research associate in sociology at the Institute of Human Relations, Yale University. Included among Dr. Dollard's published books, all of which have a bearing upon the present study, are *Criteria for the Life History*, 1935, and *Caste and Class in a Southern Town*, 1937. He was also a co-author of *Frustration and Aggression*, 1939.

ROBERT L. SUTHERLAND
Associate Director for Studies of Negro Youth

AUTHOR'S NOTE

Allison Davis

THE RESEARCH on which this book is founded was assisted by the cooperation of many individuals and institutions to whom the authors are indebted. The basic interviewing during a period of thirteen months was the work of Kacillious Bridges, Mrs. Elizabeth Stubbs Davis, Claude Haydel, John Lee Nealy, and Miss Thelma K. Shelby. I cannot here fully express my indebtedness to these persons for their conscientious and skillful work in a very difficult kind of interviewing. To my wife, I am indebted not only for gathering life histories, but also for her constant aid in the analysis of the Negro class modes of behavior, a work she began with me in 1933 in the social anthropological study of Old City. Mrs. Rosamond Spicer and Frederick D. Jenkins helped with important details of the work. The contribution of my secretary, Miss Dorothy Anderson, to this study has been so extensive, ranging from assistance in the organization of the staff to the analysis of field materials, that I can only express my feeling by saying that her energy and intelligence have been my mainstay. To Miss Rosella Senders we are grateful for her work in the revision of the manuscript and for the making of a final copy.

The public school systems of Natchez and New Orleans gave us their full cooperation, both in allowing us free access to the pupils and in furnishing rooms where the students could be interviewed alone. Our thanks are due A. S. Sonntag, assistant superintendent of public schools in New Orleans, and the following principals of Negro junior high and high schools: Lucien V. Alexis, Mrs. Margaret Davis Bowen, Lawrence D. Crocker, Samuel J. Green, George Longe, and Miss Sadie Thompson. Mr. Longe has given us extremely helpful advice. Dr. and Mrs. A. W.

Dumas, Sr., and Dr. A. W. Dumas, Jr., of Natchez, have been of invaluable aid and have proved themselves the kindest of friends.

Several private institutions have given us their help: Dillard University, the Guidance Center of New Orleans, and the Institute of Human Relations of Yale University. We are also indebted to A. W. Dent, superintendent of the Flint-Goodridge Hospital in New Orleans; to Dr. C. H. D. Bowers, university physician, Dillard University, and senior associate in the department of medicine on the Flint-Goodridge Hospital Staff, who arranged medical examinations for the students and furnished us with full reports; and to W. Mason Matthews of the Guidance Center, who had Stanford-Binet intelligence tests administered to the pupils. I wish to express my personal gratitude to Dr. William Stuart Nelson, president of Dillard University, for having made possible my participation in the research, and to Mark A. May, director of the Institute of Human Relations of Yale University, who invited me to the Institute for the period of the writing of the book, furnished me with generous office space there, and admitted me to the *sanctum sanctorum* of the meetings of the Monday Night Group of faculty and research workers.

For the conception that social class and caste form the underlying structure of southern society, and for the theoretical application of this conception to the problem of personality typing, the authors are indebted to W. Lloyd Warner of the University of Chicago. The view that the relationships of whites and Negroes in the South are systematically ordered and maintained by a caste structure, and that the status of individuals within each of these groups is further determined by a system of social classes existing within each color-caste, was the creation of Warner. Working simultaneously, Dollard in one area in the South and Davis and Gardner in another, helped develop these theoretical concepts by extended sociological field work. It is a great pleasure to express my indebtedness to Professor Warner as my teacher; also to Dr. and Mrs. Burleigh Gardner for their instruction on the modes of class behavior in the white society of a southern city.

John Dollard, my colleague in this research, has given unselfishly of his time and energy to instruct me in those elementary principles of Freudian and of stimulus-response psychology which I was able to absorb. Together, we have examined and analyzed every part of the life histories in the effort to achieve a genuine integration of psychoanalytical and sociological under-standing. Every interpretation of the data has been the result of the simultaneous play of both methods, not juxtaposed as discrete viewpoints, but united into one joint approach used by each author.

I am also indebted to Clark L. Hull, Neal E. Miller, O. H. Mowrer, and John W. M. Whiting, all of the Institute of Human Relations, for applications of stimulus-response principles to the study of social behavior. None of these people, however, may be held responsible for my inadequacies in the use of their ideas.

AUTHOR'S NOTE

John Dollard

I T FALLS to me here in this personal note to make acknowledgment to my new teachers, those who have aided me since 1937. They are: G. P. Murdock of Yale University, who has made accessible to me the Sumner-Keller theory of societal adjustment; Clark L. Hull and Neal E. Miller, both of Yale, who have given me a very short course in behavioristic psychology; Allison Davis of Dillard University, who has given me actual practice in perceiving American social class relationships; Mark A. May of Yale, who has been instructing me at odd moments on matters concerning the logic of scientific inquiry; and my colleagues at the Institute of Human Relations who have sharpened my thought in many a fervid discussion. Miss Alice M. White has given aid of greatest value both in the conduct of the research and in preparing the manuscript. No blame is due any of these if the result is not all that might be hoped.

The working relationship with Mr. Davis has been a valuable experience in cooperative effort. I suspect that his willingness to do his share and more, his ability at self-criticism, and his warmth have aided the work to go smoothly. As the senior author of the book, he has had to organize the research and carry the brunt of the work.

For Mr. Davis this joint work brings his former research on social stratification to bear upon the study of personality formation. For me, the book carries on the type of inquiry which was opened in my *Criteria for the Life History*. I have often, and justly, been reproached for not presenting life-history materials which would approximate the standard set in the *Criteria*. This is an attempt to make myself less vulnerable to this reproach. In fact, although I did not know it, it was impossible to gain ground without solving the problem of criterion six, that is, the concrete definition of the social situation. Help has come from the outside from the work done by Warner, Davis, and Gardner on social class. With the knowledge of the class typing of the pressures exerted on a person in the course of his life, it has, I hope, been possible to improve the writing of life histories.

An analyst will regard our material on personality growth as somewhat imperfect in that, for example, we were seldom able to get the critical data on the Oedipus complex phase of development. It was not possible under the conditions of this particular research to use psychoanalytic interviewing methods. We had to train our interviewers rapidly, and they were persons unskilled from the socio-psychological standpoint. It has been a compensation of our sociological interviewing methods that we were able to get good data from the family on basic training and to get converging reactions to the subject from family and clique associates. In a further study some actual data based on free associational interviewing would undoubtedly increase the accuracy of our personality analyses.

If this book is useful in social science, it will be least of all because it deals with the lives of Negroes; much more important, to me at least, seems the attempt to add something to our knowledge of human socialization. We want to know what forces are at work in training a child to participate in social life and what variables operate when the attempt is made to re-socialize, that is, to alter the habits of adults. A theory of socialization thus seems critical for a theory of social change and indirectly for the attempt of men to assume conscious control of their society's development.

CONTENTS

FOREWORD vii

PREFACE xi

AUTHOR'S NOTE, *Allison Davis* xv

AUTHOR'S NOTE, *John Dollard* xix

THE SUBJECT AND ITS SETTING xxiii

Part I
Personality Development and Status Controls

    I. THE MYSTERY OF PERSONALITY 3

THE LOWER CLASSES

    II. FRIGHTENED AMAZON 23

    III. LAUGHING GIRL 44

    IV. NAMELESS BOY 68

THE MIDDLE CLASSES

    V. SELF-MADE MAN 99

    VI. CREOLE MISS 127

    VII. ELLEN HILL, THE WINNER 156

THE UPPER CLASS

    VIII. THE BLACK SHEEP 185

PRACTICE IN ANALYSIS

    IX. A CASE FOR THE READER TO TRY 207

Part II
Class and Caste as Training

X. How It Feels to Be Lower Caste 237

XI. What Is Social Class? 256

XII. Child Training and Class 263

XIII. Social Class and School Learning 279

Appendix 291

Index 296

THE SUBJECT AND ITS SETTING

THIS BOOK is an attempt to recreate the personalities and to describe the socialization of eight Negro adolescents in the Deep South of this country. Their cases were selected from thirty life histories of Negro children between the ages of twelve and sixteen who live in New Orleans, Louisiana, and in Natchez, Mississippi. These thirty adolescents were interviewed several times weekly over a period of from four to seven months. The interview situation was informal and friendly, with only the child and the interviewer present in the room. The child's friends, his teachers, and his parents and their friends were likewise interviewed concerning their relationships with the pupil.

In order to learn the methods of training to which Negro children are subjected in the family and school, 123 children and their parents, representing all the social classes in numbers proportionate to the estimated size of the classes, were interviewed in the same way. As a further check upon the representative nature of the chosen cases, these and 74 additional Negro adolescents were interviewed concerning their relationships with, and attitudes toward, white people.

Through the operation of a system of color caste the eight children whose personalities are studied in this book are excluded from full human opportunity and status in the South. What effect does this American caste system, issuing out of slavery, have upon the personality development of such lower-caste children? What degree of character torsion does systematic oppression exert upon human personality? An effort is here made to analyze this problem, full of human bitterness and resentment, with the most recent techniques which have been developed by social anthropology and social psychology. Through these intimate life histories, the well-intentioned and socially minded reader may share the experiences of Negro children from each of the social classes in Negro society.

New Orleans and Natchez, the settings for the study, are old cities located in the Deep South where the caste pressure of whites upon Negroes is greatest. The city of New Orleans, located on the Mississippi River, a little more than 100 miles from the Gulf of Mexico, has the largest Negro population in any southern city; it is the only city south of Washington, D.C. which has more than 100,000 colored inhabitants.

The Negro population bears the brunt of the social and economic backwardness of this area. In spite of the fleeting, holiday-maker's impression of New Orleans, there is no romantic glamour in the social and economic environment of the Negro masses in this largest of southern cities.

The rate of home-owning families among all Negro families (13.2 per cent) was lower in 1930 in New Orleans than in any other large southern city. More than one-third of the homes owned by Negroes were valued at less than $2,000. The average income of colored families was less than $500 a year. Today the average wage for Negroes in New Orleans is estimated to be lower than in any large southern city. Only six out of every 100 Negro men in 1930 had white-collar employment, whereas almost half of all white male workers had such positions. Even the foreign-born whites in New Orleans enjoyed a tremendously superior economic status as compared with the Negro inhabitants. Although they had been in America for a comparatively short time, seven out of ten of these whites held white-collar or skilled jobs as compared with only two out of every ten Negroes.

A major effect of the caste system upon the Negro family in New Orleans has been to force almost half of the married Negro women to work, chiefly in domestic service, whereas less than one-tenth of the married white women work out of the home. Four of every ten Negro children, aged sixteen to seventeen years in New Orleans, were at work in 1930; only seven of the eighty-three largest cities in the United States had a higher rate. In spite of the fact that colored people were only one-fourth of the population, there were as many unemployed Negro adults in 1938 as white. In the most thickly populated Negro areas, two-thirds of all colored families were receiving some form of public relief.

Illegitimacy, nurtured by slavery and still tolerated by the white society, is very high in the Negro population; in New Orleans, one-tenth of all Negro births were illegitimate in 1938, and in Natchez one-third. The rates for both illegitimacy and juvenile deliquency were much greater for Negroes than for whites. In Louisiana as a whole, the rate of illiteracy in 1930 for Negro adults (28 per cent) was almost three times as high as that for white adults (10 per cent). The amount of money invested by this state in each Negro child's education represented only a small proportion of that expended upon the white child's.

The social and economic subordination of Negroes to whites is even more severe in Natchez than in New Orleans. Located in an area of cotton plantations, about 180 miles north of New Orleans, Natchez claims to be the oldest city on the Mississippi River. Half of its 14,000 inhabitants, and more than 80 per cent of the surrounding rural population, are colored people. In the city, the great majority of Negroes obtain only unskilled and domestic work; in the rural area, they are chiefly farm tenants. With the reduction of the cotton yield by almost 90 per cent since 1908, owing to the boll weevil, and with the recent drop in the price of cotton, the income of most Negroes has been reduced to the starvation level. Negro families on the plantation have an average cash income of only $100 a year. In Natchez, the average daily income of colored families is about $1.00 a day; for white families it is almost $3.00.

The majority of colored families in Natchez live in cabins of two rooms, or of one room and a "lean-to" kitchen. The average monthly rental paid by Negroes of the lower class, who constitute more than 90 per cent of all Negroes in Natchez, is $4.00.

Residential segregation by color is highly developed. About one-third of the Negro adults are illiterate, and one-third of the Negro children are illegitimate.

A third group of colored children has been included in this study: the colored Creoles of New Orleans. In this city, a color line now exists between white and colored Creoles. The latter are the children or grandchildren of colored persons who spoke or speak a French *patois;* they constitute about one-sixth of the Negro population of New Orleans. Their language is disappearing very rapidly, and the colored Creole group is merging socially and biologically with the American Negro group.

The colored Creoles have acute problems of adjustment to their present lower-caste position, for they once were a caste which had status intermediate between that of whites and Negroes. Now, however, they are treated in all respects like Negroes by the local whites. They attend the Negro schools, churches, and associations; and they intermarry with Negroes. Although they are highly "color conscious," there have always been some dark brown and black Creoles. The great majority of the colored Creoles, however, are light brown with wavy or curly hair. As a result of the white society's stringent maintenance of the "color barrier" against them in recent years, the colored Creoles have undergone the socially traumatic experience of being forced, like American Negroes, to assume the role of a lower-caste population.

Following W. Lloyd Warner's research in "Yankee City" in New England,[1] social anthropologists have identified social classes empirically in Natchez and New Orleans. One of the authors of the present book applied the analysis of social stratification to the study of the typical psychological mechanisms in class and color-caste groups in the Deep South.[2] Working at the same time, Dr. and Mrs. Burleigh Gardner and Allison Davis studied the entire social structure of an urban and rural society

[1] This work in several volumes is to be published by the Yale University Press, beginning this year.

[2] John Dollard, *Caste and Class in a Southern Town* (New Haven: Yale University Press, 1937).

in Mississippi and analyzed the typical behaviors of the Negro and white social classes.[3]

The present work depends upon all three of these field studies, as well as upon research by one of its authors on the Negro society in New Orleans. It takes from these earlier studies their definitions, empirically established, of the typical habits, modes of psychological adjustment, and child training found in each social class of the white and Negro groups.

At the same time, four chapters dealing with the social classes and the color castes in the Deep South have been placed after the personality studies in this book. These later chapters present the theoretical conclusions of this and earlier field studies. In the organization of this book, the personality studies have been placed first so that one may meet the impact of social class and of color caste head-on as does the individual born into the society. In order to understand the force of these pressures upon the personality formation of Negro children it is necessary, however, to read both the cases and the theoretical chapters.

Children were selected for these studies upon the basis of their class position. The eight whose personalities are examined in greatest detail represent all of the class positions in Negro society, and their experiences illustrate the fundamental controls which each class exercises over the socialization of its members. To learn the social-class technique for the study of human behavior, the reader may begin with the first life, that of a lower-class girl, and read the cases in succession. In this way, he will also vicariously experience life in each of the class positions. Following the personality studies, a case is presented in interview form. It is hoped that the reader will try his hand at analyzing this case, using the techniques he has learned in reading the preceding chapters.

In selecting sample cases for intensive interviewing, attention was given to class position, but it was not possible to base the selection upon different personality types. As the studies progressed it was found that with the exception of two cases

[3] Allison and Elizabeth Davis and Burleigh and Mary Gardner, *Deep South.* To be published by the University of Chicago Press.

all of the individuals reported in this book exhibited unusually aggressive behavior in their schools and cliques. In some
cases these traits reflect the class and caste experiences of the
child, but in no instance is an attempt made to interpret personality types by any one set of factors. Various childhood experiences, family relationships, physical conditions, and other factors
play their part in shaping the developing personality. Because
the process is so complex this study has purposely progressed
from the extensive, superficial types of personality surveys to the
more intensive analysis of a limited number of individuals. To
guard against one-sided interpretations these cases were examined from every angle. Since this project was originally directed
at the special factor of "being a Negro," special attention was
given to the pressures of caste-like limitations and to the related
influences of social class position, but not to the exclusion of
many other individual experiences in the lives of these youth.

PART I

PERSONALITY DEVELOPMENT
AND STATUS CONTROLS

CHAPTER I

THE MYSTERY OF PERSONALITY

SUPPOSE THAT an observer is idly twirling a globe similar to the one that is used in schoolrooms except that this globe is so constructed as to show the primitive societies of man, those societies which have been engulfed or destroyed by the expansion of Western European states. This earth-as-an-anthropologist-sees-it would be a remarkable affair; for example, instead of the United States one would see perhaps two hundred small separate groups each with a language and way of life peculiar to itself. Instead of the Dominion of Canada, there would be about a hundred separate and often competing tribes. Over the globe as a whole would be found thousands of societies, each in essential respects unique and self-contained.

Before such a globe had been fashioned by anthropologists and while the existence and nature of other human groups was only dimly visualized by people in our own, there was a misapprehension afloat in our society concerning the nature of the others. It was believed that the men of our society were of a special biological breed destined by sheer gift of nature to rule the world; it was further felt that men of other societies were intrinsically inferior and that nature had been niggardly to them. Peoples, it was thought, had that degree of social development which was appropriate to their biological constitutions, and it was futile to challenge the fact.

This was a comfortable belief for the conqueror, but it has not stood the test of research. First, the biologists observed the essential similarity of men's bodies the earth over and the relatively superficial differences among them. The anthropologists then noticed the striking psychic similarities among all men, their community of passion, action, and primary goals. Sociologists saw how readily persons of one race will take on pattern-perfect the social characteristics of a group other than that in

3

which they were born; it was seen, for instance, that American
Negroes, though often dark in skin, are nevertheless essentially
white in culture and social habits.

Finally it became clear that the structure of men's bodies
is for all practical purposes the same everywhere; the difference
between groups is in their cultures, their social heritage. Men
behave differently as adults because their cultures are different;
they are born into different habitual ways of life, and these they
must follow because they have no choice.

With this fact established, the attention of scientists is becoming centered on an entirely different problem. What are the
techniques by which men, originally similar, learn as adults to
behave differently—in short, what is the nature of the learning
process? For it is clear that learning, not biological constitu-
tion, accounts for the differing modes of action of men in varying societies.

How are the different ways of life characteristic of different
societies taught to the naïve children born into those societies?
A study of the effect of color caste on the personalities of Negro
children involves exactly this problem. First, one must determine what stereotyped forms of behavior are characteristic of
the Negro caste as contrasted with white and, then, how the social classes within Negro society differ in the behavior which
they demand of children born into them. Once these differing
aspects of social structure have become clear, one must consider
the nature of the learning process by which children are induced
and compelled to take on the behavior appropriate to a Negro
in a specified class position.

To learn about learning one must turn to the students of this
subject, such as Pavlov, Watson, Thorndike, Hull, Freud, and
their students; here, the need is merely to summarize the findings which are pertinent as a preparation for reading the life
histories which are to follow. The amount one may know technically in this field is great, but the main ideas are simple and
easily accessible.

The first important fact is that social learning takes place
only where there is a dilemma. People must be in some kind of

squeeze to learn; no squeeze, no learning. Prosperous and comfortable individuals, for instance, do not readily change their social habits.

Take, for example, a white rat in a cage—and let no one out of vanity despise what we have discovered about human learning from the rat. There seems to be no difference in the most basic processes by which rats and humans learn, although human learning is vastly aided by superior talents and devices; among the latter are the capacity to react adaptively after long-time intervals, and the ability to combine the results of past learning.

The rat in the problem box is in a dilemma. One of the elements in this dilemma is that he has been hungry for twenty-four hours. This hunger excites, impels, instigates him. He must behave so as to escape it.

When the gloved hand of the experimenter first puts the animal in the little problem cage, he appears lost. He starts to explore the box *at random;* any port in a storm, he seems to feel.[1] First he will nose around the box, trying to smell or touch his way to some act that will still his gnawing hunger. He will sip from the water that is dripping into the box. That seems to help, but not enough. He will wash his face, with no result. He will go through the routine again, canvassing the situation, jumping, nosing, pawing. Finally, *by chance,* he will strike a little bar which the experimenter has exposed at one end of the cage, and lo! a pellet of food will fall into a cup underneath the bar. At first the rat does not notice the food, and continues his random behavior; finally he spies the pellet, *the goal,* falls on it greedily, and eats it. He has made the eating response, or (one kind of) *goal response.*

But one pellet is not enough—far from it. A hundred would hardly serve to satisfy that rapacious hunger; and he takes up the quest again with renewed hope. At least he is sure now that food can somehow be obtained in the box.

Again the rat noses and pokes at random, smells, licks the

---

[1] Although the behavioristic mode of thought is followed, anthropomorphic expressions like the above will occasionally be used for the sake of vividness.

water, washes his face, examines all corners of the box. Again he strikes the bar, that is, performs the correct *instrumental act,* and the sympathetic watcher gasps with disappointment. Why does he not notice that the pellet has fallen? But he does not, and once more he must find the pellet blindly.

After four or five tries and random successes, the rat seems to come to the conclusion that there is something about the end of the box where the lever is that leads to success, and he confines his efforts to this part of the box. Then he drops directly from pushing the bar to eating the food, repeats this sequence several times, and the trick is done. Bar-pushing is firmly associated with getting food. Bar-pushing has been *reinforced;* that is, it has been recognized as an instrumental act that leads to the goal response. Random behavior now disappears. The problem box has lost its problem character. The rat can run to the bar, push, and eat to satiety whenever he is put in the box. He has firmly and permanently learned something, that is, what to do when put into this particular box, in case he is hungry.

The sequence at the end of learning runs like this: hunger is the impulsion; running to the bar, standing up, batting the bar, are the instrumental acts; the eating of the pellet is the goal response. Out of all the performed acts, reinforcement selects and stabilizes those action units which lead to the final response of eating. Most perfectly learned are those units of behavior which stand nearest in time to the final tension-reducing response.

The case just cited is often described as an instance of *reward.* The situation is so arranged that the animal has been rewarded for its activity. Reward may be thought of as strengthening the tendency to approach a goal. But what happens to the instrumental acts (running, pushing bar) in case the rewarding food is withdrawn? This problem has been carefully studied. For some time the rat will run to the bar and push. No food comes. He does not stop pushing the first time the pellet does not appear, but continues vainly for a while. Then he seems to give up for the moment and resumes random exploration of the problem box. Shortly, however, he returns and pushes hopefully on the bar; again no food. This time he does not push so many times, and he resumes exploratory behavior more quickly. This process continues for some time with the periods of random behavior increasing in length and the flurries of bar-pushing decreasing. Finally he will not press the bar at all, but devotes full time to random exploration. His previous learning, that is, that bar-pushing brings food, is said to be extinguished.

Withdrawing reward is a very effective way of breaking up an action sequence. There is, however, another and more rapid way. It is to insert *punishment* in the action sequence before goal response takes place. In the case of the baffled but energetic rat described above, one could insert a sharp electric shock just before the rat touches the bar. Thereafter the shocked rat will show a different behavior; he will run toward the bar as if to push, but before reaching the lever his behavior will break down; he will stop, and then *run away* from the bar. If an alternative way of getting food is possible, he will follow it and avoid the painful bar altogether. From this behavior it is concluded that punishment will reinforce *antagonistic modes of behavior;* that is, the spanked child will keep out of the flower bed, and he will be reinforced in "going by the walk" as an alternative. In contrast to reward, therefore, punishment is said to lead to *withdrawal responses.*

Both punishment and reward cast their shadows forward. If one is moving toward a known punishment, he suffers from *anxiety,* a powerful governor of behavior, the importance of which was emphasized by Freud. If one is moving with increasing alacrity toward reward, he may be said to experience *pleasure.* Both of these responses fall in a class which is called *anticipatory.*

These concepts will be used many times in the life histories that follow, and there will be ample opportunity to practice this mode of analyzing behavior. Once the pattern of thought and analysis has been learned, it can be applied as well to the behavior of babies as to that of rats. The infant too is driven by hunger. It is moving toward the goal of breast or bottle. It makes greedily the goal response of suckling. This response serves to stamp in the instrumental acts by which the bottle is reached, such as crying, stretching out its arms to be picked up, hearing its mother's step, identifying her face. It behaves at first at random, only gradually perfecting a mode of action which leads to reward. The suckling response can be extinguished by withdrawal of the bottle, and by trial and error the infant will gradually learn to accept other foods. Its eating behavior can be interrupted and even entirely broken down by painful states, such as the intestinal cramps which may come with disease. It can show anxiety and love as a result of painful or pleasant experiences.

There is probably one important difference, however, between learning in babies and learning in rats. Rats must find their way to the goal by circumventing the barriers imposed by raw nature. Babies, on the other hand, have considerable aid in finding a correct goal. Their parents know what the desired goal response is and may move the goal toward the baby, thus cutting down the amount of time required for random action. This is another way of saying that the baby comes into a systematic way of life, whereas the rat does not. Human parents aid their offspring to find a solution; this solution itself has been evolved over centuries by the society into which the child comes. With human beings, one can say that the group learns, conserves problem solutions, and offers them to the incoming organism; perhaps one should make the statement stronger and say that the group *forces* its traditional solutions on the learning child.

In this book, much use will also be made of the basic conceptions of Freud, although his terms will not be used to any great extent. The reason for not using those terms is that the scheme of thought outlined above seems a superior one for descriptive purposes to that utilized by Freud. It is oriented behavioristically and is systematically more useful. Many ideas which are present in Freud's system, however, cannot yet be presented in these behavioristic terms, and in these cases we shall use Freud's terms. Freud was a great innovator in the study of human behavior, and his findings parallel those of behaviorism at many points and anticipate them at others.

One of Freud's best ideas is that the first learning is the most critical, and stands as a kind of model for later learning. He has stressed the durability of habits developed in childhood and their orienting effect in later life. He has, in a sense, discovered childhood.

Freud has also stressed the great role of animal impulse in childhood in determining the nature of the human habit structure. Where behaviorists saw the problem box, the action sequence, and the bar, Freud saw the hungry rat and the food pellet. Freud's psychology gives vitality and body to our conception of behavior; he has seen life as the ceaseless rise and fall of elemental drives.

Freud noticed the great role of punishment, either infliction of pain or withdrawal of goal, in the formation of habit. Behaviorists saw, for the most part, only reward; Freud saw pain also as a chisel to shape human habit. Freud has shown the roles of pain and anxiety at their true worth because he has studied personalities where the empirical evidence for these forces was abundant.

Freud, and here the behaviorist joins him firmly, has noted also the role of conflict in human life. He has observed that the human being is never or rarely a smoothly compacted group of habits, but is rather a creature whose habit systems are constantly in conflict. The primitive drives may occasionally again take over the helm of personality and excite random behavior, even in sophisticated adults. *The habit tendencies of which a person is conscious are not the whole of personality; the punished and aborted habits of childhood often have to be taken into account if human behavior is to be intelligible.* He has called the latter habits "unconscious" and has noted the role of repression in keeping them from expression in adult behavior.

Freud has also noted those critical dilemmas of childhood where important new learning must take place. He has estimated at its true worth the change in habit structures accompanying weaning and the dangerous possibilities for human stability that attend this learning. He has also seen similar possibilities in the cleanliness training and sex training situations.

The great task of verifying and correcting the structure of Freud's theory has still to be carried out by scientific men. Until this is done, his theories give us our best tentative conception of the important and often fateful early phases of the learning process. Freud's thought is often used in this study even when his language is omitted.

It seems to the students of human learning, therefore, that the behavior of any human being must be looked upon primarily as a complex of acquired habits. Each of these has been learned in a dilemma where society has punished the individual's attempts to follow other courses of action, and has rewarded his learning the prescribed method of attaining his goal response (for example, eating at table, excreting in the bathroom, and so forth). At first, the child is driven by simple biological tensions, such as hunger and pain, to learn the acts leading to a desired goal response of eating, or of removal of pain. From the time of weaning, however, and increasingly thereafter, he is taught to react to his biological tensions in socially defined ways. For example, a child in our society is trained to regard only certain meats and plants as edible, that is, as goals for his hunger. He must learn, furthermore, that he cannot eat whenever he wants to (that is, he cannot go to the goal directly by the shortest route), but must accept the alternative response of eating at regular appointed hours. The intricate sequence of actions which the socialized human being has been taught to substitute for the direct biological response appears to be simply a longer route to the same biological goals, with lanes and hurdles to teach him that the responses may be obtained only under certain conditions.

The lengthy process of training the human animal does not take place, however, without leaving distinguishing marks upon the individual. To train a child not to soil himself usually requires a rather severe battle, repeated several times a day over a period of years. Human beings emerge from these long training experiences showing characteristic degrees of ease (speed and frequency) both in making the learned responses and in acquiring new behavior.

The learning of new habits after earliest infancy is always a slow and difficult process of re-education because it involves the changing of old habits. Punishment is one of the most important methods used in our society to extinguish undesired habits, and to impel the individual to new behavior. Most individuals therefore come to anticipate punishment in new learning situations; anxiety thus appears as a constant mark left upon many individuals by the processes of their socialization.

Personality is perceived in that behavior of an individual which distinguishes him from other individuals *trained by similar social controls*. Persons who show relatively little anxiety and who make new social adjustments easily may consequently be distinguished, upon a psychological basis, from other individuals of roughly similar social training who exhibit great difficulty in learning new habits, or who are unable to learn at all. Differences in personality are most clearly revealed in learning situations, for the degree of generalized anxiety experienced by an individual greatly affects his learning time.

Except in individuals with organic pathology, therefore, the origin of personality must be sought in the history of the individual's training. It is a question of how his socialization "took" with him, as compared with other individuals. In a society with the technical and social complexity of ours, the controls by which individuals are trained and their resultant habits are found to differ, in certain fundamental respects, according to the part of the social structure in which they live.

In spite of certain universal similarities (in language, dress, familial structure, and technical adaptations) which appear in our society, the conditions under which persons have access to fundamental biological and social goals are defined by a system of privilege. When this system is examined in detail, as it recently has been studied in New England and in the lower South by social anthropologists who lived in these communities for extended periods, it is found to be a system of socially ranked groups, with varying degrees of social movement existing between them. Each of these groups consists of people who associate or may associate freely with each other, but who do not associate freely with the groups "above" and "below" them.

In our society, an individual is born into a family which is a member of such a socially ranked group. His family's economic, social, and sexual participation is largely limited to its own group. He is controlled by his social position, not simply in the formation of his early habits, but throughout his life. He is controlled by the punishment which he receives from groups above and below him to restrict his participation, that is, to "keep him in his (social) place." The effect of such punishment is usually to prevent him from learning new habits, and thus from increasing his privileges. Barriers upon interclass participation thus set up differential reinforcements for each group; the nature of these social reinforcements is ultimately determined by the kind of privileges (goal responses) which the group is allowed to attain.

The systems of social rank which exist in American society differ in degree; that is, they differ with respect to the opportunity allowed an individual living within the system to move into a stratum other than that in which he was born. The most effective ways to restrict intergroup movement in any Western society are (1) to prevent the individual from marrying out of his birth group, and (2) to restrict his opportunities to earn money. When one looks at the systems of privilege in our society thus, in terms of their rigidity, one may group them into systems of *social classes* (which allow social mobility between groups) and into *caste systems* (which allow no movement at all, or practically none, out of one's birth group). The most important fact about society in the South is that it consists of a dual system: there is a system of white and of Negro castes, and also a system of social classes *within each caste,* further stratifying groups and defining privileges. In order to understand the behavior of each Negro informant who appears in this study, therefore, we need to learn the systematic demands upon him both of his caste position and of the particular social class into which he was born.

Social classes may be determined objectively by using records of intimate social participation between the inhabitants. Such a system of ranked groups, between which there are habitual controls upon free participation, exists within both the Negro and the white societies. Throughout the following studies of personality and of the social class controls upon behavior, it is to be remembered that social classes overlap somewhat in their membership. Participation lines are not rigidly drawn. In this respect, social classes are to be contrasted with the color castes, of Negroes and whites, which are mutually exclusive in their social life.

As here identified, a social class is to be thought of as the largest group of people whose members have intimate social access to one another. A class is composed of families and of social cliques. The interrelationships between these families and cliques, in such informal activities as visiting, dances, receptions, teas, and larger informal affairs, constitute the structure of a social class.

The forms of participation of the social clique and class are of an intimate type which implies that the individuals included have *equal status in the sense that they may visit one another, have interfamily rituals such as meals or tea together, and may intermarry*. Other types of cliques and larger groups which are organized upon a different basis, such as by common occupation, or recreation (card-playing, golfing, etc.), or church membership, or lodge membership, are not necessarily class-typed. Social participation of this kind, therefore, may not be used by the observer as a reliable index of class position.

The intimate, social clique relationships are the class unit, therefore. Most of the individuals in a social class may be identified by using records of their participation in intimate social relations of the kind cited above. *A person is then found to be a member of that social class with which most of his participations of this intimate kind occur.* The same basis is used by members of the local communities in New Orleans and Natchez for "placing" an individual in his social class.

Whether a class of people is regarded as superordinate ("higher") or subordinate ("lower") in relation to another class is likewise determined empirically by observing the status evaluations of the classes themselves. A lower-class or a middle-class person usually recognizes both implicitly and explicitly that an upper-class person has higher social status than himself; moreover, a lower-class person evaluates middle-class status as superior to his own. Conversely, upper-class and middle-class individuals regard lower-class people as inferior in status, and restrict their intimate participation accordingly. The upper-class likewise subordinates middle-class persons and evaluates their class behavior as a mark of an inferior status group.

Although the great majority of Negroes or whites usually associate in their intimate life with members of only one class, there is some flexibility in the social class systems which have been studied in New England and in the deep South. In contrast to a caste system, a social class system provides mechanisms for social mobility from one status group to another. An individual and a family may be downward mobile from the class position in which they were born and end by participating usually on a lower class level. On the other hand, they may acquire the social and economic symbols which will enable them to associate with a class ranked above that in which they were born. Such a change of class position usually requires a lifetime.

Social classes overlap in their membership, therefore, because there are always individuals who participate intimately with two classes. These mobile individuals are men of two social worlds. Frequently they are the children of mixed-class marriages whose parents subject them to conflicting types of class training. In American society, white or Negro, there is a relatively large number of socially mobile persons, "who look both up and down" in the class system. As a Negro informant in

Natchez said of the members of an upward mobile family, they are "jus' betwixt and between" one status group and another. Half of the personalities studied in this book are those of socially mobile individuals.

Institutions likewise cut across social class lines in Negro and in white societies. Neither the church, the school, nor the organizations are rigidly class-typed. Most churches include members of several classes in their congregations, and the Negro secret societies often include persons from all social classes. Even the college fraternities and sororities have members from two or three subclasses, although within these groups social cliques tend to separate upon the basis of class positions.

Within European and American urban societies with similar occupational and social systems, the rigidity of the social class structure apparently increases with the age of the society. American class systems allow a faster rate of mobility than European. In this country, social mobility seems to be more frequent and rapid in the West than it is in the East and old South. The complexity of stratification within a class system likewise appears to increase with the size and with the degree of socio-economic differentiation of the community. In Yankee City and Old City, each of which has a population of about 15,000, six subclasses were identified in the white society. The small Negro community of Natchez, with a population of 7,000 located in a plantation environment, has differentiated only five social classes, while the Negro society of New Orleans is stratified into six classes. Other large old cities may have seven or eight subclasses.

Those readers of this work who are teachers, social workers, or members of the liberal intelligentsia may find it difficult to realize that our society, Negro or white, possesses a complex system of social stratification. It is to be expected that these groups would be relatively unaware of the degree of status variation in the larger society, for they lead their intimate social lives in groups whose status-symbols and restrictions are somewhat deviant from the American mode. Generally speaking, in the social worlds of the academic, the "artistic," the "radical," and the "Bohemian," the range of classes is narrower, the symbols somewhat different, and upward mobility more rapid and frequent than in the status world of the great majority of church-going, lodge-joining, conservative members of American society.

In the study of human motivation in our society, the analysis of the social class pressures and rewards is of major importance. A child is trained principally by his family, his family's social clique, and his own social clique; the goals and sanctions of both the family and the intimate social clique are determined principally by the class-ways, that is, by the criteria of status in *their part of the society*. Although the evidence shows that much, perhaps most, of the behavior of adolescents in the cities studied is class-typed, it is not apparent that personality, in the sense of the emotional and adaptive disposition of the individual, is principally typed by social classes. Nor is it maintained that the adolescents studied in this book represent the usual personality types in their respective social classes. Our evidence on the nature and application of early training controls makes it impossible to claim that personality is class-typed in the rigid sense in which some social anthropologists have claimed that personality, in more homogeneous primitive societies, is culturally patterned. Such a position is not taken with regard to the following lives. It is simply held that they reveal the interplay in personality formation between those factors which arise from the general family, age, and sex controls, and those which are systematically reinforced by the class or caste environment. In the use of the designations, "lower," "middle," and "upper" for social classes no evaluation of class habits is implied. The terms simply recognize the conceptions of class rank shared by Negroes in all parts of the social hierarchy. From the sociological viewpoint, the classes might be called "1," "2," "3," and so on.[2]

[2] As has been previously mentioned, the modes of behavior, the dogmas, and the typical evaluations of each social class within the white and Negro societies have been defined in field studies by John Dollard (*Caste and Class in a Southern Town*), and by Davis and Gardner, working in the same areas of the Deep South where the following personality studies were made. For the empirical identification of the class-ways of behavior and of training, the present book uses chiefly the findings of the Davis-Gardner study of Old City (*Deep South*, to be published by the University of Chicago Press). In the last three chapters of the

In studying the status controls operating upon an individual one finds that most persons in our society are disposed to conceal, even from themselves, any inferiority in their social rank. This effort to "hide" status is caused by anxiety; such protectiveness must be understood in terms of the long and systematic punishment suffered by the individual from persons of the next higher social rank—not merely for attempting to change his status, but for occupying the one that he actually holds. Refusal to acknowledge one's inferior status, and the building of defenses to decrease anxiety on this score are especially complex with regard to class status, and must be considered at length in a later chapter. Color caste, however, is so clearly and so rigidly defined that persons in the lower-caste society (as well as the general American reader of this book) will exhibit much less psychological resistance to the fact of caste status than to that of class position. A colored person of the lower-middle class in New Orleans, for example, will state very early in the interview situation that he belongs to a subordinated color group. He will very seldom admit, however (though he will inadvertently imply), that he cannot associate intimately with Negroes of a higher social class. In learning the controls upon human behavior which are associated with the various positions in the American social hierarchy, it is simpler to begin therefore with caste training.

Even if one frequently travels between the North and the South, it is always revealing to observe the differences in the formalized relations between Negroes and whites in the two areas. Perhaps the reader has never been in the South, or it may be that the first sharp impressions of the trip have become blurred in his memory. If he lives there, he has possibly come

present book, moreover, the standards of child training for the Negro social classes in New Orleans and Natchez are described, upon the basis of the interviews gathered in the present study from 123 Negro adolescents and their parents.

The last chapters of this book, which deal in a systematic manner with the class and caste training of the Negro child, should be read in order to do justice to the personality interpretations. It is hoped that then the teacher or the social worker, if not the general reader, will review the cases themselves.

to accept the caste system without ever having visualized it. It will be helpful, therefore, to accompany a Midwesterner on his first trip to Natchez or New Orleans.

When such a "foreigner" approaches his train in Chicago, he may attempt to board that passenger coach which is immediately behind the last baggage car. In this case, if he is white, he will probably be told by the porter that this is not "his" coach; if he asks questions, he will learn that it is the "Negro" coach. Although the segregation of passengers according to their color is not legally required until the train crosses the Ohio River at Cairo and enters Tennessee, it is more convenient, presumably, for both white and colored passengers to follow this arrangement when leaving Chicago. If the traveler comes from New York, and has ridden in a coach with colored passengers as far as Washington, D.C., he will find that all Negroes disappear from his coach at the nation's capital.

As the train stops at town and city depots in the South, the newcomer (who has already begun to receive his training as a caste man) will notice that the clothes of most Negroes at the stations are markedly inferior to those of most whites. The sociologist could inform him that a tremendous difference also exists between the two color groups in other economic and social indices: in average income and in occupational level, for example, and consequently in the rate of home ownership; in per capita expenditures by the state and federal governments for schools, in the rates of registered voters, in the rates of child and female labor, of dependency, of juvenile delinquency, and of illegitimacy. If our visitor should then be motivated to visit the schools where Negro children must go, or to attend the trial of a colored defendant in a court conducted, inevitably, by a white judge, white lawyer, and white jury, or if he were bold enough to examine the community's books of registered voters, he would not long be left in doubt as to the systematic subordination of the Negro group by severe limitations of its social and economic privileges, as well as by the threat and at times the use of physical punishment.

Once our white traveler had begun to live in a southern city

like Natchez or New Orleans, moreover, he would receive daily
training in his caste behavior. He would learn that he must not
sit behind Negroes in a streetcar or bus, that he must not sit in
the same section with them in the theater, that he must not allow
them to eat with him, that he must not invite them to his home
for a social visit, that he must not address them as "Mr." or
"Mrs." or "Miss," and that generally he must not shake hands
with them. He would be learning the behavior required of an upper caste man; he would *have* to learn it to avoid the legal penalties provided for violators or to escape the economic and social
punishments which his own caste applies to enforce such behavior.

Perhaps we may now abandon our personally conducted tour
of the "foreigner," and try to look at Negro-white relationships
more objectively. We wish to examine these relationships systematically, as the anthropologist has learned to do by observing primitive societies with which he has formed no particular
emotional bonds.

The field studies of Old City, Southerntown, and their plantation environments in the lower South, have shown that the
Negro and white groups there have the positions of castes; that
is, there is no social or familial participation between members
of different color groups. The rank of these color castes is defined by their privileges with respect to occupation, wages, public
gatherings, politics, and education. It is this complex of relative
privileges which establishes the subordination of the Negro
caste, and the superordination of the white caste. (It must always
be remembered that one's social status is defined by a *group*
of privileges and traits, and that we see these several variables
acting together and at the same time, when we accord a certain
social rank to a given person or group.) Although the caste sanctions differ in minor details, as between urban and rural areas
and as between the border states and the southern states, the
basic restrictions upon marriage, occupation, public gatherings,
and education exist everywhere in this area.

Caste in the South is nothing more nor less, in fine, than a
system for limiting social participation between color groups,

and of thus differentiating between these groups with regard to the most fundamental opportunities in human society. In this latter respect, it is quite like our system of social classes. It differs from the class system in its arbitrary and final definition of the individual's status, a definition without possibility of change during his lifetime if the system persists. In southern society, for example, it is possible for an individual to raise or lower his class position, although it is a lengthy process. No individual may change his caste position, however.[3] He is born into his caste, and he must die in it, if he remains in the area and the system is not changed.

[3] In New Orleans, and in most of the largest cities, it is possible for those colored people who can "pass" as white to change their caste position in certain fields of behavior. It practically never happens today, however, that such persons marry white individuals. There are still a few white men who establish common-law marriages with colored women, and live part of their day in a house with the colored mate and children. They are usually outcastes as far as intimate association with whites or Negroes is concerned. The colored women in such open unions are likewise barred from intimate association with Negroes; in Natchez, for example, these women associate chiefly with each other, and are not invited to the homes of members of their former social class.

THE LOWER CLASSES

The Lower Classes

The first three personality studies are of adolescents whose families, friends, and intimate acquaintances are members of the Negro lower class. The colored lower-class society in New Orleans and Natchez divides itself into two levels, or ranks, between which free social participation is checked by restrictive controls: an upper-lower class, and a lower-lower class. Upper- and middle-class Negroes refer to these groups as "common, ignorant people" or "the worst class of Negroes." The first case, "Frightened Amazon," is that of a girl who is "falling" (downward mobile) into lower class, from the lower-middle-class position into which her mother was born and for which she attempted to train the daughter. The second life is that of a girl whose habits and goals are very similar to those of her upper-lower-class parents and grandparents. The concluding study in this section deals with a lower-lower-class boy, who is "falling" into the declassed group of criminals.

CHAPTER II

FRIGHTENED AMAZON

JULIA WILSON is one of those individuals who seems to have an insatiable claim against life. Driven by strange and unpredictable animosities and by equally mysterious and uncontrollable fears, these individuals are the children of wrath and of self-love. We have all met such people, and the interviewer could not avoid Julia Wilson.

Of the thirty students[1] who were interviewed at length, Julia Wilson was the only one who insisted upon being included in the study. In what proved later to be her characteristic mode of attack upon both men and women, Julia interrupted the male interviewer in his preliminary talks with several other girls and demanded that he begin interviewing her at once. By tracking him down and pushing other girls aside, she literally shoved herself into the study. After his first talk with her, the interviewer commented mildly that she was "quite talkative" and "very aggressive."

Once having isolated her man in the interview situation, Julia immediately began to talk to him of her "boy friends," and to conduct a systematic campaign against him, with practiced skills and highly conscious lures. She was indeed a master of men, as she often boasted, but in the interviewer she met a man who was not only of a higher class position, but who kept his money close to his pocket. Since gifts are the very essence of love to Julia and none were forthcoming, she soon extinguished her exploitative hopes toward the interviewer, and gradually came to regard him as a kind of neutral-sexed creature to whom she could confide her contempt and hostility toward both sexes.

Julia is a "good-looking," dark-skinned girl of sixteen with a

---

[1] This term is used for adolescents interviewed in the study. Since the interviewee was not only giving us information but also *learning something about himself and his social relations*, we have referred to him or her as a "student."

slender figure which she regards as a handicap in her campaign against men. She attends the first year of high school but shows little or no interest in her work. Her family is upper-lower class, having fallen from lower-middle-class position. She lives with her mother, father, and two younger brothers in a four-room house near the railroad tracks in New Orleans. Her parents own the house, one room of which they rent to male lodgers. She also has two older sisters who are married and live in New Orleans. Julia is the third child; there is a difference of about two years in age between each child and the next younger. She was interviewed by a dark-skinned man, twenty-five years old, who is of middle-middle-class position. The social distance between them is great; under usual circumstances it would require at least two generations for Julia's family to attain the position and behavior of the interviewer.

At school, Julia's acquaintances (she has only one intimate friend and does not believe in forming a circle of close associates) call her not Julia, but "Raddie" Wilson. Her nickname means "rowdy," or "troublemaker," and she is regarded by both pupils and teachers as a "show-off." Julia herself boasts that the people at school, as well as the boy friends whom she curses and fights, think she is "crazy"; that is, that she will do "anything"—fight a man, curse a teacher, or kiss a boy in the schoolyard—without regard for the usual restrictions upon a girl and upon a pupil.

Her own mother says that Julia thinks of herself as the "Big I am," and that she has never been able to play cooperatively with other girls or to get along congenially with anyone except her next older sister. But Julia is a fighter and she does not bar even her mother. She replies that her mother does not like her and has never liked her. Nor does she pretend to like her mother. Her mother, Julia insists, likes only her son Earl, who is two years younger than Julia.

In spite of her rather pleasant smile and her somewhat middle-class "front," there is no doubt that Julia deserves her reputation as a fighter. A slender but tigerish Amazon, who fights with her fists rather than with a knife, she harasses her boy friends with insatiable aggression until a curse and a slap lead to a knockdown drag-out fight. She fights not only the bantams at school but even the white girls who "meddle" with her; she curses and slaps the older boy friends who drive her to school in their cars; and she engages grown men in public fights and cursing duels in her own neighborhood.

As a child, she was a favorite with the "across-the-tracks" gang of boys and girls. They fought with rocks, knives, and sometimes with pistols. At fourteen she saw a boy badly stabbed by another in an argument over her at a school picnic. She married at sixteen, and had a fist and chair fight with her husband the first time she saw him after her marriage. There is little exaggeration in her claim, "I don't run from nobody—girl or boy. I either beat or get beat. I ain't scared of nobody. When James (a man thirty years old) hits me, I hit him back. I don't care where I am, either. I curse him just as much as he curses me." She retreats only when severe punishment is certain—when her opponent has a knife or pistol, or when a teacher threatens her with expulsion from school.

Julia is not only a chronic fighter, she is a clever and unrelenting exploiter of men. What she wants from men is their money. To attain this goal, which to her is all important, she holds out her sexual lures to a great variety of men but she has sex relations with few or none. Over a period of four months she furnished the interviewer with detailed accounts of fourteen boys and men whom she remembers having successfully gouged of money and presents. In this list is her father, whom she values more highly than her mother "because he has always given me things," but whom she nevertheless has blackmailed for years with the threat of revealing his love affairs to her mother. There is also an easily gullible married man of about thirty, from whom Julia has been extracting rather large sums of money since she was fourteen. She boasts that she has kept him under control by her "craziness" (her constant fight-picking) and her refusal to have sex relations with him. "That's the way to do," Julia triumphantly points out. "When you get a sucker, bump his head."

To Julia, men are a class of people who have more money than women and who are therefore capable of giving one the more vital needs of life: candy and clothes and money and automobile rides. They are beings who also have a strange and apparently headlong desire for sexual responses from women, a weakness in their nature which Julia regards as universal to their sex, and as originally designed for her specific aggrandizement. It is this curious and simple-minded passion of men, she feels, which makes them susceptible to her various baits and lures; it enables her to use them and at the same time to keep them writhing at a safe distance. As she sums up the case of Fred, her married suitor, "I know he likes me 'cause I can get anything I want out of him. I can get things when his wife can't. Yes, I know he loves me, but I don't care for him, and he knows it, too. He told me that once. He said, 'I know you don't love me, but I'm crazy about you.'" Men are apparently not sex objects to Julia; they are necessary instrumental steps to the attainment of money and gifts.

This thirst of hers to be given things, or to take them, is not directed only toward men, however. She wishes to use women in the same way—to extract presents from them, for example, and to cajole or browbeat her mother into giving her more attention or gifts than the other children in her family. Since women have little money to give and since they are competitors with Julia for the rich haul which men do have, she spends relatively little time with girls. Instead, she takes their boy friends from them and taunts them with the fact that it is their hard luck if they are unable to keep them.

In the face of the convincing evidence that Julia is really a "tough" girl who fights anything two-footed, and that she is a persistent exploiter of both men and women, there are nevertheless strange inconsistencies both in her report of her life and in her overt behavior. She is extremely afraid of the unpredictable pain of illness or accident. She has no hesitation in admitting that she cannot bear much pain and that she still cries "for the least little thing that hurts me." Except for the memories of her father's gifts to her, moreover, all of her earliest childhood recollections are of terrifying experiences: of a flood in which she and her family were swept out of their house, of her childhood diseases, of the illness of her mother, of the fights between her parents, and of accidents and sudden deaths which came to relatively unknown people. She has exceedingly vivid and lacerating memories of the killing of an uncle and three white children by snakes and she claims to have seen their dead bodies with the snakes around their necks.

Even more unexpected, in view of her continual pursuit of men, is the strong aversion which she expresses to exposing her body to any man, or to having full sexual relationships. She gives as the worst experience of her life the times when she was compelled to submit to medical examinations; she says that she turned her head in shame on each occasion and was always afraid thereafter that she would meet the physicians on the street. Unlike most lower-class girls of her age, she insists that she has never had sex relations, except with her husband; there have been only three such occasions, she claims, in their year of courtship and marriage. At these times, she always felt ashamed of her action and could not face her husband afterward. Dreams and strange accounts of attempts by unknown men to attack her or to abduct her are as numerous in her record as are her stories of sex fights.

There are even more puzzling aspects of Julia's behavior than her fear of accidents, sickness, and sexual attack. This Amazon from the battlefield of "across-the-tracks," who has had boys stabbed for her and has fought men and women on the streets, displays behavior which is often childlike, almost infantile. At times, even now at the age of sixteen, she plays "dolls" and "keeping house" with the little children in her neighborhood. Until she was twelve or thirteen, she regularly played with dolls, and even at that age played "mamma and children" with much younger girls, always forcing them to grant her the position of "mamma." Julia says, furthermore, "I am always trying to get my mamma to do things for me. She does them for me, too. I rub up against her and feel her breasts until she does." She adds that she likes to play with her mother's breasts, and that she attempts the same behavior toward her next older sister, who slaps her hands. Mrs. Wilson herself says that Julia insisted upon keeping her pacifier until she was eight or nine years old, although the mother had tried to break her of this infantile habit when she was two years old.

Our initial view of Julia is that of a girl who is self-centered, exploitative, and chronically aggressive. At the same time, she shows unmistakable fear and deep distrust of life, and is curiously infantile in certain fields of her behavior. If we wish to understand this Julia, whom we now experience as a rather unpleasant and dangerous member of our society, we must obtain a detailed record of her training from the earliest days. We must also attempt to trace her developmental history as a member of a particular family, living in a specific status, in Negro society.

There is strong evidence both from the clinic and from the laboratory of the experimental psychologist to indicate that the earliest learning of human beings is the most basic learning. In Julia's case, we may say at once that her earliest experiences were of suffering, of punishment, and of deprivation, and that these hostile and noxious aspects of life struck her when she was as yet completely unaware of their causes. When she was barely one month old, her method of eating, which was the prime activity and the very basis of her life, was sharply interrupted. The breast of the mother was suddenly no longer there. Instead, she was handed a bottle. This new method of feeding not only deprived her of her mother's breast, which to her was a necessary condition for the activity of eating, but it also interrupted violently her already established habit of getting food. To her, it may have appeared as a permanent withdrawal of food. Since she had not been gradually taught to substitute the bottle for the breast, she starved for two days. To attempt to understand this experience in our adult terms, we must imagine the punishment and the actual suffering of starving through two and a half days (eight mealtimes); we must add to that trauma the condition that we could not understand *why* we were being starved, and to that we must still add the necessity for learning an absolutely new method of eating, if we wished to end our starvation. It seems likely that Julia learned from this experience that even the most gratifying and well-fixed habits could be inexplicably interrupted by deprivation and suffering. She learned in a scarcely conscious manner that the "world," which to her was the mother, could not be depended upon *to bring necessary things to you*.

Apparently she came to anticipate undeserved pain as a constant aspect of eating. Her mother did not consult a physician with regard to any of her babies, for in the lower class one must learn to do without expensive doctors. As the result of an incorrect formula for bottle feeding, Julia had persistent colic during her first year of life. Colic in babies is evidently severely painful. Julia learned to expect pain after sucking and developed an ambivalent[2] feeling toward eating and toward people. Not only must one expect his habits to be interrupted painfully and his food withdrawn; not only will good things not be brought to him, but pain (and consequently the anticipation of pain) appears to be a steadily recurrent aspect of living. For a child with colic the pleasure of eating is constantly followed by physical suffering, and he can therefore only expect that all fixed habits, no matter how basic to life, will be interrupted by loss and suffering.

In addition to feeding, there are at least two other fundamental types of early training in a child's life; they center around the child's soiling of himself, and his discovery and manipulation of his genitals. In the course of this training, Mrs. Wilson subjected Julia to systematic whipping and terrorization. She began by spanking her, when she was about three months old, for rolling off the bed pad and wetting the bed. "I did that for a couple of months till she wouldn't roll off that pad." Julia experienced not only feeding pains, therefore, but also severe physical punishment as an infant and small child.

---

[2] "Ambivalence denotes contradictory emotional attitudes toward the same object arising alternately, or existing side by side without either one interfering necessarily or inhibiting the expression of the other." Healy, Bronner, and Bowers, *The Structure and Meaning of Psychoanalysis* (New York: Alfred A. Knopf, 1930), p. 30.

Julia experienced extremely harmful and traumatic punishment from her mother and her oldest sister in connection with her discovery of her genital and her efforts to handle it. In the second year of life, children seem to complete a systematic exploration of their bodies and of the external world with their hands, and it is to be expected that in the course of this exploration most young children will discover and manipulate their genitals. It must be remembered that the feelings of extreme guilt and self-revulsion which adults experience on this score are not native with the child, any more than revulsion for the excreta of his body is innate with the child. The guilt of the child concerning masturbation is established by a powerful taboo, which is instilled by parents, relatives, maids, and other children, and is enforced by whipping, terror stories, and social contempt.

There were no scientific witnesses to this early period of Julia's socialization. The best that can be done, therefore, is a reconstruction based on available fact. It seems that Julia underwent punishment for her childish sex-play in an especially violent and unforgettable form. Her little brother, Earl, was born just at the time when her mother and sister were actively scorning and rejecting her for an infantile habit whose adult social meaning she did not know. To the two-year-old Julia, the mother was suddenly thrown into strong and ominous relief. She was a person who not only took away one's forms of gratification (as she had done long ago in the past), but who also permitted them to another child, the baby. At the same instant when, as a result of the baby's sudden appearance, Julia was being denied her former privileges of sitting in the mother's lap and having the mother's attention and care, she was also being frightened, punished, and severely rejected because she continued her gratifying but (for some reason unknown to her) disapproved behavior. Mrs. Wilson tells us that Julia's behavior changed very markedly at this time, and that these changes later became strongly fixed in her habits.

Before hearing her mother's testimony, however, it is important to visualize the dilemma in which Julia found herself. At

the age of two years, she was apparently facing an urgent demand
from her mother for new learning, for a change in another basic
habit, which involved the giving up of a source of gratification
which was constantly accessible to her. But her mother offered
her no adequate recompense for the effort required to break an
established habit. Instead she *took away* most of the privileges
and rewards which Julia already possessed, and gave them to
another child. What Julia learned in this situation was not what
her mother tried to teach her. She learned always to associate
pain and terror with her genitals. She was confirmed, moreover,
in her feeling that people will not let you have gratifying habits;
they will stop them by punishment. In this world where any
habit, no matter how pleasant or well fixed it may be, can be
interrupted arbitrarily, you must fight for and take what you
want.

What Julia actually did, according to her mother, was: (1) to
begin to cling to and cry for the mother, as an infant does; (2)
to insist upon keeping her pacifier, and to try to take the mother's breast again; (3) to push the baby out of the mother's lap, to
beat it when the mother's back was turned, and to criticize and
attack the mother. Mrs. Wilson reports, "Julia never did like
Earl—ever since he was born. She was a good girl till my boy
came, an' then she started acting more like a baby than she did
when she was younger. She hated him. An' ever since then, my
biggest trouble was tryin' to keep Julia from beating Earl every
time my back wuz turned. She would always take things from
him and beat him." She also states that Julia called her names
and attacked her, when she tried to protect Earl from Julia's
blows.

During this period, Julia refused to give up her pacifier. The
mother tried to break her of the habit by putting red pepper on
the nipple, but Julia fought for the pacifier and often tried to
suck the mother's breast. Finally Mrs. Wilson, in order to mollify
Julia's constant aggression, and probably to reach some compro-
mise with her on the injustice which had been done her, allowed
the child to keep the pacifier. In spite of the fact that Julia now
prefers the father and expresses openly her hostility to her

mother, she still clung to the mother during the years from three to eight, showing great dependence upon her, and still carried her pacifier.

It seems likely, therefore, that Julia solved her dilemma over masturbation by retreating to an earlier and less strongly tabooed form of gratification—that of sucking. She took a substitute, infantile form of pleasure, and gave up open masturbation. She still shows marked genital fears, and she still prefers the oral-indulgent gratifications of the period to which she retreated during her third year. It seems probable, moreover, that she hung upon her mother until she was nine years old, not only to obtain the protection and privileges of a baby but also to shield herself from the punishments which the mother had imposed upon her for masturbation and to defend herself from her own urge to renew this behavior. It is inferred that as a result of the extreme violence with which the genital training was administered Julia was terrorized concerning the use of her sexual resources and confirmed in her infantile, oral habits.

Julia did not accept this crippling deprivation without fighting back. She could not fight the real source of the injustice, the mother. Her hostility seems to have been displaced to the baby brother, whom she could successfully attack. As she grew older, however, she became increasingly aggressive toward the mother. "My mamma don't like me, and I don't like her, 'cause she's too mean to me—I don't do what she says noway."

Later, Julia was confirmed in this hostility by experiencing another frightening deprivation and punishment at the hands of her mother. In a fit of rage, Mrs. Wilson suddenly jerked the pacifier from Julia's neck and frightened the child so terribly that she never asked for the nipple again. Julia was nine years old at this time. For six years after the birth of her brother, she had insisted upon keeping a pacifier; indeed she had fought her mother, her oldest sister, and her teasing, contemptuous schoolmates in order to keep it. Moreover, her mother had consented to her using it and was continually buying her new pacifiers because she lost them regularly. At the age of seven, she had also been allowed by her mother to stop the first grade because she was afraid of school and would leave the building whenever the teacher's back was turned. The mother taught her at home for two years. Then at the age of nine, Julia was suddenly confronted with a mother who was no longer indulgent and protecting, but unaccountably enraged and violent.

"I tell you how I stopped her, an' I wish I would've did that before. One day I had jus' finished whippin' some of my children an' wuz tired an' mad, too. Julia came up and jumped up on my lap an' started cryin'. I jus' jerked that string from aroun' her neck an' threw that nipple so far! An' then I tol' her, 'You'd bettuh not ask for no nipple no more!' An' she never did. She ain't asked for that nipple from that day on. When I jerked that nipple from aroun' her neck, she jus' looked at me an' trembled —she was so scared!"

Through her whole early training, therefore, Julia was constantly driven back upon herself for approval and support. Her mother denied her those habits which were gratifying and left her without substitutes. Her oldest sister, who had control of her during the long periods when her mother was at work, also rejected her by strictly enforcing the mother's training demands. Her brother, Earl, replaced her in the mother's favor, and there was no peace between them. Her father was away on jobs in other towns so she very seldom saw him. She valued him simply for the gifts he brought her and for the shopping "splurges" on which he took her against her mother's wishes. The only person for whom she ever expresses love and approval is her next older sister, Mary, who was too young to help the mother train Julia, and who also fought against the mother's control.

Upon the basis of her long and hard experience that even the people closest to her would not give her what she needed or let her keep it, Julia began to depend upon herself alone. She took what she wanted and fought to get it. Since she expected only hostility and deprivation from her family, she acted not as they wanted her to, but as they—especially her mother and Earl—did *not* want her to act. She was henceforth in business for herself.

She would not be a "good girl" in school, as the mother insisted, nor would she attend church as the mother regularly did.

(On the latter point, she still says that she will not go to church because she does not like to go with her mother.) Her mother did not receive her confidences, nor did Julia ever tell her mother of the father's affairs with other women. During her mother's illness she slipped away from her duties as nurse in order to go to a night club and now she boasts of the trick. She expects nothing good from her mother, but shows chronic hostility and fear of her. In her earliest years she virtually adopted a neighbor as her mother, eating and sleeping at her house; she often eats there still, claiming that her mother will not cook what she wants but only what Earl wants.

Julia also dislikes her oldest sister who helped train her and who still criticizes her rowdy and headstrong behavior. Toward Earl, the baby, her behavior is still revengeful. She boasts that she used to beat him and take everything she could from him, "even if I didn't want it." She also used to make faces at Earl, when the mother was whipping him. In order to harass him now, she insists that he be made to escort her home from parties or visits, even when he has just "come home from work, an' be so tired." When she fights with Earl, she tries "to kick him where I can ruin him for life."

Julia and her father were at one time united in their common flight from the mother's control, but Julia emphasizes only one point in her feeling toward her father. He gave her money and presents. She still extracts this booty from him by threatening to reveal to the mother his latest affair with a woman. The father was also a free spender and a "good-timer"; through her experience with him, Julia learned that men have the most to give or to have taken from them. This early relation appears to have set the pattern for her later exploitation of men.

In view of the early sexual intimidation which apparently befell Julia, it is difficult to see how she could have become the present "Raddie" Wilson, not only a two-fisted Amazon, but an open hunter of men. To understand this development in her later behavior, we must examine the modes of behavior allowed her by her family and her social clique, as members of lower-class society. The influence of her class position has already appeared in Julia's early life. Since her mother was at work during the day, she was not able to supervise Julia's training carefully, but had to entrust it in large measure to a daughter who was only four years older than Julia. Her father was only a transient member of the household because he was compelled to follow the itinerant life of a roustabout and laborer on the river. The use of the pacifier until she was nine is a thoroughly class-typed form of behavior. This practice is permitted at a late age in the lower class where mothers do not have pediatricians and where any device to quiet a child whose mother is away all day may be used—from sucking a meat skin to smoking the grandmother's pipe. In the middle class even a mother who was as unpredictable as Mrs. Wilson appeared to be to Julia, would not have been able to let a child keep a pacifier until she was nine years old. The gossip and open criticism of outraged neighbors and friends would have forced her to conform to middle-class methods of child rearing. But Julia and her parents live in a lower-class world and behave in accordance with the systematic expectations of their part of society.

In the rural area in Louisiana where Julia's mother was born, she was of lower-middle-class position. Her status was somewhat anomalous, however, because her father was a white man who had married her mother during Reconstruction days.[3] He was a small landowner and trapper who was a good provider for his colored family; he still visits Mrs. Wilson in New Orleans and gives his granddaughter, Julia, presents. Mrs. Wilson completed the graded school in her parish (seven grades) and her manners, speech, and dress are those of a lower-middle-class, rather than of a lower-class, woman. Her husband, however, was the son of a farm laborer; both he and his brothers were lower-lower-class people who cut and shot, went to "breakdowns," had their women, and are still known as "bad niggers." One of his brothers stabbed a man badly and a second brother shot a man to death.

[3] Legal marriages between Negroes and whites existed in the early days of the Reconstruction period.

Mr. Wilson was a good worker, however, and with his wife's aid he began to buy a modest but better than ordinary house of four rooms and outfitted it with gumwood veneered furniture. Like many upper-lower-class families, the Wilsons have a piano and a radio and they live well as compared with most lower-class families. During Prohibition, Mr. Wilson made and sold whisky in his home.

The divergent class training of Julia's parents was a source of conflict within her family from the very beginning. Mrs. Wilson did not want to "work out" at domestic labor as her lower-class husband believed a wife should do. The struggle between them over this fundamental point burst into open conflict when Mrs. Wilson later stopped work. One day Mrs. Wilson boasted in her husband's hearing that she would never work again for any man. There was a fight; the father tried to choke the mother. She left with her children, but the father pursued her and would have shot her but for her sister's intervention. Mrs. Wilson had her husband arrested, but he was later acquitted upon the basis of the pleading letters written to the judge by his children.

Julia's father is not only a fighter and a bootlegger who allowed his customers to give Julia drinks at the age of ten, he not only curses freely in his home and threatens to "stomp" his children to death, but he is pre-eminently a "woman chaser." Julia remembers many free-for-all fights in her home over this point, with the mother and all the children joining in against the father. One Christmas, when her mother and father were shopping downtown, her father met one of his "girl friends" and had a fight with her in the mother's presence. When he came home, Julia's next older sister hit him on the head with an axe, and all the family except Julia tried to "beat him good." He is like a stranger in the house now, and is barely spoken to by his wife or children.

Although Julia shares her mother's feeling that the father has disgraced them and now exhibits some hostility to him on this account, she used to get along with him excellently and to prize his free spending and violent living. She constantly emphasized to the interviewer the "free-heartedness" of her father, as contrasted with the stinginess of her mother. Equally constant is her insistence that the father was lenient with her; he allowed her to go out at night, did not try to discipline her, and aligned with her against the mother's discipline. Even now Julia goes to night clubs with her father and his "girl friends."

In the father's way of life, and under his protection and tutelage, Julia found a socially approved outlet in lower-class life for her cursing, fighting, and exploitation of men. She expected nothing good from her mother, and resisted her efforts to make her "respectable." At one time her mother had hopes of preparing Julia for middle-class status, and sent her to a private school. But Julia soon punctured these hopes and ended her mother's attempts to raise her social status. She was discovered gambling and drinking in the boys' dormitory, and was expelled for these offenses.

Even more important than the example of her father in reinforcing her overt aggression were Julia's childhood fight-gangs, her cliques. The children from "across-the-tracks," with whom she played, maintained a continuous feud with the children from the River Side of town. They had a well-organized system of terrorizing the unlucky children from the River Side who strayed into their province. Julia helped to beat up strange girls and to blackmail them for protection. She put River Side boys "on the spot" by leading them into traps and whistling for her gang of boys. She was friendly with boys who carried knives and sometimes pistols, who broke street lights so that they could beat up "outside" boys under cover of darkness, and who "turned out" house parties by hurling bricks through the windows. This warfare continued into late adolescence. Her brother, Earl, at the age of fourteen carries a pistol to and from school and leaves it for safekeeping during school hours with a relative who lives opposite the school.

Unlike some of our upper-lower-class and lower-middle-class students who were thrown into contact with similar fight-gangs, Julia was not intimidated by this warfare. She did not flee from lower-class life. Instead she entered into it with such zest that

she earned the honorific nickname, "Raddie," and the reputation from students and teachers alike of being "crazy" and capable of doing "anything." Coming out of her early family training with basic frustrations and violent aggressiveness issuing
from a deep sense of rejection, Julia found in the life of her
lower-class gangs and cliques not simply approval of habitual
aggression, but a demand for it.

We know, however, that Julia is subject to chronic irrational
fears. What becomes of her dread of hurt and pain in this violent lower-class world? We recall that the pain which Julia fears
and "never could stand" is that of illness, that pain which is unpredictable, and which to a child, has no prospect of ending. In
the fighting and cutting of lower-class life, however, she finds
that people rarely die of sticks, or stones, or even knives. She has
seen her own parents recover rapidly. She herself has been hit
on the head with a brick thrown by a jealous woman. She has
seen men and women beaten, severely cut, and has stood beside
a man when his hat was shot through. She has seen a boy beaten
by another for talking to her and has enjoyed the fame of having
a boy stabbed for her. She knows that blows and cuts seldom
kill and she has become habituated to giving and taking them.
To her, the danger and punishment are slight compared with
the reward, which is the goal response of hitting and hurting
others. Rage is one of the two passions which are real and deep
in Julia's personality. The other is her passion for exploiting—
to be given "good things" or to take them away from others;
sex pleasure is not included. We remember the sadistic streak in
Julia. She enjoys beating people. When she tells of a stabbing
duel between a man and a woman, she comments excitedly,
"And then she pulled out her long knife and started stabbing
him all in the face and on the neck, and she really was putting
it to him, too. She'd put it back in as fast as she could pull it
out." Early experiences like those which Julia had do not make
pleasant people. They make people who want to hurt.

In her fight-gangs Julia found a ready outlet for her chronic
hostility to people. She was constantly reinforced in her resentful attack on life. Embracing a lower-class role, she became more

aggressive and rowdy in her behavior than are most lower-class children. She had no desire to be trained by her mother into middle-class "goodness" and respectability, because she was, above all, instigated to express her animosity against her mother and against life in revenge for the frightful "injustice" which had been done to her when she was incapable of protecting herself. She flees not up but down the class ladder, therefore, because in lower-class modes of action she can shout out her grudge, her unrequited claim against the world.

In addition, her deep-seated fear of all new situations and new learning impels her to flee from the demands for new habits which middle-class contacts would require of her. Just as she left the first grade because she was afraid of school, and later refused to change to a new school, so now she wishes to leave junior high school and to return to the graded school "across-the-tracks," because there she led an unchallenged lower-class existence. This graded school is one of the two Negro schools in the city having an almost homogeneous lower-class student body. Julia remembers with great longing the freedom of her life there and contrasts it with the "stiffness" and class humiliations of her life in the private school where most of the children are "light" and of middle-class families. Her fear of the strange behavioral demands of middle-class and upper-class people and of the punishments which she suffers in relations with them has now carried to the point where she was unwilling to come to the research headquarters at a Negro university. She also refused an invitation to a banquet there because "you have to know how to use your knife and fork."

In the weakness of its controls upon cross-sex relations, lower-class society also provided Julia with a virtually unlimited field for her exploitative passion. In the lower class, a girl cannot depend upon her parents or upon the law to control the fighting, slashing, and promiscuous male. Only a woman's wits, her cunning in playing off one man against another—in exploiting before she is exploited—can protect her. Julia welcomed this pattern of behavior. To her, the world of men appears as a dangerous but booty-laden field of conquest and she counts her trophies proudly and often. She not only seeks a "sucker," but she "bumps his head." "He tells me that he's just a fool. I know he is, and I'm using him for one, too."

But Julia is an Amazon in her coldness toward men, as well as on the field of battle. In this one respect she is not willing to adopt the lower-class modes of behavior. Although she has known exactly how babies are made and born since she was a child of six, she does not now have, nor has she ever had, any enthusiasm for men as sex objects. Her fears of attack are extreme and appear in repeated tales of attempted attacks. Her dreams are full of similar incidents and show a definite fear of penetration. We recall that her worst experience, as she remembers it, was her examination by a physician. This fear has actually had tragic consequences in her case for it led her to marry a man against her will. After one premarital relation, which occurred, she says, at a time when she was drunk, she was frightened by a pain in her stomach. Her present husband told her it was a baby coming. "I was scared. And I didn't want to go to a doctor, I told him, 'cause I didn't like to let them look at me. So I married him. When I found that I wasn't going to have a baby, I got mad at him, and I ain't liked him no more." The husband works out of the city; Julia will not answer his letters, nor does she show any sexual interest in him.

As with all men whom she has known, beginning with her father, Julia was first interested in her husband as a source of money and gifts. She always seeks men out in order to use them, to take from them. Her skill is great and her thirst unquenchable. She takes the lead in sexual advances, next she asks favors and presents, and then she repeats the process without permitting consummation. To Julia, sex is not a reward in itself as it is to most people. The genuine reinforcement to Julia is to "get something"—candy, clothes, money. All her approaches to men are simply instrumental acts toward her real goal, money, and the childish satisfactions which it brings. In the lower class, men are accustomed to giving money to girls, but they are not accustomed to having the sequence stop there. Here Julia's aggression comes to her aid. In fact, this is now the chief use which she makes of her facility in cursing and fighting. After she has been given her presents, she drives off the man by what she calls her "craziness." To men, she is a strange mixture, first a Circe and then a raging Amazon.

The sexual intimidation of this lower-class Negro girl must appear startling to those who think of all Negroes in terms of the American stereotypes concerning "racial" traits. But it has been clear for some time that the conception of "race" as a hereditary control upon behavior must be abandoned. Julia must be understood, therefore, as a human being trained in and restricted by a peculiar social position. In the South, all Negroes are members of a rigidly subordinated lower caste. The fact that Julia was born into this severely underprivileged group means that the social and economic world available to her has been arbitrarily limited. She goes to schools which are inferior even to those which lower-class white children attend. She and her parents constantly face a thoroughly organized occupational blockade which is directed against them as Negroes. Even the fact that her playmates and her neighbors can make a battlefield of "across-the-tracks" and that they can all fight without fear of the white law, is caste controlled. For, as an upper-class white woman in Old City stated, cutting and shooting among Negroes are not regarded as crimes by the white law. A Negro's fighting becomes really criminal and punishable only if he fights a white man.

Julia's adjustment to her caste position is in accord with the basic structure of her personality. Caste is another form of rejection to her and she responds to this, as to all other deprivations, with marked aggression. Within her own family, she explains her abiding hostility to her mother on the grounds that her mother rejects her because "all the rest of the children are lighter than me," and she goes on immediately to say that she was glad when one boy stabbed another over her because she felt "that would make my mama see that somebody does want me." As a matter of fact, Earl, the mother's favorite, is the darkest child. It is true, however, that the mother is light brown, while Julia is quite dark. Julia seizes upon this presumed source of invidious distinction, twists the facts, and asserts that the mother herself makes color the gauge of her love. She can thus avoid admitting even to herself the deeper injustice which the mother has done her and can rationalize, upon this superficial level, her own unrelenting hostility to her mother. But this fear and this hatred have their real source in the early deprivation and traumatic punishment which she suffered at the mother's hands.

In her relations with the white world, Julia feels the sting of systematic deprivation. She says that she wishes that she were white "because white people got all the money." She remembers that when she was a little girl she always sat in the front of the streetcar (in the section for whites), and that her mother had to bring her back to the rear of the car. White boys have called her "nigger" and once when she cursed at them they cut her leg with a stone.

But Julia is not a person to be controlled by force, or to accept rejection meekly. She fights back and returns hate for contempt. "I hate white people," she repeats many times. "I just like to beat on white people. I hate white people. They don't like us, so I don't see why we should like them." She says that she fights white girls on every occasion she can find; she was a member of a clique of girls which regularly fought white school girls until the white principal complained.

In the theater she not only is a trouble-maker in the colored gallery, but as she says, "Sometimes I lean over the banister and spit down on them ol' white people's head." On a bus, when a white girl called her "nigger," Julia began to hit her and was stopped by a colored teacher who was on the bus. On another occasion, in a crowded bus, Julia was called "nigger" by a white woman who was standing beside her. She threatened to "beat up" the white woman, and was prevented by the bus driver himself.

There is strong ambivalence in Julia's feelings toward "white people," however, which constantly leads her to make important reservations with regard to her general creed of hatred. In this respect, her white grandfather occupies a very pleasant niche in her early memories. He not only gave her money and took her to stores, but he actually sat with her on streetcars until the conductor forced him to sit in the white section. The strong positive feeling which she has for this white grandfather has been transferred to other white people who have befriended her and has reinforced her in having pleasant relations with a few "good white people." Side by side with her expressions of hatred for "all white people" and her accounts of fights with whites, there are happy memories not only of her white grandfather but of a white woman who gave Julia's family food and shelter during the flood, of two white children in the country who played with her and let her ride their horse, of a white ticket seller at a theater who even now gives her tickets on credit, and of a white lady who let Julia take her little girl to a theater where only those Negroes who act as nursemaids for white children are admitted.

Her white grandfather and her next older sister have been the only people in her life for whom Julia expresses a warm and abiding human regard, however. Essentially, Julia is a person with a grudge against life itself. It seems in the very beginning to have starved her and robbed her of gratifying and necessary habits, when she was incapable of protecting herself and unable to understand what was asked of her. Her deep animosity toward people stems from the hostile demands and the abrupt, traumatic training which she received from her mother and oldest sister. She has a just, but never to be requited, claim against the universe. Therefore she can never expect anything good of most human beings, nor can she absolve them and her mother from having taken the good things of life away. Long ago, she learned not to expect support and guidance and love, and therefore not to move unless driven. Restitution is not to be made. She must take what will not be given. She must abstract from people, by wile or force, what was taken from her. She will love, genuinely love, only herself.

CHAPTER III

LAUGHING GIRL

MARY HOPKINS comes of a family of laughers, hearty belly-laughers who slap the thigh and raise the roof. Her father is always telling stories and jokes which amuse the family. Mary often laughs when she tells some of the funny things that have happened, such as her grandfather's being drunk and the beatings he got from her grandmother. In a group picture of the family, they are all smiling, down to the smallest boy, and they appear to have natural smiles that come easily.

Mary is a dark-skinned girl of fifteen, slim and strong, with a sweet, mild expression. She has short "bad" hair, a broad nose, and thick lips. She comes from a countrified suburb of New Orleans where all the residents are laboring people. Her father, mother, grandfather, grandmother, and four younger brothers make up the family. Considering that she is a lower-class girl, she is unusually fortunate in having both her parents alive and together.

Mary was uneventfully interviewed by a light, upper-class Negro woman. She was asked to help on the study and was offered friendship and personal aid, if need be, in return. If Mary had any resentment toward her new friend it did not show on the surface; she always insisted that "many bright[1] people are nice to dark people and don't seem stuck up," and implied that the present interviewing situation was a case in point.

Upper-class and middle-class Negroes often criticize lower-class Negroes for being loud, ignorant, black, or dirty persons. If this charge does not appear in a case record, it is safe to assume that the individuals concerned are of lower-class origin. It does not appear in any of Mary's comments or those of her family. In the Hopkins family three generations are found living in the

[1] The term "bright" is used by Negroes in this region to describe light-colored members of their own group.

44

same house and all are of one class position, namely, upper-lower class. There is no rise from grandmother to granddaughter but neither is there any loss. No part of the family has escaped lower-class position and none seems likely to. Mary's family has been on relief since her father broke his arm; the mother did not mind applying for relief nor does Mary mind talking about it.

In the lower class, a child usually knows the mother's side of the family quite well and is able to give adequate information concerning relatives on this side, but he knows little of the father or his people even when the home is intact. This was the case with Mary, and a special interview with the father himself was required to learn something of his parents.

If people have claims of high status to make, they seem bound to make them as soon as occasion offers. Sister's husband is president of the bank; that old piece of furniture belonged to my great-aunt who was the wife of General So-and-so; mother taught school until she was married. Something that grand-father said—"the Doctor, you know"—comes to mind. Only the father in the Hopkins family makes any such claims, and they apply to his father who enjoyed a certain transitory distinction during Reconstruction days. The rest of the family shows an unrelieved record of women working in domestic service and men on common labor jobs, of low school achievement, and of unbroken lower-class participation. Of five uncles on both sides of the family, three are on relief. The other two work, one as a salesman and one as a blacksmith.

People usually live in a residential area with their own social class group, and so it is with the Hopkins family. They live down near the tracks and they know the whiff of coal smoke and the slow pant of the stalled locomotive. In their block there are three saloons and three establishments which sell lottery tickets. Mary says that the colored people in the neighborhood "are noisy and be fighting." One of the few things she is afraid of is going out in this area at night by herself. She has heard much talk of kidnappers and the "gown man," and "besides there is always a mess of drunks on the street, and it just ain't safe."

Mary lives in a narrow, "shot-gun"[2] type of house with her brothers, her father and her mother, and her mother's parents. The grandmother owns the house which has six rooms, three on each side. The house has a toilet, dining room, front room, and three bedrooms for the nine members of the family. There is no bathroom in the house and electricity is provided on one side only. Mary sleeps in one room with her two smallest brothers, aged three and one. The house has a radio and a piano; "the piano was mamma's wedding present."

Mary's maternal grandmother is a lively woman of forty-seven. She married at sixteen, became a grandmother at thirty-two, and still does not take her age too seriously. Her father died when she was young, and she was taken out of school early but not until she had reached the sixth grade. She has been in domestic service all her life; at the present time she owns property, has money in the bank, and has taken out insurance on all members of the immediate family. She has at least one doubtful habit—she plays the lottery consistently, getting her numbers from her little grandson John, aged ten. Mrs. Hopkins says that playing the lottery is foolish and Mary says it is gambling but the grandmother apparently is not bothered by either consideration, or even by the inconsistency of the habit with her religious beliefs.

Mr. Hopkins gives some surprising information about his father, who died a few years ago at the age of ninety-two. He had "been to" college, had practiced law, and had been a policeman and a part-time watch repairer in a neighboring town. This information would be confusing in view of the present state of the Hopkins family but for the reflections that the eldest known Hopkins must have grown to young manhood as a slave (if he were free, it would certainly have been claimed as a mark of distinction); that the "college" of so long ago probably was a graded school by our standards, and that the legal and law-

---

[2] A rectangular, one-story building with two apartments separated by a common wall. The rooms in each apartment are placed one behind the other. The front of such a house points on the street like the muzzle of a double-barreled shot gun.

enforcing aspects of his career probably took place in the un-
settled atmosphere of Reconstruction days. The father evidently settled down to the position of laborer in later life with
a part-time avocation of watch repairing.

On her mother's side, Mary has two living grandfathers, one
the step-grandfather who lives with them now and is married
to her grandmother, the other her real grandfather. Not much
is known about him except that he murdered a man in Mississippi and that the police are after him. He is at present hiding
out in a near-by town. He is said to be a man of fearful temper
who curses dreadfully, but "just can't help it." The grandmother's present husband, known as "grandfather," is sixty-six
years old, is on relief, and is a Baptist like the grandmother.

Mary is not the child of a mixed-class marriage. Her father
and mother come from the same level in the lower-class group
and are well matched as to outlook and habits. Mrs. Hopkins
reached the tenth grade in school and then married at the age
of fifteen. In the early years of her marriage she worked in
domestic service "to he'p her husband out," as a good lower-
class wife should do. After the children came it was more difficult, but she still worked sporadically.

Mr. Hopkins has probably put a deceptively high value on
his class origins, since his present behavior accords so badly
with his alleged start in life. He quit school when he was in the
third grade and even today can read and write only a little, but
he has recently been going to night school to catch up in this
field. When he was a youngster his father tried to teach him
watch repairing but he refused to learn; later he decided to
acquire this trade and worked during spare time for a white
watchmaker. He now has a watch repair shop in the front room
of his house, just as his father did before him. He has never
done "just watch repairing" for a living but has always had some
other, major kind of work on which he depended for support.
He has been a laborer on the railway tracks and on this job got
his finger cut off. Later he worked as a dock worker and according to Mary, "A barrel rolled and hit him in the mouth and
knocked all his front teeth out and now he has gold front

teeth." He is a dark-skinned man who smiles often. Mrs. Hopkins says he is a steady man and a "good provider." He does not drink excessively, or play the lottery, or curse around the house. He shows some interest in a wider social life, as when recently he "got all dressed up, put on plenty of mother's creams and lotions, and came to the P.T.A. meeting." He reported that he enjoyed the meeting very much and wanted Mrs. Hopkins to come with him the next time. In the social ranking order which lower-class people recognize among themselves, he would probably be placed at the top of his class group.

Hopkins may be a solid citizen in his own class but he is not the boss in his own house. This prerogative belongs to Mrs. Hopkins and her mother. Mr. Hopkins explains that he is living in his mother-in-law's house because he had a "little difference" (woman trouble) with Mrs. Hopkins. She left him and came to live with her mother, taking the children with her. When he came to get her, the grandmother refused to let her daughter go back to him because she felt that he might not "treat her right." So Hopkins swallowed his pride and moved in with them. Mary knew all about this situation, and she was asked if she had not been afraid she would not see her father again. She answered, "I was not worried. I knew I would see him again 'cause he always come and get us and I know my mamma always take him back."

Mary had a younger sister who died at the age of nine; the grandmother "took" this child and brought her up. The old lady also tried to make the other children call her "mamma" and in general put in claims as the queen mother. When Mary was small, there was still another important woman in the extended family; this was an aunt of the father's. This aunt used to say, "Mary is my chile," and she claimed to have raised Mary and her sister. Mary indeed puts her mother and grandmother first in her affections and after them her father and grandfather, thus following the hierarchy of their actual authority in the family.

For such a jolly-seeming group there is a surprising amount of aggression shown in the Hopkins family, and it is not at all the exclusive province of the male head of the family. Mary says the mother is always "fussing"—that is, fighting—with the father, "picking on him" about something. Grandmother sets a firm example in this case. It seems that grandfather is a drinking man, sometimes ugly but often jolly when drunk. Recently he came home on a Saturday night much "under the influence," and grandmother "kep' bopping on him all night." The next morning one of the small grandsons asked him how he felt, and the other children all laughed at him. Some years ago the parents used to fight much more than they do now. The children always sided with the mother. Asked if she was scared when they fought, Mary answered, "No, indeed. We be gettin' our licks in too. He got to fight all of us." Once her mother hit her father over the head with a skillet; Mary commented, "When my mamma hit him, we laughed plenty." In the fighting lower class, a well-placed blow does not pass without appreciation. Mary was not ashamed of her parents' fighting and talked about it without emotion; she explained, "Everybody was always fighting." She implies that, in her class, family fighting is conventional. Mr. Hopkins has a sister who is a drunkard and who occasionally comes around to his house in a drunken state; he resents this and beats her up soundly before sending her home.

Mary gets along well with her smaller brothers, though she likes to tease them, but she fights with the two older ones. The oldest one, John, is "mean," and the second, Jimmy, is "tough"; indeed, Mary says, "Jimmy is really bad. He and John have terrible fights. He hates school and don't do good in his work either. He gets left back all the time." At nine years of age he is still only in the second grade and seems a defiant and retarded lower-class boy. Mary herself does not get many whippings and does not, in fact, deserve them; she says her parents do not believe in them, though they whip their children occasionally. Mary affirms that she herself does not like to fight but repeats the lower-class cliché that "she won't take nothin' off nobody." Once when another girl threatened Mary, Mrs. Hopkins told her "if she didn't beat that girl she would give *her* a licking." Mary beat the girl. The training of children for actual self-defense is one of the most necessary teachings in the lower-class family, and the parents usually see to it that children learn to rely on themselves and not on their absent parents, or an apathetic policeman for defense.

There survive in the Hopkins family magical beliefs which have been transmitted to Mary, and continue to affect her attitudes in spite of the teaching against magic carried on by the public schools. The finger of suspicion is pointed at her grandfather, that loud and often amiable man who regularly comes rolling home on Saturday nights. At times he is a sinister figure to Mary. For example, when she is housecleaning she always cleans his room with particular care, "'cause he ain't gonna put no powder in his room and have it working on me." It is further believed in the family that he once tried to poison the grandmother for her insurance. Mary says, "He likes to cook, but I won't eat none of his cooking." It may be that the grandfather, out-generaled by the women in the family, has taken to magical acts as a surreptitious form of counteraggression. Certainly his behavior illustrates a form of outmoded dogma and practice that still persists in the lower class.

A difference in the sexual mores between the lower class and middle class has been widely noticed by students of Negro life. These differences are real, not just the product of a romantic wish on the part of biased observers. The lower class has a sexual code of its own, though, to be sure, it is a code and not a mandate to license, as many middle-class people think.

It was nevertheless somewhat surprising to discover from gentle Mary that grandmother has a "boy friend," and that Mary knows all about this affair. Some neighbors assert that the Reverend Jackson, the biggest Negro minister in the community, is the man; gossips even say that grandmother feeds him chicken dinners every day. But Mary doubts this "'cause Brother Ira was her boy friend, and he comes to her house all the time." Mary knows for a fact also that "Brother" Ira came to live at the house when the grandfather was "gone" and he comes frequently now when "grandpa ain't home." As for Reverend Jackson, Mary hears that he has at least three girl friends. He drinks too, she knows, because "he sends down to the beer parlor for beer and sets up and gets drunk with grandfather."

Mr. Hopkins is not suffering deprivation in this field either. He, too, has a girl friend. Mary often hears her mother tell him to "get out and get over to that little gal you're going with." Mrs. Hopkins has left him several times for short periods on this account. Mr. Hopkins also has two older daughters by another woman; these girls live in New York but write to him all the time. Mary does not know whether Mr. Hopkins and their mother were married or not, and it is to be suspected that they were not. Although the father does not drink or gamble, sex relations outside of marriage are obviously not objectionable to him.

Mary also knows her mother's boy friend. He is "Brother" Butler. Butler comes to the house frequently when the father is away. Mary tries not to overhear his conversations with her mother and often has to play the piano very loud when they are around in order not to hear them. Mary appeared to sympathize with her mother's actions but also profited from the situation herself by blackmailing "Brother" Butler. "I told him to pay me to keep my mouth shut and he give me a nickel." Asked how she felt about her mother and father having "friends," Mary answered, "It don' make no difference to me 'cause all the rest got 'em."

It is not uncommon in Mary's neighborhood for girls to become pregnant before marriage. She named six or seven girls between the ages of thirteen and seventeen who had babies before they were married. Some were "saved" and some were "sinners," but the churchgoers among them were not punished by the church in any way. Some of the parents of the pregnant girls want them to get married but some do not attempt to make them marry if the girls are unwilling. Mary's objection to premarital pregnancy has a practical rather than a moral turn; for her, it means the end of carefree girlhood and the adoption of adult status. She says she does not see much of those girls from her play group who become pregnant because "they don't have no more time to play and be runnin' around"; but she

does not think that association with such girls would be de
clined by her friends for moral reasons.

Mary's own sexual behavior will be discussed in connection
with her personality, but it will be noted for the moment that
her brothers, aged nine and ten, are apparently already having
intercourse. Mary does not know this for a fact, but she knows
the little girls they go with, and considers them "fast."

There is one form of sexual behavior which the lower class
does not countenance, namely, association between colored
women and white men. Colored women who behave in this
way are isolated by the lower class and expelled from the group
into a subsociety of their own. Mary notes, for instance, that
there was a white man "going with a lady" who lived next door
to her family. Asked if this lady were a friend of her mother's,
Mary denied it. "They talked, but she wasn't nice, and my
mother don't go with them." Mary added, however, that the
white man, a bus driver, does not beat the girl as some colored
men do their wives, but "people talks about her all the time."
This "talking" is the group mode of directing scorn at her and
isolating her from the society of upper-lower-class people.

Mary and all the other Hopkins children go to the local
Baptist church. Grandmother, who is a strong Baptist, sees to
this. Mary, however, does not "belong" to the church; she is
still in the status of a "sinner" or person who has not undergone
the ritual of joining the church. The reason is that she does not
feel herself a good enough person to join. The church denounces gambling, dancing, and card playing, but Mary dances
nevertheless, and says that it is old-fashioned to forbid dancing;
"anyway, everybody dance." But she does not play cards because "that's gambling." Mary reported that she went to a
dance on Sunday, a fact which emphasizes the difference between her and a middle-class Protestant child to whom Sunday
would be sacred and Sunday dancing forbidden.

Mary's grandmother "gets happy" all the time in church and
"shouts," and Mary has seen her in these states repeatedly. Mary
is too shy to shout herself but she thoroughly approves this be-

havior and perhaps she will shout one day. Mr. Hopkins attends the Church of the Living God (Sanctified) and goes into religious transports; Mary has seen him "dance" in front of the church and was startled to hear him speak in an unknown tongue. At first, she says, she was inclined to laugh, but not later, as she grasped the full meaning of this behavior. The mother is an uncertain church member; she used to be devout, but no longer is interested. Mary says, "She done got out. An' my grandmother, she be always after her and fussing for getting out of the church." It is an impressive fact that the mother can resign from the church as if it were a club. No lower-middle-class person could do this, because in the middle class it would mean a rejection of personal ethical values. But for Mrs. Hopkins and most lower-class people, ethics and religion are separated; the church is a social ritual. A sign of her present nonconformity is the fact that she dances. Perhaps she will join again some day and if she does, it will make no drastic change in her daily life.

One of the most striking differences between lower-lower-class and upper-lower-class people is the great role that organizations and associations play in the lives of the latter. The upper-lower-class people are churchgoers and lodge members, and thereby they achieve a wider and more solid type of social participation. This is well shown in Mary's community. When asked who the leading Negro in her area was, she indicated a preacher, saying, "Reverend Young. I guess he's the biggest. Everybody goes to him for everything. Anybody in trouble, they go to him—when they sick or in jail or need money or anything. And it don't make no difference if they belong to his church or not. Half the people go to him ain't members of his church." The Reverend Young is a genuine leader of his class; and it is noteworthy that he is not a doctor, lawyer, or teacher, but the head of a religious organization.

Mr. Hopkins shows the tendencies of his class in this respect. He is a "jack-leg," or fill-in, preacher himself. He is a member of the National Association for the Advancement of Colored People and as we have already noted he has been known to turn up at a P.T.A. meeting. He tries also to encourage the others in his family to copy his forms of participation and thus sets an example for Mary.

The mother and grandmother are said to have recourse to church and society meetings "for fun." Both belong to the "Young Ladies" club, the chief function of which is described by Mary as follows: "They all dress up and turn out when you die, and you pay your dues and they pay for your funeral." The "Young Ladies" should not be contemptuously dismissed by anyone; many are those who are ashamed that they have never been able to join.

Everyone lives his actual personal life in relation to a small circle of intimate friends, that is, his clique. This clique is very likely to be composed of persons of the same class status. The banker may be a man of fine human sensibilities but he rarely invites the ditch-digger to dinner. The members of Mary's clique are as like as the proverbial peas so far as class status is concerned. She named seven girls who are members of her intimate group. All but two of them live within two blocks of her own house. Their mothers are friends and co-religionists of Mrs. Hopkins, and their fathers are or have been laborers on local jobs. They rank in age from thirteen to seventeen, and are in grades from fifth to ninth. Like Mary, they are on the average somewhat retarded in school. Sara Belle is Mary's best friend. She finished the sixth grade last year at the age of sixteen, then left school to get married. Sara Belle "has religion" and sings in the choir. Before her marriage she lived with her aunt who is a good friend and former schoolmate of Mrs. Hopkins. Three of Mary's seven girl friends are called "real nice," meaning that they do not permit sexual approaches from boy friends and that they approach middle-class standards. One girl is known to have intercourse with her boy friend and she is teased about it but not rejected in any other way. The clique meets often at Mary's house to play games and dance. The boys in the group are evidently members of the upper-lower-class group; they are factory workers, lottery agents, and the like. The clique is primarily based on area and does not seem to include

Mary's schoolmates; perhaps the reason for this is that she attends a school outside the area in which she lives.

The story of Sara Belle's marriage indicates the kind of life that Mary herself looks forward to. Sara Belle still lives near the tracks. Her husband works in the mill. She got a new bedroom set from her husband as a wedding present; it is almost paid for. Sara Belle was courted for some time, and her marriage was not forced. She had a regular wedding at which Mary was present and wore pink. Sara Belle got presents in abundance; "my mamma gave her some perfume to smell sweet when she was married, and I gave her some powder and a comb for her hair. Mos' everybody gave her something."

On the other hand, Mary described two of her friends who got married recently but not until "they were showing plenty"; and Phoebe, a third friend, who "was going to get married, but her husband he got put in the pen." These intimates of the clique are important because it is they who reward or punish behavior, who make evaluations in terms of which their fellow clique member sees himself. These examples show the actual behavior patterns which are expected of Mary.

Mary, who, like her friends, is a child of a domestic servant, knows how to do all kinds of work such as cooking, scrubbing, cleaning, washing, and ironing. She helps her mother with the housework as much as her school requirements permit. She is in grade 8B at school, indicating some retardation for her age of fifteen years. Like other lower-class people, she has a vague faith in education, but the passionate drive for "schooling" so characteristic of middle-class parents and children is simply not there.

Scientists have shown that when a brood of chicks is hatched and allowed to move freely in quest of food, a "pecking order" is rapidly established; this pecking order is a scale of dominance or superiority in which all the chicks are ranked. The chick at the top of the order will scare away any other chick from a morsel of food, and the chick below will yield without resistance to the superior one. The Hopkins family has a social rank which has been described as "upper-lower class." Far above them they see the "big Negroes" of the upper group; in their own neighborhood, they look down upon the people of lower-lower class. Their main wish seems to be to stay where they are, not to go up and certainly not to go down. Only a large amount of unexpected money, or the development of skills difficult to acquire, could start them on the road upward. They have suffered pinched circumstances with the rest of the lower class since the advent of the depression, but have maintained their relative position in the structure. There is no push from the family toward upward mobility, no mixed-class marriage to hold up ideals of a higher status to be gained. As it was in the beginning, so it is now, and so it shall be for generations to come; there is no one to teach them the strange habits of another class when their contacts with middle-class people are so few.

The security of the family is well shown by the fact that there are no complaints about the "tough going" of present times. They would prefer not to live on relief, but what can they do? The family is secure also in having ready and unhindered access to the basic goals: food, shelter, clothes, sex, and aggressive responses can all be made; these goal responses in turn reinforce the Hopkins' lower-class folkways. There is no bothersome goal of high status to lure them into anxious days and wakeful nights. Mary shares in this confident atmosphere. Her grandmother assures her that even should her parents desert her, which is highly improbable, she could always count on Granny to take care of her. Another element in the family security lies in the fact that the parents are not thinking of sending the children to college and do not imagine for their children a status much higher than their own. The insurance agent may say, "Madam, have you considered the advantages of one of our educational savings policies in educating your child?" but the door slams in his face on a gale of laughter.

Mary seems to have only two wishes that might be described as evidence of mobility strivings, that is, of a yearning to change her class position. She would like to have long hair like her mother and she would like to finish high school and be a nurse. Long, straight hair is, of course, a class mark, since it is often found on lighter Negroes of higher status; Mary's hair is short and kinky. She says her hair "started out" to be long, but she cut it off once and "it didn't never grow back right." But for this mischance, she feels, it might have been longer than it is now. The grandmother would like to see Mary finish high school and become a nurse if she wants to; after all, there is no tuition for nurses in her city, and high school is the top of the academic mobility ladder visible to these people. Mr. Hopkins says he has no ambitions for Mary. Her future, he remarked a little obliquely, "will be taken care of by Mrs. Hopkins and her mother." If Mary wishes to be a nurse, he would not mind. "That wouldn't cost much money and wouldn't take long." Mary herself would like to be a nurse; a number of surgical operations in the family have called her attention to this profession. But she is evidently not certain she will be able to finish high school and qualify, for she says, "If I can't be a nurse, I guess I'll learn to sew."

An alternative and much more probable solution for Mary is to marry. She does not expect to marry until she is nineteen and has finished school. She would like to marry a man with "plenty money and good education." The man must be able to "look after her," for she does not want to marry and then have to go back to her family. Plenty of money, she specified, would be the $20 a week which is paid at the mill, and a good education, presumably, would be one equivalent to her own. None of those boys who can barely read and write for her! She hopes she will not have to work after marriage, but her husband will certainly expect her to work in case of need; this necessity will not seem so bitter a blow as it would to a middle-class woman. Mary was surprised when the interviewer asked her if she expected her husband to give her a better home than her parents had provided, and reminded the worker that she was "living in a six-room house now." The only thing her husband could give her that her parents did not have "would be better furniture and that would be just 'cause it's new." Mary will make a good marriage according to her standards because she does not expect anything that is not easily accessible in her world.

Asked to express her three strongest wishes, Mary said, "A gold front tooth; a twin sweater and roller skates; and to finish high school." The first two seem much nearer of attainment than the third, but all three are possible and practical; by their modest character they indicate also the outlook of her class group.

In passing, it is noted that the five children, formerly seven, in the Hopkins family are a hindrance to mobility. Parents of any status who wish to "push" their children do well not to have too many of them. There must be a little platform of capital to shove under the feet of the mobile children, for higher status costs money to acquire as well as to maintain. Money is, of course, not "everything" but it is often translated gradually into class behavior on which the society places high value.

Perhaps the strongest element in the immobility of the Hopkins family is the fact that they are not punished by discriminatory attention from, and invidious comparison with, the group next above them in the social scheme. Their immunity to punishment is a result of their physical and social isolation from lower-middle-class people. On the other hand, in their neighborhood, there are lower-lower-class people; in contrast to them the Hopkinses have a comfortable feeling of being well placed and secure. The upper-lower class is economically better off, more highly organized as to church and lodge, and well connected with white people who can and will aid in an emergency; in comparison, the lower-lower class is economically insecure, poorly organized, and unbefriended. Since upper-lower-class people are quite conscious of how well off (relatively) they already are, there is little incentive to change.

The Hopkinses rank high in their class, and they are aware of being a "nice" family. Although much like lower-lower class in some of their behavior patterns, such as sexual behavior, they are also conscious that Mr. Hopkins does not curse around the house, does not gamble, and does not drink. The grandmother is very well placed in the community, having as her friends, and even "boy friends," the leading people of the neighborhood. Mary knows that she will have as a legacy these

times. Her grandmother, by intuition or training, was especially solicitous of her at this time and would try to relieve her
pain and soothe her. A pacifier was given the child, sometimes
a sugar teat, sometimes a piece of fat tied to a string. Apparently
Mary learned then that when she cried someone would come to
help because she still cries in conflict situations.

A new child was born when Mary was fifteen or sixteen
months old; Mary was especially "bad" for many months thereafter. She began to cry more, eventually learned to take the
baby's bottle and drink from it, and would sometimes pinch
the baby. Her mother treated this misbehavior by spanking
her and "hollering at her." Two acts at the age of about two
and a half years are remembered by her mother which may be
an evidence that this dislike for the baby was displaced to other
objects: first, she disliked dolls and promptly smashed one that
was given her; second, she took her pet poodle and threw it
into the water closet, where it drowned horribly. She bitterly
mourned this dog even though her mother told her it would
come back. She may have learned at this time to be frightened
by the consequences of aggression and may have begun the attempt to check it before it could lead to dangerous results.

Cleanliness training was begun at one year; the mother
spanked her or shouted at her for failures, but the grandmother
apparently rewarded her for success. The grandmother says
that at this time, and from this time on, Mary seemed to prefer
to be with her rather than her mother; the grandmother says
that her daughter had little patience in training Mary and that
therefore Mary's devotion shifted to her.

The mother and grandmother also carried out their respective techniques with regard to sexual training. The mother
spanked and shouted at her whenever she found Mary was
"playing with herself"; the grandmother also discouraged her,
but more gently. Mrs. Hopkins thinks that probably Mary "did
it" when she was alone, however, because a good deal of dis-
couragement was required. It seems possible that this training
laid the foundation for a passive and frightened character so
far as sex matters are concerned, although we have not enough

detailed knowledge of the early events to relate them exactly to her present life. Since Mary slept with her parents up to a late age, and since her parents had sex relations during this time, she must have been aware of them, but we do not know with what effect. Many children are both frightened and excited by this experience.

She was spanked for peeking at her little brothers, as well as for allowing little boys to examine her; to this day she locks all doors leading into her room when she is dressing or undressing and denies that she knows what males "are like." She received no sex information from her mother directly (more middle-class than lower-class in this respect), but did have secret access to a "book" around the house which she read behind her mother's back. On the whole, her experiences with sex seem to have had painful and forbidding consequences, of which the worst was loss of favor with the much-prized mother and grandmother.

After the first years of training, which, of course, Mary does not remember, she was not whipped much. She says that her parents did not believe in indiscriminate whipping, a detail which probably differentiates their behavior from that of a lower-lower-class family. The latter seem to beat their children daily whether they need it or not. The worst whipping Mary remembers getting from her mother was at the time when she knocked a vase off a mantelpiece. Her father whipped her when she was about six for taking his watch-making tools. Evidently destruction of property was a matter on which the parents were willing to be severe. Mary does not, however, view her childhood as one long misery. On the contrary, she remembers "lots of parties" at which she had a wonderful time. She always had a birthday party with ice cream and cake, and everybody gave her presents. She seems to have no complaints or regrets.

It has already been noted that when she is teased, Mary cries rather than fights, and this trait has been tentatively attributed to the stern taboo upon aggression to which she was subjected as a small child. Both the fear of losing her mother's favor if she showed aggression, and the early-appearing relief from adults which usually followed her crying, helped to reinforce her nonaggressive behavior. She still has "cry-baby ways" and they seem to have been intensified a few years ago when she was twelve or thirteen. The current impression she gives is one of timidity. She admits that she is moved to cry and "shout" at funerals, but gets up and leaves the church rather than yield to the impulse. She is evidently too shy to express emotion publicly. Mrs. Hopkins says that no one has any trouble with Mary. All the teachers praise her as a very good child.

The only one who seems to disapprove of her is her father, and she quarrels with him all the time. Mary says her father is mean and she intimates that he is a tightwad. To have this kind of father is evidently a surprise to a lower-class girl; a father ought to be more of a "good-timey" man, more free with his money. To her father, Mary is evidently the symbol of the embattled females in the family, a fact particularly irritating to him because she ought to be subordinate to him on the ground of both age and filial relationship. Nevertheless, Mary helps her father with another of his sidelines, umbrella mending, and "goes everywhere with him." He has money and she can always be sure of wheedling or teasing some out of him. As a smaller child, she was evidently fonder of him. Once when he was to have an operation, they all cried when he left, "'n his hat was hangin' on the wall, 'n every time we'd look at it we'd cry, so mamma had to take it down 'til he came back." Evidently the father is not so deprived of the affection of his family as he might seem to be at first. It is always possible, too, that he and Mary quarrel just to show that they are less fond of each other than they really are. People have been known to act so.

On class grounds, Mary ought to have a boy friend and not be ashamed of it. Evidently, however, her early training on sex and personality grounds does not permit her to make full use of the freedom which her lower-class position allows her. At first, she denied that she had a boy friend at all, saying, "I don't like no ole boy kissin' me or nothin' like that." Later she admitted that she had had two boy friends, Louis and Claude, both workers in the local factory. Her current friend is Joe, a lottery writer. Mary does not drink ("seen enough drinking, the way my grandpa he get drunk all the time"), and will not kiss a boy except in one of the kissing games which her clique plays. The group evidently foregathers at her house, and her parents pay no attention to what they do. Boys occasionally approach her for sexual intercourse, but she says, "No, I ain't doing that." She admits she might say "Yes" before she gets married, but thinks it improbable because "it don't interest me." The dilemma of the lower-class girl with regard to sex is that there is no one to police her a good part of the time when she is at home—the parents are gone and the boys come around. But Mary knows how to meet this situation too; she says, "I don't never let them inside the house unless someone is home. Even if you don't do nothin', people talk about you, and my mother says to keep 'em out." Her mother has told her that intercourse "might ruin you for life and you don't ever be well again."

In spite of these instructions it is still a puzzle why Mary shows so little interest in boys. Judging from the behavior of her parents and clique associates, it would be almost a matter of social conformity for her to begin her sex life at this time. Is she perhaps not telling the truth? This seems unlikely, since everything else she has told us seems to be true. More probably the answer lies in her appearance and her personality history. Mary is not a good-looking girl and has "bad" traits of color, feature, and hair. She is also a rather passive type of girl. Apparently she does none of the teasing which men invariably recognize as a sex lure. She puts the total burden of sexual aggression upon the boys, who probably consider it too much of a job to pursue her vigorously enough to overcome her resistance. There seems little doubt, however, that this state of affairs is transitory and that she will eventually follow the customs of her class—if not before, then after, marriage. This may well occur just at that time when the authority of her beloved mother and grandmother is reduced, and she attains the full status of a woman who no longer expects to have time "just to play."

A final word about her health and intelligence. According

to the medical report she shows no evidence of syphilis, a statement necessary to make in respect to any lower-class child, however jarring the detail may be with respect to gentle Mary. On the Stanford-Binet she showed an I.Q. of 91. It seems likely that this is a measure of her class opportunity for attainment as much as of her native endowment.

One must remember that there is a white lower class also, and that in it there are millions of people whose behavior is very similar to that of Mary and her family. There is little that is peculiar to Negroes in the description of Mary's life and class. The critical fact is that a much larger proportion of all Negroes are lower class than is the case with whites. This is where caste comes to bear. It puts the overwhelming majority of Negroes in the lowest class group, and keeps them there.

What cannot be cured, for the moment at least, must be endured. Let us see how the Hopkins family and Mary have learned to adjust to their color-caste subordination. Their policy may be stated in a word, "submit"—to all but the most violent and most direct of physical assaults. When Mary was asked how she felt about being colored, she said, "I don't mind being jes' like Gawd made me. He made colored people so I guess He must want 'em, and so I don't mind being colored." Mary knew that a policeman had shot a Negro man from her neighborhood while he was in jail, but she did not express anger or protest. Asked if she minded riding in the back of the bus, she said, "I jes' go on to the back. That's the place they got for us. You don't never get in trouble like that." She says that she has never fought with white children but just leaves them alone and pays no attention. Queried as to whether she minded white people's addressing grown-up colored people as "Girl," and "Boy," or calling them by their first names, she answered, "No, because you know they ain't going to call you nothing else."

Mrs. Hopkins has carefully instructed Mary in caste etiquette as she understands it. Mary is to avoid temptations to fight white people. "Don't pay any attention, come on home—sit in the rear of the bus 'cause that's their bus anyhow!" Mary says, "Two blocks from us they was a whole bunch of white children and every time we'd walk that way they'd call us names, and so my mother she made us stop going down there 'cause my little brothers they would fight 'em, and my mother don't want us gettin' in no fights with white children." (Mother knew that a small colored boy, victor in a gang fight, might be punished as an adult criminal!) Mary reports also that white people live on the same street with her family, but they do not mix. "Sometimes I hear 'em say 'Nigger,' but I wouldn't do nothing. Jes' act like you don't hear 'em." Asked further if this made her angry, Mary said, "No ma'am, I don't think about it." In examining this aspect of her life, of course, we must remember Mary's passive character and her lack of aggression within her own class group; a more aggressive lower-class child would undoubtedly respond with more spirit than she does. Her small brother Jimmy, for instance, is more of a fighter. "He ain't scared of nobody, 'n he'll call white children names quick as not."

A strong example of self-defensive rage against whites has been furnished to the Hopkins children by their father. Once a drunken white man picked a fight with him; he knocked the man down and went home to get his gun, expecting to have to shoot it out, but the police came and, when a tavern keeper also complained against the white man, they took the white man home. They did not lock him up for assaulting Mr. Hopkins, however. "Father was real mad that time." Lower-class Negroes are accustomed to fighting in their own group and will fight whites in case of direct assault.

Mary says that the "white folks" for whom her mother and grandmother work are nice. They all sent her presents at Christmas time. She works occasional Saturdays herself and once made eighty cents for a day's work; she says the people were "nice" to her. Negroes who work as domestic servants do have many pleasant contacts with white people and tend to be bound to them by services mutually rendered. They have the best chance to know middle-class and upper-class white people and to form opinions concerning them. Probably the white people in return have a chance to experience the full humanity and sympathy of their Negro servants, and to learn how exceptionally "nice" a Negro can be.

Mary also says that the white adults who live in her block are nice; they never call the police even though there is much disorderly conduct among Negroes in the area. She seems to be particularly impressed by this fact, as if the reverse were rather to be expected.

Regarding light-skinned people, Mary claims to have no resentment. She says that her father has "plenty of bright kinfolk, but I don't see 'em that often to know 'em good." Is this perhaps a veiled criticism of the lighter people, after all? About light Negroes who "pass for white," she says phlegmatically, "Gawd made 'em colored, but if they want to pass, that ain' my business. I can't pass." She thinks nevertheless that some, but not all, light-skinned people are prejudiced against dark-skinned Negroes. Even against those light-skinned Negroes who are "uppity," she seems to feel no resentment. Here again, her unprotesting personality makes itself evident in her judgment of people above her on the status scale; many dark Negroes hate their lighter castemates and feel the pressure of their discrimination more keenly than Mary does.

And yet, even into the placid spirit of Mary Hopkins, there has come the vision of the promised land, of escape from the chains of caste. She would prefer to live in New York, where her father's other daughters live, or in Chicago with her grandmother's sister. There "white and colored can go to school together, and sit together on the streetcars, and a colored person is just as good as a white person. I'd like that."

CHAPTER IV

NAMELESS BOY

THE SCENE, as the dramatist says, was an empty classroom; the time, midsummer. Three small Negro boys, among them Edward Dodge, were awaiting an interview. The secretary reports:

The three boys sat in my office talking to me while they waited for the interviewer. "Do you lock everything up at night? You don't leave nothin' around, do you?" one boy asked.

"Oh, no. Everything is either locked up or taken out of the building," I answered. "Why?"

"The boys 'round here will take anything. Not so much big stuff like a typewriter or desk maybe, but do you-all leave desks here at night?"

"Why, yes. Nobody could slip a desk under his coat and run, you know," I laughed.

"But they'd do anything. They used to get in here and steal stuff out of that closet right behind you."

"How do they do it?" I asked.

"Well," answered Lester, "one of them talks to the guy and then the others get the stuff. 'Course me, I don't do it, me!" The other boys laughed. "Boys go to the stores 'round here, and they get all kinda stuff like that and little stuff like candy." (It was obvious that he spoke from experience.) "But when the police catch ya, I jes say I ain't seen nothin'. I don't know nothin', and I'm careful. I ain't gonna get myself in jail."

This should have been fair warning, but middle-class white interviewers learn slowly. The Doc, as the boys called him, finished the first day of hard work, listened to the dying swish of his new fan, and left for home, grateful to be free of the bare, scrubbed interior of his classroom "office" in a Negro public school. The moment he left, so excellently prearranged, there was a patter of bare feet, a brown hand yanked the fan wire from its socket, and in two minutes the fan was gone and the schoolyard clear. The janitor came in after ten minutes, but thought the secretary had locked the fan up in the cabinet; the secretary had left it to the janitor.

Next morning everyone agreed, at least, that the fan was gone. Suspicion centered on Edward and his two pals. They firmly denied the charge. The Doc was helpless; how could he use boys as informants when he first had to convict them of a theft? There were interviews and interrogations. Finally, Charlie, the janitor, broke the case by securing partial confession from the weakest and most stupid boy. Charlie emphasized particularly the dangers of a boy's falling into the hands of the police, how he was beaten, and so forth. With the three boys in one room, surrounded by determined adults (mostly middle-class Negroes, proud of their school and its reputation), the boys gave in bit by bit. An admission by one was followed by an accusation from another. The truth appeared to be that Lester actually took the fan. Edward got a bathing suit in which it was wrapped up while being carried off the school grounds. The three boys tried to sell it to several laymen, but all were suspicious that it was useless or stolen. Finally they went to "The Greek's," a well-known "fence" in the area. The Greek evidently suspected that the article was stolen, but nevertheless ran it for an hour to make sure it was not damaged. Meanwhile the boys waited, visions of movies, ice cream cones, and snowballs ever brighter in their minds. For some reason, the Greek became suspicious and called the police. As the squad car drove up, the boys spotted it and ran. The police gave enthusiastic chase but could not catch the thieves in their familiar alleys. The Greek then took the fan to police headquarters, where it was later retrieved by its saddened owner.

This was, to say the least, a stirring introduction to Edward Dodge. Before interviewing could proceed, Edward had to tell the truth about the fan affair, and he did, confirming the account here given. He added that he had wanted a pair of tennis shoes and that "the boys" told him that his share would be a dollar. With this sum he could have bought a pair. By way of defense he stated that it was not his idea to steal the fan and that he had never been sent to the "Home" (Detention Home for Juvenile Offenders), while the other boys had.

Edward is a slim, strong boy of thirteen. He has brown skin with a coppery underglow, kinky hair, and Negroid features. His clothes seem to consist of odds and ends of apparel. They were ragged and patched, but clean, when he came for interviews. He was always barefooted in summer. He is the only child of a hearty woman who has never been married to any man, though she has been common-law wife of two. When questioned about his family, Edward talked readily enough about his mother and "stepfather," but when he was asked what his "real daddy" was like, he broke into tears. He managed to say that his father had left home when Edward was a year and a half old, that he had then gone somewhere else to work, and had died. He talked brokenly between sobs and said he always cried when anyone asked about his "real" father. Edward's behavior was so arresting that the interviewer changed the subject at the time, but came back to it many days later; on the second occasion, as on the first, Edward cried and became incoherent.

There were inevitable questions in the Doc's mind: Why should a boy show such grief about a father whom he had never known as a social being? Should not Edward have been too tough to have such sentimental feelings? Here was a mystery, and mysteries are not avoided by the conscientious historian of human lives, rather they are the cues that point the way to important, though perhaps concealed, information. The solution had to wait, however, and the work with Edward was continued.

It cannot be said that Edward was a good informant or that he ever told his most intimate thoughts or feelings, but fortunately for the interviewer, he had never learned to conceal them as adults do. Three factors conspired to make the relationship a difficult one. First, there was the social gulf between the lower-class boy and the middle-class white interviewer. This was concretely expressed in the white linen clothes the Doc wore, the university he came from, the automobile he drove, the spending money he had in his pocket, the strangeness of his speech, and a thousand other details. For example, Edward once accepted a cigarette from his friend but smoked only a third of it, then crushed it out and put the butt in his pocket; he next inquired how much the Doc's cigarettes cost (more than his, of course), and showed some of the envy in his soul that the Doc could spend more for cigarettes and smoke them so freely. Every class comparison of this kind is a jolt to the self-esteem of the person with "inferior" status; it does not increase rapport in the interviewing situation. The relationship was made still more difficult by the age difference between the two persons. Lower-class children have learned by hard knocks to expect punishment and betrayal from adults in whom they confide. The interviewing took place in the very school building which Edward attended in winter; for him it was undoubtedly full of the ghosts of authority. These circumstances of age and authority served to make him suspicious and uncommunicative. Finally, Edward was a gang boy and was himself implicated in illegal operations. He was afraid he might disclose information which would put him at the Doc's mercy; then he would be accused of "ratting" on the other boys if the Doc should betray him. Ratting often brings serious penalties from the members of the gang.

The result was what might have been expected. Edward kept several appointments and then stopped coming. But the Doc understood what was going on and did not blame Edward; instead he tried to make him "want" to come. Knowing the great value lower-class Negro boys put upon passes to the movies and Coca-Colas, he decided to use these as rewards. He told Edward and the other boys that he would issue a card good for one Coca-Cola after each hour of interviewing, and further, that if a boy came all five days of the week, he would receive two movie passes on Saturday morning. This was not to be considered as payment (since a boy ought to help with the study out of self-interest), but to be merely a "treat." At any rate it worked, after a fashion. Edward came regularly.

Unfortunately, however, the reward seemed to reinforce only his coming to the interview; it did not succeed in making him talk spontaneously while there. As a result, the work had to proceed by badgering Edward with questions, and its success depended entirely on the Doc's ingenuity in thinking up things to ask, rather than on Edward's genuine cooperation. It continued on this basis. Another handicap, not appreciated until after the research was finished, was Charlie, the janitor. Charlie himself was something of an expert with boys, and thought he knew better than the Doc what the boys should talk about. He instructed them not to give certain family and personal information on the ground that it was not really pertinent to the research; since Charlie was a powerful adult, and near at hand, his advice was followed in part. Charlie was supposed at first to be a friend of the project, but he proved not to be so and to his duplicity may be laid many of the defects of the case.

The discussion may now safely shift to what was learned about Edward, rather than how it was learned. Although Edward was forced to change his living arrangements before the interviews were over, at the time they began it was found that he lived in a two-room "apartment" which is reached by walking down a long alley between two ramshackle houses. Directly before the front door hung a clothesline, on which were a pair of step-ins, a pair of men's overalls, and other articles of clothing. The unscreened windows of the house were an invitation to flocks of mosquitoes. But the place was clean and pleasant smelling. Edward and his mother and her boy friend, when he was there, lived in the one room and kitchen. There was no telephone, bath tub, running water, or electric light in the house. There was a fenced-in toilet in the yard, and a tap for running water near it. Edward's mother, Mrs. Martin, paid $1.75 per week as rent for the two rooms, a lower-lower-class rental. Through the thin walls of the apartment, one could easily hear what the neighbors next door were saying and doing. Privacy is indeed a class-typed luxury!

The Doc was informed that Edward slept with his mother in the one (double) bed. Where he slept when his stepfather

was residing in the house was not indicated. The neighborhood
is a hive of such apartments—hot, bare, ill-equipped. The surrounding streets are unpaved, dusty in summer and muddy
gulches in spring and winter. There are a great many saloons
and beer parlors, the social clubs of lower-lower-class people.
Edward once remarked, "When the men get drunk over there,"
pointing to the saloon near by, "they do plenty cutting." In
this neighborhood one is seldom out of range of an automatic
victrola; it seemed most incongruous to hear the sensuous voice
of Ella Fitzgerald blaring forth a nursery rhyme early in the
morning from a beer parlor near Edward's house. "A tiss-kit,
A tass-kit, A green-and-yellow bass-kit, I sent a let-tuh . . . ."

Edward had no information to offer about his "real" daddy
nor yet about Mr. Martin, his stepfather. Lower-class children
rarely know much about the male line in the family. But the
mother and her people are more important and are known.
Both maternal grandparents came from rural Louisiana and
both were tenants in the cane fields. Both were Baptists, and
the grandmother, at least, could read and write. Later the
grandmother was a domestic servant, first in New Orleans and
then in New York. Mrs. Martin's sister was also a servant; she
was sent as a child to work for a "white lady" in New York.
There was no mention whatsoever of notable ancestors in Edward's family, and it is to be inferred that he comes of a most
inconspicuous line.

Mrs. Martin is herself a domestic servant and has been such
throughout Edward's life. She is a dark-brown woman of marked
Negroid type. Her wide and ready smile reveals a number of
gold teeth in the front of her mouth. At the time of the first
interview she had on blue slacks with a white polo shirt, somewhat torn but clean, and a pair of felt slippers. She made no
apology for her dress. She accepted the Doc's cigarettes, but
made no effort to get him an ashtray when he smoked. She
seemed a competent, independent woman from near the bottom of lower class, and not very sorry for herself.

Martin, consort to Mrs. Martin for the last nine years, is tall
and dark, much darker than his wife. When interviewed, he

wore no coat, and his shirt was tieless and open at the throat. His wife has complaints about him: he drinks and gambles; he is jealous of her and tries to prevent her going to dances and beer places (where she could meet other men). She said she had kicked him out a number of times for his jealous quarreling, but that he kept coming around every few days, trying to get back with her. She said that she often thought, "What's the use havin' a fussin' man around when you're earning your own livin' anyway?" He does not get much respect from her, for she commented, "My husband is dumber than Edward." During the two months of interviewing, Martin was banished, but appeared to be reinstated with his wife just at the end. Mrs. Martin knows her value well, and knows, too, exactly what she will put up with in a man.

Edward says there is a good deal of fighting in his home, and that it usually occurs when his stepfather comes home drunk and starts to criticize his mother; it is certain to happen if his father knocks things over or breaks glasses. Usually, he says, they try to get him out of the house when a fight is beginning; they will give him money and send him to the movies, and then will have it out. Sometimes his mother gets disgusted and tells Martin to "take your clothes and get out." This has happened a number of times, the last one very recently. The lower-class boy faces constant violence in the home from earliest years on; his is not the controlled and suppressed atmosphere of the middle-class home where violence is a prerogative of the father.

Mrs. Martin is the undoubted head of the house; she pays the piper and calls the tune. When Edward is to be "licked," his mother does it. His stepfather never puts a finger on him; but if he objects to anything Edward does, he tells the mother and she does the punishing. Nor may anyone else, except the teachers, beat Edward without facing his panther-like mother. Recently when a man slapped Edward's face, he came home crying to his mother; she seized a broomstick, went out on the street, found the man and told him she would kill him if he so much as touched Edward again. She became so angry while talking to him that she raised the stick to hit him over the head right there on the street but somebody held her arms.

Mrs. Martin has no idea, however, of having a disobedient child on her hands. She says that she has "plenty of trouble to get Edward to do right," and that she has to beat him constantly. Two issues which are chronic are Edward's staying out late, as when he stays to see the show a second time at the movies and does not get home till twelve o'clock, and his truancy from school. He seems to take the beatings meekly and never fights back; he is shocked at the mere idea of retaliation. It is probable that in a more conventional lower-class home, the father would play a greater role than he does in the Martin family; Martin has been there on probation himself and does not dare exercise the privileges of a more firmly established father.

Another useful index of the class of a child is the group of intimate associates of his parents. Mrs. Martin named four close friends, all between the ages of twenty-five and thirty-seven. She herself is now twenty-nine years old; apparently her friends are within the age group still interested in "good times" at dances and beer parlors. All of them have low-paid jobs as domestic servants. One of them cannot read and write, and another went only as far as the fifth grade in school. All are married. All are medium- to dark-brown. All are technically Baptists, but none seems to belong to an organization of any kind. Three of the four have no children, and the other has only one child, a fact which makes a carefree life the more possible. All live within a few blocks of the Martin home but they do not exchange visits very frequently. All rent their lodgings. They exhibit a complex of habits which may be designated as those of the lower-lower class.

The matter of church and organizational participation is particularly tell-tale. Mrs. Martin says she is a "Baptist" and was baptized as a young girl "in a river in the country." But she is not actually welded into the life of her community through her church. Indeed, she is not a "member" of any church, in the sense of going regularly, being known to the congregation, holding church office, or paying dues. She just "goes once in a while" to a neighboring Baptist church, and then again to a Sanctified church around the corner. If she should stop going, no one would miss her officially. The case is quite different with the upper-lower-class person who is the very staff of the church.

Membership in clubs and societies tends also to bind a person into his community and give him a broad base of participation. Mrs. Martin differs from the "joining and belonging" upper-lower-class Negroes in this respect also. She does not belong to any clubs or associations because she does not have the time or money for them. The beer parlor, rather than the "Busy Bees," is her club.

Edward's participation will inevitably follow that of his mother, but for the moment she seems to think that church is a good thing for him and will help to keep him a nice boy. He goes to Bible school on Sunday for a different reason, however. "You go to school from nine to eleven-thirty on Sunday," he explains, "then on Friday you get ice cream and cake and a ride to the lake for a picnic, all for ten cents a week." It may be seen that the reinforcement to Edward's religious behavior is concrete and visceral. Edward has not been baptized, that is, joined the church. He argues against it because one is bound to become a sinner again, and this would be "triflin' wid the Lawd." Behind the excuse is seen again the feeble organizational impulse that characterizes his mother's participation.

Aside from the two already identified, Edward named seven others as members of his larger group of intimate associates or clique. All of these boys are three to four years retarded in school, a striking fact about lower-class children. All are from his neighborhood. He met all but one either at the public swimming pool, at the Community Center, or at the school. Apparently his mother does not know the parents of most of Edward's friends; this is an important point, since middle-class parents are always careful to identify the class of the parents of their children's playmates. Two of Edward's closest pals have been in the home for delinquent juveniles, one of them six times and the other four. Edward followed gang etiquette carefully in the interviews and would not talk about these boys, both of whom are maturing criminals. Their biggest exploit has been to steal $30, which they used to purchase identical suits of clothing. For this they were given a long term in the "Home." It was amazing how rapidly Edward and his gang would scatter and take cover if one came on them at any of their forbidden activities, such as gambling. An unexpected knock on the door would be followed by a rush, and the newcomer would look into a silent room swept clean of boys.

Edward never goes to his friends' houses to spend the night or to play. This is Pollyanna stuff; anyway it does not work out well because whenever the boys go home they are put to some kind of work. They play, therefore, on the streets or in public places like the playground or the Community Center. When asked about the games they play, Edward recited only the pious ones, such as mark and fate, chalk the rabbit, and humpty head. In this game, a gang of seven boys run off, and when they get to the corner they holler, "Ready!"; then another gang of seven boys chase the first group. If the captain and one man of the pursued gang are caught, they are then "it" and must chase the others. There is, of course, nothing "lower-class" about such games; they are rather the general cross-class property of children in our society.

But the talk in Edward's bunch indicates sports that are by no means so innocent. They recounted with strong disapproval the story of a boy who was always robbing the little fellows of their movie money when they were on the way to the theater. In fact, Meatball was sent to the Home on this charge the last time. Two of the boys argued also on how long they had been "in" the last time; it was finally settled at eleven months for Lester and six months for Meatball. This led to a derisive discussion of punishments at the Home. One "caught" such punishments for smoking in the dormitory, having sex books in one's possession, breaking rules, and the like. Lester told of the severest punishment administered there: it seems they strip your back and tie your hands up; then they put hot or cold water on you (your choice) so that the strap will sting more; every time the strap lands, a little piece of flesh pops off the boy's buttocks. This was followed by other stories of stealing and of outwitting the authorities and getting away with it, all accompanied by laughter and pride in dishonest achievement.

Edward's mother is by no means happy about this state of affairs. She says that Edward used to like to go to school but after he started "goin' 'round with a no-good bunch of li'l niggers," he took to playing hooky. As a lower-lower-class woman, she has her own standards, and these do not countenance criminal behavior. She saw herself losing Edward to a criminal gang in the neighborhood and found herself powerless to do much about it; even her nightly beatings, so long and hopefully administered, were of no use; perhaps, indeed, they only toughened Edward and prepared him for the fight gang and the sadistic guard.

Edward knows some girls in the area, although his significant clique includes only boys. His cousin Genevieve said she did not know Edward very well and had as little to do with him as possible because he was a bad boy. Of the five girls Edward named, all are retarded in school as much as two or three years. He met them all through casual neighborhood contacts, and no parental supervision of his choice of girl friends was seen. They are apparently all lower-class girls, as one would expect. He does not play much with girls " 'cause if you do, the boys call you a sissy." The struggle of boys at this age in all classes seems to be to differentiate themselves from girls and to become males instead of just "children."

Edward is an ardent movie fan, as are his clique-mates, and he seems free to go as often as he likes and to see whatever pictures he chooses. No middle-class injunctions like, "You can go Sunday and see 'Alice in Wonderland,' " for him. His mother complains mildly that he goes three and four nights in succession, but seems to be disturbed only by his staying out late after the movie. Probably she feels relieved to be rid of him at the movies if he does not stay up too late; at the movies he is safe at least, and does not interfere with her dropping in for a glass of beer at the corner.

Edward likes his movies rough and tough. Favorites are gangster pictures, horror pictures, and westerns (with plenty of shooting). He particularly liked "Penitentiary," which he summarized as follows: A boy killed someone with a bottle and then was put in the pen. He tried to escape and one of the prisoners squealed. Another convict killed the squealer, and the boy saw it. He refused to "rat" on the murderer and was put in solitary. When the murderer tried to rescue him, the warden intervened and was stabbed by the murderer, who was in turn shot. Asked about the point of the picture, Edward said it was that you shouldn't murder people, which seemed quite correct to the Doc. Such movies evidently match the aggressive tone of life in the neighborhood and confirm Edward's impressions from daily life; they are not a "sublimation" as they might be with a middle-class or upper-class child, but represent the world of actual behavior as he may soon come to know it himself.

Before and after the theater, Edward hangs around with his gang on the streets—playing, fighting, talking, learning "life" from the older boys and men. His mother warns him not to come home later than ten-thirty and beats him if he is later than that; however, he knows that story well and does not fear the beating. A middle-class mother would not stand for such behavior in her son.

Edward gets a great deal from the Community Center in his slum area. He has become a very good swimmer in its pool; he boxes in the gym; he plays baseball and horseshoes. He is one of the snappiest dancers at the weekly parties held there for young people. But the Center cannot fight the whole weight of class and economic conditions in the slums.

With his gang Edward goes on picnics too. They go to the lake and sometimes to swim in the canal, a dangerous pastime for small boys. The mothers make up lunches for the boys and then go off to work, glad of the assurance that the boys are doing nothing more mischievous or dangerous. Middle-class mothers would be unlikely to permit such jaunts without supervision, perhaps by a Scout leader; Edward, however, has never been a Scout, nor, he says, has he ever been asked to join. Edward lives in what might be called a "fish-fry" area; he often goes on fish-fry picnics and eats fish and potato salad sandwiches.

It has already been suggested that Edward lives in an atmosphere of violence. He lives, in fact, on a sort of frontier of American life where the man with the most courage and the most invulnerable arteries survives. In his childhood, Edward saw many terrifying sights. Recently, he came along a street near his home and saw two men lying on the ground after a gun fight. One man was bleeding from the mouth, where he had been shot; he had also been shot in the back while trying to run away. He died on the spot. The other man had a belly wound and was taken to a hospital. Eventually he recovered. Edward did not know what the fight was about but he must have absorbed the lesson that he himself would grow up into a world of adults where shooting and killing would be a natural recourse in a quarrel, and he must not have been too frightened by it. After all, only one of the men died!

Violence in the lower-lower class is not confined to men. Once Edward saw a "lady in black" drive up in a car, call a girl over to her from the curb, then get out and slash the girl with a razor. Evidently the girl had not expected trouble or she would have run. The lady cut her on the back, around the neck, and across the breasts. Then the lady got in her car and drove away. The girl who had been attacked was left lying on the ground, bleeding and whimpering. They took her to the hospital, and she *recovered*. The lesson again was clear: the manly or womanly thing is violence, and it is not so dangerous either.

Edward explained that "li'l" boys like himself do not carry knives much but that all the big boys do, and are always "juggin'" each other. He illustrated with the story of a fight that occurred near the theater one night. A man named Doug was pitching car checks with the boys. Another man came into the game and lost; he then accused Doug of cheating. Doug said, "Nigger, don't tell me I'm cheating." The other man ran to get his gun and came back threatening to shoot Doug. Doug got out his six-inch, spring-blade knife and told him he had better shoot straight because if he didn't kill Doug the first time, he was going "to get butchered up plenty." The man with the gun then retreated. Edward added that the big boys fight a lot about girls, following the "you let my girl alone" pattern, but that the little boys do not feel this way about girls. Their sex activity is surreptitious and does not imply possession.

If Edward sees constant aggressive behavior at home and among adults in the neighborhood, he has also been well trained in it by personal practice. His mother says he has been fighting all his life with other children in the neighborhood. She deplores this mildly but seems to accept it as inevitable, as indeed it is, in the training of a lower-lower-class child. She says that the older children would pit the younger ones against one another. In fact, Mrs. Martin said she had got herself into a lot of trouble for slapping an eleven-year-old girl who was "setting Edward up to fight" another child when Edward was three. Edward has been fighting ever since—for his rights, for dominance, and sometimes truly for his life. He is becoming very skillful at it, as are all his friends; what they couldn't do to a bunch of middle-class boys! Only a short time ago, Mrs. Martin reported, Edward knocked out a boy much bigger than himself. The only thing she will not stand for is his "picking on" younger children, but she has always encouraged him to defend himself against all others if they "meddle" him.

Edward has a clearly visible scar over one eye. It is a battle trophy. He quarreled with a boy and a girl during school hours and they attacked him after school; the boy knocked him down and the girl gouged him in the eye, making a long tear in the flesh. A few days before the interview, he had fought with a boy who tried to take his bathing suit away from him. Edward hit the boy in the mouth and the boy bit him; he exhibited a heavy scab on his right index finger, and a series of sharp little scars, like tooth marks. One day, Edward tried to promote a fight in the Doc's office between Meatball and Lucian and almost succeeded; another time he jeered at Lester until they began to make threatening gestures toward each other and were on the point of fighting.

It must be clear that instead of talking about how high his grades are, what clubs he is secretary of, what possessions the family has, or what a high social mark he is aiming for, Edward filled the interviewing hours with talk of conniving, fighting, violence, and crime. His folkways are different from middle-class ways; they are the ways of the lower-lower class and the only ones he knows. He is proud of being a leader along his own lines; instead of being president of the Hi-Y, he is the best fighter in his gang. After a long series of trial-and-error fights, he has finally climbed to the top fighting rank of his clique; by general agreement he can lick any of them and he stands at the head of the "pecking order" within the group. This position of dominance is obviously sweet to him and he uses it ruthlessly, provoking a fight when he wishes to see one and stamping it out if he is not in the mood.

When authority is wielded against Edward by Negroes, it is generally by middle-class Negroes; in his anti-authoritarian attitudes, therefore, there may be an element of class antagonism. This was illustrated by an altercation which the Doc watched one day. The boys were teasing one of the play supervisors at the Center, intimating in no uncertain way that they considered him a sissy. He responded by pushing one of them around. "Steamboat" responded by calling the supervisor an "ole nigger." The head of the Center took up the case and said he was "going to get respect for the supervisor." The boys obviously enjoyed the situation and were not intimidated by his threat to tell their mothers or to forbid them the use of the Center. They knew the sensitiveness of the middle-class man to the use of the term "nigger" and were twitting him with it. Edward said the boys called each other "nigger" all the time and did not mind being called it. They were exhibiting a trait of their class.

Lower-lower-class boys are familiar with, and most of them take part in, the game called "the Dozens." This is a method of tormenting another person by making unwelcome allusions to him or his family. Each sally draws a retort from the person addressed, and the procedure goes on interactively until one party withdraws or the participants fight. Sometimes the insults are couched in rhymes and sometimes in prose. Edward, Lester, and Meatball gave a great many examples of the play in their daily reactions to one another. For example, Edward mocked Lester in a whining, effeminate voice, to show how Lester assured the guard in the Home that he had not stolen something. "You're not going to whip me, Mr. Walter, are you? I'm not a bad boy." Meatball goaded Lester about his stealing, saying he was so light-fingered he would steal the sugar off a sugar bun. Lester twitted Edward for never having been in the Home, saying, "He's a *nice* boy; he even goes to church." Edward admitted that he did not steal, but added that when he was with a bunch that did steal he would not "squeal" as Lester does. Both boys accused Lester of having squealed on them in the fan episode, saying that he was "weak to the jive" of some older person. Edward accused Lester of effeminacy and of gaining favors by personal concessions to an older man. Lester accused Meatball of playing with himself in the lavatory. At this Meatball became really angry and seemed about to fight, but finally withdrew and went away, at which point Edward called him "yellow."

It was plain that not all of these taunts were without foundation; indeed, it seems likely that the Dozens player seeks out the true weakness of the other person and jabs just where the skin is thinnest. It was also clear that this game is part of the pattern of free aggressive expression which is characteristic of the lowest stratum in lower class. "Kidding" there is, of course, in every class, but this game in its dirtiest and most aggressive forms is the province of lower-lower-class people.

Marked sexual freedom has often been noticed in the pattern of lower-class Negro life. The data from Edward and his friends serves to confirm the observation. He knew all the usual obscene words and a number that the Doc had never heard. Among themselves the boys talked freely and openly about sexual matters, and they often made obscene remarks about girls passing on the street or girls who visited the office. But with the Doc, Edward was more reticent. After all, how far can one trust an older man—even an amiable one who does not send you to the Home when he has a good excuse to do so? Edward answered questions, apparently truthfully, but volunteered nothing. He said he had learned the difference between boys and girls very early, in fact had always known it. He had heard the fellows talking about such things. He himself had started "doing it" with girls when he was about eight. He had first done it with a girl with whom he was playing house. He thought that a lot of boys of his age had never done it yet because they were "sissies." Apparently it is manly in his circle for small boys to have intercourse, but not all are equal to the demand. He had had intercourse last about a month ago but could not remember much about it except that it had occurred in the schoolyard. He had "done it" only with little girls, never with big ones, but with quite a number of the former. The likelihood that Edward was boasting is reduced by comments from his mother; she apparently opposed his early sexual activities but could not make her opposition effective. She said that recently Edward got into a fight with a grown-up man over a girl (the occasion when he was slapped in the mouth and Mrs. Martin defended him). Mrs. Martin asked Edward if he were "courting" the girl, and Edward said he was not. The mother warned him against this girl, said she was a "little woman," that is, sexually experienced, and no "girl" at all; then she gave him a whipping for keeping such company. His mother has standards for Edward: she believes that sexual behavior of a rather free kind is all right after a certain age; at this time, however, she feels that Edward is too young. But his play associates have other views and Edward follows them, in accordance with his natural drives. He and his friends distinguish, however, between "nice" and "ratty" little girls. Nice girls are not promiscuous, although neither must they be altogether chaste; but ratty girls will have intercourse with practically anyone on any provocation. Nevertheless, the boys who may call a girl "ratty" are often willing to have intercourse with her themselves. Edward has standards of his own in the matter of sexual behavior. He has never joined a bunch of fellows to have intercourse with the same girl at one time, nor has he ever used force on a girl. He holds himself above such actions, just as he despises homosexual and perverse activities.

Who does the maid work, the dirty work, the tedious work for lower-class families? The answer must be, the children. The mother works for the "white folks" and the children work for the mother. On a typical day Edward gets up at six and goes to the grocery store to get the day's supplies for his mother; they cannot afford to put in a stock of supplies but order in daily bits; they cannot afford to have it delivered so they go and get it. The mother makes the breakfast and then goes to work. Edward washes the dishes, sweeps the house, makes the bed, and then goes over to the Center to play. Lower-lower-class boys work both inside and outside the home. Edward sold coal and wood at a general store last year after school. People would come in to buy twenty-five cents worth of wood or coal, which Edward would put in a sack and take to their back yards in a wheelbarrow. With their small incomes, they must buy fuel, as they do food, in small quantities from day to day. On Saturdays and Sundays, Edward shines shoes, often making a dollar, which he gives to his mother; she returns twenty-five cents to him, keeping the other seventy-five cents for rent and food. Shoeshining is a kind of menial work which a middle-class boy would not ordinarily undertake, especially on Sunday, as Edward does, but neither the meniality of the work nor the significance of the Sabbath means much to a lower-class boy. Another item of family economics is that Edward has been to the doctor only for major illnesses and injuries and to the dentist only twice in his life, both times for extractions.

There is a battle in progress for the possession of Edward's mind. The ancient world of ghosts and spooks was first made real to him by his family and friends; they gave him beliefs that have held sway over English minds since the most ancient times. The schools, on the other hand, stand for the modern rational world of sience and they teach Edward to decry such notions. Edward stands in the middle, influenced by both, and not wholly the creature of either. Although he had reached only the fifth grade when the interviews began, and was therefore retarded at least two years, his schooling had still taken effect to the extent of shaking his faith in the superstitions of his class. However, the folk society seems likely to win the struggle for Edward's mind. It seems doubtful that he will get far enough in school to have a consolidated position against magical beliefs. In this he is a true child of his class.

Edward claims that he does not believe in the "gown man" legend, although most of his clique do; he says that his mother told him this story to scare him about being out after dark. He said a "gown man" is supposed to go around in a white gown at night. Sometimes he would get up in a tree, drop down on you, and then stick a needle into you. This would kill you, and then he would take you to the hospital and cut you up. Several of Edward's pals reported direct experience with the "gown man" in the most lively detail; after seeing him, they usually ran, hotly pursued, and just managed to gain the safety of their parents' presence. Asked what the "gown" was like, Edward described quite clearly a doctor's hospital coat, buttoned down the front. Edward is wavering, but will probably end up by believing completely in this homespun demon.

Edward also denied believing in ghosts or "sperrits," and added that he thought his mother told him about these just to scare him or punish him; but he displayed a surprising amount of information about them for a boy who does not believe in them. He said that a ghost might, for instance, shake your bed when you were getting into it, or open the gate in front of you when you were going into the yard. He volunteered that if the ghost was friendly it might not harm you, but if not, it would. It seems to depend partly on your attitude; for instance, if you see the ghost and walk around it, it will not slap you, but if you see it and do not avoid it, it will certainly hit you. He stated that ghosts came from people who had died. This is probably only a hint of the extent to which Edward and his gang believe in magic; since they are punished by the ridicule of the classes above them in Negro society for such beliefs, they probably tend to conceal them except from other lower-lower-class people.

Edward and his bunch hold firmly to the idea that a boy can have a baby, a certain kind of a baby called "blood baby." They do not know much about the circumstances except that it comes out of the boy's stomach and the stomach has to be cut open to get it out. How it gets into the stomach, Edward could not say.

Although apparently not much afraid of death, Edward is fearful of the dead, a reversal of his supposed position on ghosts and spirits. He said, "When I come home late from the shows, I'm plenty scared of dead." It is clear that his mother has done her work well, and that his fear is of the spooky and supernatural rather than of direct violence, toward which he has the indifference born of familiarity. Edward also believes in fortune-tellers and described how one directed a man to go to the pawnshop where he would find his lost radio; he went, and sure enough, there it was. He also has some perhaps more rational fears; one of them is of hospitals and particularly of the Negro hospital in his area. He agrees with his mother that everyone who goes there for an operation dies; they will never take *him* there for an operation. With many other lower-lower-class Negroes, he shares a distrust of the Negro middle class, and prefers white doctors and hospitals. Lower-class Negroes have had historically a close contact with upper-class whites and have come to trust and depend upon them. They still have such contact and often feel nearer to the remote upper-class whites than they do to the middle-class and upper-class people in their own caste, whose rivalry with them is more open and immediate.

Does Edward not have a secret itch to be up and doing? Does he not envy the better homes and softer ways of those above him in class position? Apparently he neither itches nor envies; he is fairly happy where he is, he is isolated from the prodding scorn of those above him, and he is held tight in the vise of his lower-lower-class folkways. As a small boy, he was taught by his mother to tap dance and later he performed before her white employers. They thought him "cute," liked him, and paid him well. The role of entertainer and clown is a familiar one to lower-class people, and Edward received his class training early.

Evidently Edward has no clear picture of what he wants, a fatal defect if a person wishes to be mobile. He said that he might be a mail carrier when he grows up, and to this end he wanted to finish eighth grade so that he could take the examinations. (As a matter of fact, he would have to go at least through high school to achieve this goal, which would mean staying in school until he is twenty!) It is clear, however, from the foregoing that Edward's mobility ceiling of phantasy is a lower-middle-class job. Failing to become a mail carrier, Edward turns to a more characteristic mobility aspiration of his class, that is, to be a prize fighter. On this subject he was enthusiastic. He asked the Doc if he had ever seen Joe Louis. Edward pointed out proudly that an impression of Joe was marked on the little round cloth cap he wore, for which he had paid ten cents. He said he had seen Joe Louis twice, and affirmed that he looked like his pictures. Edward has had a lot of training in boxing at the gym as well as the informal training of the streets; he readily drops into fighting stance with the left hand out, high up in front of the retracted right. But alas, he probably has neither the physique to be a boxer nor the mentality to be a mail carrier.

Edward has never thought about getting married and has no particular plans for marriage. Mrs. Martin's plan for Edward's life is to have him finish school. She epitomizes her educational philosophy in this way: "There's too many dumb people in the world now." She realizes, more clearly than Edward does, the disadvantages of lower-lower-class status and has a strong wish to get him out of it. But she has neither a definite plan nor a very firm determination. When she says she wants "to put him through school," she is using an expression that has different meanings at different class levels; she means that she wants him to finish eighth grade or the nearest convenient unit. Beyond this she has no plans. She hopes that while he is in school he will learn a trade like carpentry or plastering, a lower-middle-class status goal. But she is openly contemptuous of the possibility of his realizing his wish to be a mail carrier; she considers this completely impractical. Nor does she have much hope for prize fighting. She remarks that Joe Louis is "one in a million," and that Edward's chances of achieving anything by this route are very remote. Mrs. Martin has accepted the probability that Edward will not be "anything," and only hopes that he will not be something so definite as a criminal.

Our data on Edward's personality come from direct observation of him and from his mother's account. She said that she worked while Edward was small (she had to support him). A sister who was living with her took care of him part of the time, and she also paid a "lady in the same block" to look after him when the sister could not. Edward's first year of life was uneventful; his mother nursed him whenever she was at home and he never had colic. He was finally weaned at the end of the second year. He rarely cried and was "a nice baby" whom she could leave with almost anyone. Cleanliness training started when he was a year old. She made him sit on the pot and would whip him if he tried to get off. She "always did whip him a lot to make sure he was a good boy." She managed to establish the connection between being near the pot and being safe from punishment so thoroughly that he would not part with it but carried it around with him all the time; it amused her to see him running around with it in his hand and sometimes putting it on his head. Mrs. Martin was one of the few mothers interviewed who reported that her son had never played with himself and that she had never had to deal with this problem. It is possible, however, that this discipline was administered by her sister or by the "lady in the same block." At any rate, today Edward shows well-embedded marks of such training.

There is apparently no effort in the lower class to spare children a knowledge of death or its meaning. Edward had an aunt who died when he was five years old. He said that they embalmed the body, then held a wake before the funeral. At the wake they sang for the corpse (a lower-class rite), served drinks, and stayed up all night. "When you die," he continued, "they take out your insides, your teeth (for the gold), and your eyeballs. Then they blow you up with air." Edward said he was not afraid of death, and his mother seems to be equally unafraid; at least she referred quite casually to the possibility of her own death.

Mrs. Martin says that Edward has always been a smart boy The psychologists disagree; they grant him an I.Q. of 71. The Doc, however, tended to agree with the mother. How shall one measure by standardized tests the skills of a boy who has learned to acquire the fruits of stealing and at the same time to escape being put into jail?

If Edward is not a very good boy, it is certainly not for lack of beatings. His mother whipped him unmercifully from the beginning but she now thinks there was something wrong with the plan. She says, "He'll go do the same thing you whipped him for doing." Of course she was not able to punish his misdeeds until she came home from work at night. Perhaps the whippings did not follow the disapproved actions closely enough to be effective. Furthermore, her plan of whipping on more or less "general principles" has the defect of not selecting from his action tendencies those which she wants to discourage, and the whippings, therefore, probably came to be regarded by Edward as a circumstance of life to be expected along with everything else. Also lacking was the vitally important example of good behavior on his mother's part, although she did as well as she could by her standards. At any rate, Edward seemed to be skidding into the status of a very bad boy in spite of all his mother's efforts. She does say for him, however, that he has good manners and always says, "Yes, sir" and "No, sir." She credits this achievement to her frequent beatings. Looking toward the future, she believes that Edward wants to be a "little tusk hog" (hard-boiled person), but she considers him a sissy in many ways. Until very recently, he would stand up on the floor and cry if she did not give him what he wanted or if she whipped him. She feels that a boy his size should not cry. On Edward's side, it seems probable that he found that he could manage his mother to some degree by crying and could occasionally soften her strenuous beatings by this means, or even do away with them en-

tirely. In his gang life, he is certainly not a sissy; he evidently
reserves this behavior for authoritative adults.

In his clique relations, Edward appeared to be calm during
the "jiving" of the Dozens game. He seemed to have a sure sense
of mastery over Lester and Meatball and to enjoy tormenting
them to suit his pleasure. When the other boys stole, he shared
the booty with them, but "kept out of trouble" himself. Meatball followed Edward gladly; Lester, however, occasionally rebelled and submitted after protest only because he was neither
strong nor bright enough to resist. In these relations, Edward
was certainly not a weak cry baby—"master mind" would describe him better.

Edward likes his mother and realizes that she has been a valuable person to him. He does not sentimentalize about her but
says that she has been nice to him. He does not seem to resent
her lickings but rather has taken them for granted when he
could not avoid them by crying first. At the end of the time of
interviewing, however, the mother was becoming quite bellicose
about Edward because her maternal authority was being challenged by him, with the aid of his clique, in no uncertain way.
For the first time, Edward was playing hooky on a large scale.
Had she been at home, she would no doubt have walloped him
to school and back every day if necessary, but she had to work
every day. She punished him but he still played hooky. A crisis
occurred when she got off a bus at an unexpected time and place
and saw Edward on the street during school hours. He ran away
and she said, "He was jumping fences just like one of them
rogues." Edward's pals, left behind, had the effrontery to tell
her that it was not Edward she had seen.

She then made up her mind to play her trump card; she would
put him in the Home, a threat she had often used but never
carried out. This time, she was as good as her word. That night
when he came home very late, she gave him a beating. The next
morning she took him to the school and found out he had not
attended his classes for about two weeks. She inferred that in the
meantime he must have been "goin' 'round with that bunch
of no-good niggers." Edward tried to escape banishment to the

Home by suddenly becoming very polite and docile, but she was not to be fooled; she said, "He got that bad, he's sly. He will say 'Yes, ma'm' and go right on and do what he promised not to do. He sure is p'lite, but he only tries to fool me with that. He a li'l liar, an' I hate liars. If a person lies, he'll steal, and I don't like no thief in my home." So she called the police and asked them to take Edward to the Home; they demurred on the ground that Edward had not done anything sufficiently reprehensible. "If he had stole something or something like that, it would be all right." But in the end they took him.

Mrs. Martin was quite satisfied with her act, regarding it as a personal as well as a sociological triumph. She said, "I don't have to worry about where he is or if he's out in the street with a bunch of bad boys. I know where he is. And he's in bed too. He might not be 'sleep, but he's in bed. And he'll go to school in there 'cause they make you go. He'll be all right when he comes out. I'll bet he'll go to school then. I bet he wish he hadda went to school now." Her personal reaction to outraged maternal authority was voiced in this way, "I just put him in there to let him know I wasn't jokin' and I meant what I said." But she is probably wrong about "saving" Edward by sending him to the Home. Sociologists agree that most boys' reformatories do not reform. Since Edward went into the Home his two closest friends have followed him there, and now they are together again, Edward furnishing the ideas and they the muscle. In the Home he has a good chance to meet experts in crime and to achieve through them a higher level of criminal accomplishment.

A telling incident of the research occurred when the Doc went to call on Edward's mother. He was a little uncertain from Edward's report just what name she used, so he asked her. She responded that her name was Geraldine, thus revealing her complete and unprotesting subordination to caste etiquette. No middle-class Negro woman would do this; she would invariably claim at least her full name, if "Mrs." were not also insisted upon. But Mrs. Martin has learned and accepted the caste code of lower-lower-class Negroes and does not deviate from it.

Edward, too, knows the code and has had the "correct" training for his class. He has played with the white children for whom his mother worked and has "gotten along all right" with them. He and his clique have had occasional fights with white boys in the public park where both groups play hockey, and boys on both sides have been badly hurt at various times. The white boys sometimes called him and his friends "niggers," but they did not mind very much; they called the white boys "dagoes" and "poor pecks" in return. In using the word "nigger," the white boys were only doing what the colored boys already did among themselves; it is not to be supposed, however, that the word "nigger" has no aggressive tone when used by lower-class colored people. It is decidedly aggressive and is likely to be used in situations where insult or banter is intended. Mrs. Martin, for instance, has repeatedly referred to Edward's gang playmates as "li'l niggers," and it is sufficiently plain that she does not like them. The fact seems to be only that there is less sting in the word for lower-class Negroes than there is for middle-class and upper-class Negroes.

Edward has heard of lynchings but he seems to understand by the word both legal and illegal killings. He said his mother had told him how a Negro was hanged from a tree over in Mississippi by being made to step off something while there was a rope around his neck; Edward showed no resentment about this story. The records of this study seem to indicate that phantasies of efficient aggression toward whites come mainly from middle-class children. After describing this real lynching, Edward referred to the legal execution of a white criminal in the Parish Prison as a "lynching." According to Edward, the man who kidnapped the Lindbergh baby was also lynched, after several stays of execution. Edward cited kidnapping, robbery, and murder as the offenses most frequently leading to lynching, but seemed to have no practical conception of the crime of rape against white women.

The Doc was shocked by the temper of his fellow whites when

he went to the police station to recover his fan. The sergeant in charge listened to the circumstances of the theft, handed over the fan, and then gave a piece of advice; he counseled the Doc to set up a machine gun in his office and use it to shoot the boys down, indicating with a swerve of his index finger how the mowing could be done. The Doc thought at first he was joking but soon realized that it was not a joke. Nevertheless, Edward says he would prefer white to Negro "cops"; he feels that the latter would be tougher on gang boys, perhaps because they would know their ways and haunts better.

Mrs. Martin carefully trained Edward to be a "good" little Negro boy. She taught him that white people were not "his kind," that there were plenty of Negro people who were, and that he was to deal with these. This assumption of basic difference between whites and Negroes was an obvious article of faith with her; on this point she has submissively accepted the view of the white caste. Mrs. Martin says that Edward has never seemed to worry about his color. He apparently has no phantasies of escape from the situation and never mentions wanting to go to school or to work in the North. Here again he seems to follow his mother who has often been urged by her mother and sister to come to New York with them; she does not go because she thinks she "would not like it."

The effect of caste on Edward is best seen in all the class marks which he bears. Caste forces him and his like into the lowest class groups in great numbers. The perils, deprivations, and privileges of lower-class life are more characteristic of Negro children than of white. There are many white boys like Edward but not in such overwhelming proportion to the total white population.

Lower-lower class is the bottom of the Negro class structure, but like many "bottoms," one can drop through it. Prostitutes, wanderers, illegitimates who cannot even identify their fathers, and colored women who regularly have intercourse with white men, are outside and "below" the lower-lower-class group; they exist either in small groups of their own, or in a kind of chaotic limbo outside the class structure. The details of their lives are not yet known. Edward is aware of the standards of the lower class and he knows it is not a criminal group; his mother cannot stand a thief around! He considers reefer smokers (drug addicts), "ratty" girls (semi-prostitutes), and gang rapers (criminals) as below him. Homosexuals, also, he views as a declassed and inferior group with whom he would not associate. It is from the circumstance that he still has something to lose from the standpoint of class status that we can solve the "mystery" referred to earlier, his crying when the Doc asked him about his "real" father.

Edward himself never did supply the answer; he was too ashamed. But his mother talked about it. She said that Edward's name is not really Dodge but that his father was named Thornton. Mrs. Martin was impregnated by Thornton but never lived with him, nor was she ever married to him. Edward's father drifted off the social scene before Edward's birth and has not been heard from for many years. Edward's mother registered the child under her maiden name, so that his official name is Edward Phillips. For three years after Edward's birth, however, she lived with a man named Dodge of whom Edward was very fond. When Edward started to school, he always insisted on giving his name as Dodge. She tried to persuade him not to do this, but he has persisted and is even now registered at the Home as Edward Dodge. She knows that Edward is very sensitive on this score but does not understand his feeling.

To understand the foregoing, one must be familiar with the forms of paternity in this class. They are four, in declining order of respectability. The first is regular marriage of the parents. The second is common-law marriage. Such marriages are relatively respectable and often quite stable; the wife may be heard to speak in this manner: "We've been living together for eighteen years. There's not a better man than my husband. We've planned to get married a number of times, but he lost his job." The third is a sexual association between the parents without marriage, but where the father admits his paternity if the matter comes up. In the fourth group are those associations in which the mother does not know who the father is, or the father will not admit his paternity nor give his name to the child. This dilemma is illustrated by the comment of a Natchez woman who said, "I asked Elizabeth who the father of her child was. She say, 'How I know?' Now, you know dat not right. When yo' ain' messin' wid no lot o' men, you kin least tell who de daddy is. De child ought to know who it kin call pappy." Both Negro and white men father such children. In the latter case, a middle-class or upper-class white man today will usually not permit the child to bear his name, whereas "white trash" do not seem to mind.

With this knowledge in mind, it became clear why Edward cried when he was asked about his "real" father. He felt that he had none. He knew he ought to give Edward Phillips as his real name because his mother had told him so; but if he did, he would risk expulsion from the lower class altogether. Even as matters stood, the other boys knew there was something wrong and twitted him sharply about it. "Wheah yo' daddy, Edward?" would bring him into fighting posture at any time. He has, therefore, to keep up a kind of pitiful masquerade, with the mask threatening to drop off and reveal his status-nakedness at any moment.

In the face of this situation, to be a bad boy and a leader of bad boys was one of the positive things that Edward could do. He could compensate for his weak social position by being a fighter and gang leader. He could hardly hope ever to be very respectable with a social blot attached to his very birth, so why not make the most of his talents in unrespectable ways? Perhaps he must leave the New Orleans area and cut all ties with his neighborhood to become inconspicuous; or perhaps he can find anonymity by allying himself with the criminal world where fewer questions are asked.

THE MIDDLE CLASSES

The Middle Classes

When one studies Negro adolescents whose families live in a middle-class position, one finds training demands upon the individual quite unlike those of the lower class. In New Orleans, the Negro society recognizes three subdivisions within the middle class: lower-middle class, middle-middle class, and upper-middle class. The first life, "Self-Made Man," is that of a boy who is attempting upward social mobility from the lower-middle-class platform provided by his family. It is followed by the study of a colored Creole girl who is in a stable middle-middle-class position. The third case in this group is that of a girl, Ellen Hill, whose family is "falling" from lower-middle-class into lower-class position. In this series, it will be possible to illustrate the constant struggle to maintain or to improve class status, which is a major concern of the middle-class individual.

CHAPTER V

SELF-MADE MAN

This is the story of a boy who built himself up and of his family who helped to build him. Taken by himself he is probably not important, for he will never be president of Harvard or sit on the Supreme Court; but the record of his growth and achievement is significant. He has made the American dream a reality and he symbolizes the essence of the American social scheme. His fight to be "up and above," as his father put it, has cost him renunciation, bitterness, and anxiety, and the long war is not yet over. We meet Chester Olivier, therefore, on the field of battle for higher status, and through the smoke we catch a glimpse of him in childhood, adolescence, and early manhood. It will be our purpose to define the field itself, the mode of warfare and the resources of our protagonist.

Chester is short and slight for his age of sixteen years. His skin is medium-brown in color and his hair woolly. Photographed with his family, his face is tense and set, but to the interviewer he seemed friendly and amenable, and anxious to give an account of himself. Mr. and Mrs. Olivier are living, and Chester has two brothers and a sister, all younger than he. He lives with his mother and the other children.

Chester was asked to cooperate in this study at the high school where he is now a junior. He assented readily and seemed flattered to be picked as a "representative boy." Our primary knowledge of him was gained through the young woman who made this first contact. This interviewer was twenty-three years old, came from about the same class level as Chester, had done graduate work in sociology and been a practice teacher at the school he attends. She is about the same color as Chester, firm and pleasant in her manner, and was able to establish the necessary rapport. She interviewed Chester at his school and later at the university. Like the rest of the informants in this study, Chester was never paid for talking about himself. Evidently he was willing to talk because he thought the connection with the research a good one from the social standpoint and because he was attracted to the interviewer on personal grounds. Once he became impertinent in his approaches, but she hewed to the line and was able to maintain effective research contact in spite of rebuffing him. With the directors of the study, he was pliant and beamingly cooperative.

A quotation from Chester will give a direct introduction to him. His words were written down thus: "Don't get the idea that I am inferior. I am far from it for I believe that I can fill any qualifications or equal any of the average boys, white or black, my age, physically, mentally, or any other way." These are fighting words, but does he perhaps protest too much? What kind of person makes such a statement when he has not been challenged? Is it a judgment of inferiority by his contemporaries that he is denying, or is there present also the echo of a long-standing self-evaluation which was set in his childhood? The reader himself must judge from the evidence.

Children take inevitably after their parents. The parents are the first teachers and they can teach only what they know themselves. Children may sometimes improve on the class position of their parents, but they always begin with it.

Chester's father is a colored Creole who "looks like a foreigner." He comes from a small town and is an artisan from a family of artisans. After finishing fifth grade he went to work as a "mud-digger" and worked up to a good job as a wire and cable setter. In good times he averaged $150 a month or better. None of Chester's paternal uncles has done better than his father, though Chester claims that the grandfather was a "well-known sugar grower and inventor of the sugar cane harvester." Since Chester, human-like, does not fail to make class claims where he can, he hastens to add that the grandfather was of Indian and French extraction and "well educated."

In reciting his genealogy Chester gives his mother less attention, less indeed than she deserves. It is clear only that she was the granddaughter of a slave, that she came from a rural district, that her family owned some property there, and that she entered, but did not finish, some kind of high school. Seen by the interviewer she proved to be a person of great weight and strength, light-brown in color with "bad" reddish hair, not recently straightened.

The parents would seem, then, to have started their married life as lower-middle-class persons. As a family, however, they began the march for higher status, driven by the stout heart and ambitious will of Mrs. Olivier. They acquired a good five-room house in a neighborhood populated by semiprofessional people. They had a piano and a radio, and cultivated a flower garden. They had a bank account and some pieces of property. They were moving, it would seem, toward middle-middle-class status, and their children, of course, were moving with them.

Mrs. Olivier had a class ideal of staying at home and caring for her children; she felt lucky that she could. She did not "run around" with men other than her husband and denounced those women of lower-class habits who did. She helped her husband save, even forced him to do so. She insisted on having well-mannered and obedient children. They were to be neat and clean, and so Chester is to this day. She always fed the children at the table, and not in their hands, as persons of lower tastes did.

Chester, her first-born, was to be a doctor, a high ambition but not out of the family reach. The children were not to bring "hoodlums," that is, lower-class children, to the house and were not to play with them. They were not to play strenuous games, lest they be injured, and were on no account to get "in trouble." They were not to go out of the yard after four in the afternoon, and when Mrs. Olivier was away from home, the neighbors acted as police. Chester was more than once belted home by his powerful mother in full sight of the neighborhood, for being "away without leave." All the children were given music lessons, even when times were hard; "Mother wanted us to know some music for our own use." The foregoing shows Mrs. Olivier in action, training her children in the class-ways familiar to her; renouncing immediate gratifications herself, she demanded the same of her children, and forced them to learn to work and wait for satisfactions.

But even such a powerful arm as Mrs. Olivier's is helpless in fighting a whole community. She could not keep Chester out of bad company. The public schools he attended contained large numbers of lower-class boys, and he had perforce to endure their company and even to join one of their cliques. This proximity to lower-class society is one of the conditions of Negro life created by the caste system, and all Negro children are subject to it. Mrs. Olivier's solution was to keep the children in the yard after school, in order to lessen such participation.

Chester's first clique in his lower-class school had standards quite different from those enjoined at home. Fighting was mandatory, sex knowledge and sex experience abundant, and music lessons sissified. Direct, man-to-man action was the ideal. Chester, however, never escaped the influence of his mother's training, and made a rather bad adaptation to his "fight gang." He was apparently intimidated and never could hold his own in fighting. His father, a two-fisted man himself, complained, "Why, every kid in the neighborhood used to run over him, and he wouldn't fight back." He always "hung around" older boys who would not expect him to fight as an equal, apparently taking a subordinate role and letting them do his fighting for him. In his first extrafamilial social contacts, therefore, he is seen associating with older people of higher privileges. Although it is likely that this behavior was primarily an escape from fear of contact with his age mates, it resulted in his acquiring knowledge above his own age level and tended to set an "upward seeking" pattern in his social behavior.

On one point his lower-class clique does seem to have determined his behavior. He always got "U" (unsatisfactory) in deportment at school even when his grades were good in other respects. Apparently he had to adopt the "fight gang" attitudes of defiance toward school and teachers. His mother did not fail to note this "U" and exercised coercion on him to change his ways. As a mobile mother should be, she was allied with the school and its discipline. She foresaw, of course, what the school could do for Chester. Though she could not shield him completely from the powerful influences of the play group, she did manage to keep him in general on the straitened path of mobility. Wedged between fear of his mother and fear of his gang, Chester chose to be a "good boy," perhaps because he also feared the rough way of life of the lower-class boys and was glad to escape from it into more refined circles of participation. An important item of class behavior learned from his mother was that of saving. She taught him how to save, took over his money, and let him experience the reward following renunciation. He still follows this pattern with his small, hard-earned wages.

Mrs. Olivier experiences great comfort from her church. She belongs to the Spiritualist group, a faith which is deplored by upper-middle-class and upper-class Negroes because of its emotionalism. Chester followed her class behavior at this point also; she is satisfied and says, "My Chester is a good little Christian." He has a record of being very religious and often edified his parents by personal prayer even when a very small boy. In one account of his day's activities, he mentions getting up at six o'clock and saying his prayers. At present he goes to his mother's church and also to a Methodist church where he teaches Sunday school. Perhaps he has to do this now in order to keep his mother as an ally in his efforts for social mobility.

The Olivier family ship seemed in the early years of the marriage to be sailing smoothly along toward the headwaters of higher status. Mrs. Olivier knew how to behave as a good lower-middle-class person, and middle-middle-class status was in sight. Mr. Olivier had a good job and under the firm guidance of his wife was saving money and acquiring property. Mrs. Olivier knew the value of occupation and education in the struggle for higher status and was determined that the four children should have a good rank in both. There seemed nothing to keep Chester from reaching her goal of becoming a physician.

The weak link in the chain was Olivier, senior. He had always been at least technical head of the house, as a middle-class husband should be. The wife reported to him the lapses of the children and threatened them in his name. But apparently there was conflict. Mr. Olivier did not like to have his money saved for him and put away where he couldn't get at it. He found his wife bossy, opinionated, and perhaps jealous. He said, "If she thought I went around with another woman, nobody could make her believe that I didn't." He alleges also, perhaps defensively, that he could not stand seeing her beat the children. He is convinced that she turned the children against him and says that she constantly disputed his authority over them. At any rate, seven years ago, Mr. Olivier deserted his family and practically abandoned their support. He now has a "second wife."

Mrs. Olivier gives a different account of his behavior. She says, "He is wild about young women—low, dirty women that he drags around from one job to another—prostitutes," and she pours forth her resentment on these women "who have fallen in the gutter." She suggests as another reason for his desertion that he has never been interested in the higher education of the children (upward mobility of the family) and that he deserted in order to escape the renunciations which would be required of him in achieving it. Mr. Olivier adheres to his rural Creole training as an artisan, and believes that a boy should go to work after he completes graded school.

His wife might have sued him for nonsupport, but this is not in accord with her lower-middle-class mores. She says, "He is awful, but I just hate to go to court and start a lot of publicity." So, after his desertion, she accepted the hard alternative for herself and her children, and set out to support the family. The proud housewife took a $7-a-week job as a domestic, where in addition she receives patronizing donations of food, second-hand clothes and medicine for herself and the children. She started taking in washing for "the man across the street." She dropped the insurance that she had carried for the children. She lost her chance to bring her children up with personal care and to continue for the others the class discipline so successfully practiced on Chester. For seven years she has had need of every bit of her energy and every ounce of her determination to keep up the house, feed and clothe the children, and keep them in school. A mother with lower-class standards might have thought it time for the boys to go to work, but not Mrs. Olivier. Little Dorothy, aged ten, has not even been allowed to drop her music lessons.

The loss of the father, however, has been a threat to status. The Olivier family is "on the skids"; it is described by scientists as downward mobile. The family is ashamed of Mr. Olivier. Chester is protective, as all people are, of his weak spots, and his father is one of these. For months after the interviewing started, he did not tell the interviewer that his father had deserted, but said merely that "he was away on a job." He was certainly trying to avoid the negative judgment that people would pass on him if they knew. How shamefully lower class to have one's father run off and live in sin! What would the parents of his polite friends at high school think?

Chester has been soured by this experience and has taken on the cares of a man. He helps his mother faithfully around the house and for some time went with her to her job to aid in washing dishes and dusting. If he wants money from his father he has to hunt him up and ask for it, and even then he does not always get it.

The mother has scaled downward her aspirations for Chester. She no longer sees any hope of sending him to college, let alone professional school. She will do the best she can, but an income of about $35 a month is not $150. Still, she has given Chester a powerful push; he has the habits and skills of a mobile person and has been able to do something for himself. His mobility, in fact, is freakish, for he seems now to have free participation with an upper-class group in his high school.

Chester is ambitious and is well aware of it. He says of himself, "I hope to hear and see my name recognized anywhere." His father has observed this characteristic and says, "Chester always tried to bring himself up and he went around with decent boys and girls, boys and girls who were up, and he tried to bring himself up like them. He wanted to be above, not below." His efforts for upward mobility were successful both before and during the time of his family's decline in status.

He had a monotonously successful record in graded school. He was school oratorical champion and runner-up in the state contest. He was editor of the school paper and received a gold medal for his services. (What a jewel in the crown of Mrs. Olivier, sitting proudly on the platform!) He was a successful athlete, having been captain of the basketball and baseball teams. He was class president one year and a member of the student council, and he was graduated from grammar school with a very good average. He is particularly proud of his record as a swimmer, "Right now I have the highest speed record for white or colored in the city." For three years he has held the Boy Scout and city-wide championships in swimming. Recently also he placed in a popularity contest as "Fifth Most Popular Negro in New Orleans" (he does not understand yet that the "best people" do not go in for this sort of thing, and that his title advertises his social weakness).

At fourteen, when he left graded school, an important event occurred. Through his own exertions and those of his indomitable mother, he was entered at the Donner Preparatory School. In graded school he had been in a group where his own class, lower-middle, was the top group represented; when he moved to Donner, he was thrown for the first time with the sons and daughters of aristocracy, and he found close at hand a class group which was markedly superior to his own. His inferiority feelings were apparently strongly activated and he took as his goal participation in this uppermost group. Not all boys who come to Donner do this; some, for instance, denounce social mobility as a sham and refuse to modify their class behavior.

At Donner, Chester began at once to exercise his talents to acquire high status, according to his familiar graded school pattern. He has earned consistently high grades (a mobile boy must be good in school), has gone out for dramatics (writing and producing a Christmas play), was vice president of the junior class and member of the student council. He belongs to the tennis and dramatic clubs, and is sports editor of the school paper. He has done well, but his achievement is not so sensational as it was in graded school. He feels a bit thwarted on this score and says grumpily, "I don't have a lot of positions around here because I don't like to be a figurehead." There are perhaps too many upper-class children, especially favored by the teachers, who stand in his way; or perhaps the competition here is keener.

Chester is keenly responsive to any imputation of his being different and inferior, and reacts immediately to recoup himself. He has experienced this punishing sense of inadequacy for two years at Donner and has modified his behavior as rapidly as he could along the lines of his ambition. It has been observed by Davis and Gardner that there is a wider spread of class membership in high school cliques than between the parents of the same clique members. Children associate freely, although their parents never see one another. This fact gives Chester his chance, and he is making the most of it. For instance, he makes a great effort to dress well and went without lunch for several weeks in order to buy a tailored suit. No $1.89 trousers for him! *Change clothes, change class* might be his slogan.

It is remarkable how successful he has been. His intimate friends are the most highly placed children in the school. He has jumped a full class, from the lower-middle-class platform provided by his family to his upper-class clique. His feat is best evaluated if the social characteristics of his mother's intimate associates are compared with his. Mrs. Olivier's six closest friends are all in domestic service or common labor. They earn on the average about $8 a week. They are all medium-brown to dark-brown in color, a fact likely to be associated with lower status. Their common interest is in the church and they are all members of low-status churches. Conversation centers around religious matters, mutual consolation, and children. In education, they vary in achievement from the fifth to the twelfth grade. Chester's friends, on the other hand, are all in the "swank" high school which he attends. Their parents are the eminent persons of the city, physicians, educated clergymen, highly paid insurance officials, and businessmen. The parents seem to be with rare exceptions people of college and professional education. They tend to be a light-skinned group, many of them indistinguishable from white. Their interests are cosmopolitan and include preoccupation with the arts, literature, and music. They are no less proud of their moral standards than is stout Mrs. Olivier.

The contrast between these two groups shows what has happened to Chester. By every reasonable standard he is out of his class, but he does not admit it, and neither do his friends at Donner. His male friends seem to fall into two groups: a social clique of upper-class boys whom he calls his "bosom" friends, and a clique of athletes who are his "closest" friends and have improved their status by exhibition of a special talent. The latter are probably the ones with whom he is more naturally allied.

It is the social clique which he stresses and refers to most often. He tells us at once in an interview what they mean to him, "We all go to the same invitational dances, and we always try to talk up invitations for the one who has none"—in particular Chester, of course. These boys evidently orient Chester socially in upper-middle-class and upper-class groups. They are also a great help in school, for they can "get away with anything at Donner." He emphasizes the loyalty of the group to one another, and this is certainly what he needs to consolidate his status.

His success in associating with a group of upper-class girls is also important; since women control polite social life, he can be mobile through them. He says indeed that his best friends are the girls, and gives as a reason that "the opposite sex are to be trusted more." He seems to be on a quite informal footing with the best placed girls in the school. One of these girls, independently interviewed about Chester, certified that he is actually a member of her clique, and indicated the reasons. She said, "He's always so neat. He don't have a lot of suits of clothes, but he sure keeps the ones he has up. . . . He is one of us. You see, he knows how to act. He's a nice boy." She goes on to say that Chester comes to her house all the time, and that his girl friend is one of her best friends. This testimony is critical and indicates that Chester is really accepted. He is neat, and he knows how to act according to upper-class standards; and then, from the standpoint of upper-class Negro girls, eligible men are hard to find!

The same girl explains how Chester gained admission to the group in the first place. She said, "He's a good athlete, a good actor, and he studies a lot, too." With these talents he was able to attract the attention of the highly placed children and to gain preliminary participation. Sensitive as he is to behavior deviations in himself, he was evidently able to plane his character very rapidly to the behavior model expected of an upper-class child.

It seems likely also that Chester did not wait meekly for an invitation to join this group but rather insistently "hung around" with them and pressed his claims. He was willing to take the risk of making the first home visit, as in the case of Phillip Randall, and to rely on his skills to get away with it. Randall accepts him but adds, "I really don't know much about Olivier other than what I've learned at school and when we're out together." He is pointing out by indirection that he does not know Chester's family, does not go to his house, and realizes there is something unusual about this situation.

The feeling among Chester's Donner clique seems to be that they don't have to be ashamed of him. After all, he is a champion swimmer, good student, vice president of the junior class, and so forth. He seems to be more aggressive than the other boys in his clique, and they find it hard to keep him out. Probably he presents a nice combination of aggressiveness and subservience: pushing himself in, but once in, showing the proper deference and conformity to the class-ways of the new group.

Chester adheres vigorously to the new conception of himself as a lower-upper-class person and rebuts any implication of lower-class status. For instance, he was asked as a matter of routine to tell some of his dreams during the course of interviewing. He refused, saying that he had dreams but could not remember them. This was remarkable since it was the only item on which he was uncooperative; no detail of his sexual life, for instance, seemed too personal to recount. The analyst might assume that his refusal was based on an unconscious fear that his

dreams would reveal too much about himself; and this interpretation cannot be absolutely dismissed. But Chester finally
gave a satisfactory explanation, saying that he has no interest in
such matters and that only the "superstitious" (that is, lower-
class) people believe in dreams. He had taken the interviewer's
request as an affront, as a suggestion that she thought him capable of behavior appropriate only to "ignorant," low-placed
people.

But Chester's social climbing campaign is not without its
complications. In addition to denying lower-class traits, Chester
must also suppress evidence of his lower-middle-class origin and,
with it, his family. No more proud sitting in graduation audi-
toriums for coarse-handed Mrs. Olivier. Chester was afraid the
interviewer would "find him out" and tried with various ex-
cuses to prevent her from seeing his mother; this behavior was
puzzling until the present analysis was worked out. He tries to
prevent his mother and other members of his family from going
to the Donner Preparatory School on any occasion, giving as a
weak excuse that he fears his mother will find out from the
teachers how mischievous he is and will punish him. His brothers, too, must be kept in the background. Sidney, aged fifteen,
says, "It just looks like it makes Chester mad for us to want to
go anywhere with him. He doesn't want us to go places with
him, especially at Donner." Sidney, who is a prize fighter, is not
to be allowed to interfere with the delicate social campaign that
Chester is conducting.

There is therefore a conflict between Chester's family loyalties and his wishes for social aggrandizement. He has outdone
his parents in school achievement, often a source of patronizing
attitudes by children toward parents, and surpassed them by far
in his social claims. In a sense, they cannot even see him on the
dizzy heights which he has achieved. The conflict is accentuated
by the fact that his family is now downward mobile, owing to the
desertion of his father. Suppose the mother should appear at
graduation, and the father too with his "second wife"? How
visible then would be the deviation of the Oliviers, and the
shame of Chester. Chester views the situation in deadly earnest

because he knows that his family cannot help him, that high school is not the end of his mobility, and that his high school friends may be a great help to him.

If the students accept Chester on the basis of his manners and his achievements, the teachers at Donner do not make the same mistake. The teachers know the stable adult world of class, and judge Chester by his parents rather than by himself. The teachers also are allied with and dependent upon the upper-middle-class and upper-class families who support the school, and they try to preserve this rank order in it. Chester does not put the situation this way, of course, because he hides and protects his weakness at every point. But the interviewer discovered that the teachers knew about his family, and knew that his mother was "Holiness," that is, a member of a low-status religious group. One teacher claimed indeed that she was a "faith healer." Chester feels the pressure of this discrimination (why was he not included in the cast of the operetta when he had specifically asked to be?) and responds with hostility toward the teachers and upper-class adults generally. "For leaders," he says, "we don't have anything." He says the De Frances (highly placed) are color struck, that they pass and will have nothing to do with dark people. The principal of the school is said to be color struck also; she will do anything for white people, he says, but insults Negroes. She is also said to favor light students (Chester is dark!). Chester continues defensively berating the principal, "She respects me just because she's got to. I don't like any fair people, or any color-struck people."

In the school, then, his campaign has met an obstacle in the social class prejudices of the teachers, and he responds with a hatred proportionate to his zeal for self-advancement. He hates upper-class and light-skinned adult Negroes because they bring into painful relief his darkness and his lower status. He does not fail, however, to denounce those below him in status, thereby showing loyalty to middle-class and upper-class standards. He says, "The majority of the colored people are of the worst type." He does not blame the authorities for threatening to exclude Negroes from the beach, or for moving them because they "cuss, dirty the place, and are noisy." He says, "Right here in this school they got plenty Negroes that will never be anything." Chester cannot understand those who do not strive for improvement and despises them.

In sum, then, Chester was very successful in graded school. In the Donner Preparatory School, under the pressure of discrimination against him, he developed a new level of status aspiration. With an adolescent clique, he has been phenomenally successful, although at a price, but not so with adults. Still there remain questions about Chester's behavior. Why is he so sensitive to derogatory comparisons? What urges him to such brash mobility? Is he pushed solely by his mother, or is there an element of personal insecurity which makes him feel that only the highest posts and places are safe for him? The following material on Chester's personality may help us on these points.

To discuss Chester's personality is to analyze his total behavior. His personality is a result, as it stands today, of his family, class, and caste training. What is to be explained primarily is Chester's boastful, defensive attitudes, his anxiety before criticism or derogatory comparison, his need to master and "be above" people. In seeking this explanation, we shall survey his early training, since the first socialization of the child is often of lasting importance.

Chester was a long-awaited child, born after five years of marriage. His mother feels that he has been, since birth, more reactive than the three younger children, struggling harder and longer for what he wants. He was breast fed, and weaned gradually at seven to eight months, the time recommended by government pediatricians. He was given a pacifier to make the problem of changing food habits still easier. Mrs. Olivier says that Chester was a good baby and seldom cried. He was not sickly; in fact he had no diseases in the early years. It might be said that he had a warm welcome from life.

He began to walk early, that is, at eight to nine months, which means at least that his personal investigation of the environment began a few months earlier than with other children. He talked somewhat early also, according to his mother's recollection, although we must keep in mind here the tendency of mothers to boast about their first-born.

The circumstances of their cleanliness training have been found to be an important learning situation for children. In this respect, Chester had a very ambitious mother. She began training him when he was three months old, trained him quickly, and says she did not wash a diaper for him after that time. She kept him on her lap over a little pot, used an enema syringe to start the act, and petted him so that he would not cry. Why she started so early, we do not know—perhaps she hated washing diapers or perhaps she wanted to make a prodigy out of Chester. At any rate, he became accustomed at an early age to having things taken away from him, rather than to giving them up out of love for the parents. It is difficult to know how to deal with these facts because there is no comparative science of character formation based in part on alternative methods of cleanliness training. It is to be noticed, however, that from early childhood on, Chester was the most selfish of the four children. He did not want others to use his things and would lock them up or stow them away; on the other hand, he always wanted to use the toys and implements of the other children. Was his fear of having things taken away based on this experience of being looted during the early sphincter training?

The mother spent a great deal of time with Chester during the first year. He preferred sleeping with her and did so until, in his second year, Sidney was born. Then he slept with his grandfather. It would seem that the mother had more time to give the first child and used it to advantage. She says she could not train the others as well as Chester because she "didn't have time for them." She seems to have wanted to be the "perfect" mother with Chester and to make him an advanced child.

Mrs. Olivier was asked if Chester had ever "played with himself," and she stated that he did as a small child. Apparently he was quite persistent about this behavior because only harsh means finally served to dissuade him. He was spanked and threat-

ened with spanking, and "finally he stopped." Mrs. Olivier did
not know that the discovery of his own genital is natural and
inevitable and not a sign of depravity in a child. She responded
according to the American mores and punished Chester, thereby
putting the first mark of pain on his exercise of sexual function.
Our observations are not sufficiently detailed to know if a change
in the character of the child was actually noticeable at the time
this taboo was imposed, but it would not be unusual if there
had been one. Perhaps some of the anxious and defensive traits
which he shows have their origin in this difficult piece of training. As to other early manifestations of interest in this sphere,
he says that he was an attentive auditor during some occasions
when his parents were having sex relations. Apparently he reacted with keen interest and sexual excitement, which leads to
the conclusion that he was advanced in sexual knowledge and
interest even as a small child.

Chester seems to have modeled himself early on his mother's
character and aspirations, a fact well brought out in his later
career. His mother was the more decisive person, but it is also
true that the father's job called for long absences from home, and
therefore he had less opportunity to influence the boy. Chester
did not imitate his father on certain major lines, such as wishing to carry out his line of work. He did not want to "get down
in the ditch" and start where his father had. When working as a
water boy with his father's gang, he collected his own wages in
defiance of his father, and at his mother's suggestion. If the
father imposed penalties for bad behavior which the children
thought unduly severe, the mother connived with them to avoid
the punishment. Since it was the mother who had the aim of
mobility for the family, it is important to notice this identification with her. Through her Chester became the banner carrier
of the family's status, and later achieved, for a time at least, the
high position which she has never been able to attain herself.

The role of early punishment and fright in Chester's life is
worth noting, for this bears on the question of his anxiety as
later manifested. It seems that infliction of pain was liberally
used as a method of training the boy. His mother still remem-

bers the great scare that he received at ten months. He was crying in an annoying manner, and a cousin put a sheet over her head to scare him. He stopped crying, but when the father came home, Chester inarticulately tried to tell him about the incident. The father's attention was arrested by the child's strange behavior, and he finally forced a confession from the mother as to what had happened. Chester led his father by the hand to his mother and her cousin and indicated that he wanted them spanked. This event can hardly have occurred as early as Mrs. Olivier indicates, but the exact date in months does not matter. What we have is a record of fright as manifested by crying being attached to one of his aggressive demands.

Mrs. Olivier was evidently quite stern in the training of her children. The father says, "You know I didn't mind her whipping or spanking the children to correct them, but when she would beat them and brutalize them I couldn't stand it. . . . I don't like nobody treating my children like animals." Evidently the father's Creole standards of training children were rather indulgent, and he was offended by the harsh methods of the mother. Mrs. Olivier did her job well because Chester was, by all testimony, a very good boy indeed; she did too good a job, however, for the father's taste. He says, "Chester was the best boy you'd want to see. . . . He listened to us like a trained animal and never did speak back." The father, in fact, denounces Chester for a coward and evidently felt he was no chip off the old block. Chester, according to the father, would never fight back "because he feared something terrible would happen to him." Mrs. Olivier says also that Chester has never had any fights and that "he isn't the fighting type." Sidney, on the other hand, likes fighting and has been practicing for years to be a prize fighter. Chester has a permanent anxiety in the face of physical pain such as must be suffered in fighting, and, though he is bellicose enough in the verbal field, he cannot "take it" when it comes to man-to-man encounters. Perhaps he found his "fight gang" less satisfying than did Sidney for this very reason, and was glad to escape into more refined company.

Chester is quite competitive with his brothers and sisters, and his relations with them are not very good. At the present time he is smaller than either of his younger brothers; he may have a tendency to assert himself against the ignominy of being the shortest. But this cannot be a major factor because he has been antagonistic to them for some years. He has quarreled constantly with Sidney, though he can no longer beat him in a fight. Melvin, four years younger, began to develop skill as a swimmer and once defeated Chester. Chester then exhausted himself completely in the effort to beat Melvin. Melvin also made more money at shoe-shining than Chester until Chester proposed a "divvy-up" treaty which enabled him at least not to be left behind. Sidney calls Chester, by inference, a snob; and Chester in turn says that Sidney is "deceitful and a tattler." This same competitiveness of Chester's is shown also in his school cliques, where he tries to outdo all others. The effect of these rivalries seems to have been to make him compete for, and often to win, his mother's approbation and preference over the other children.

It is no news now that Chester was the most religious one of Mrs. Olivier's children. His father, who disapproved, said, "He wouldn't destroy anything with . . . any saint picture [on it]. He was afraid if he'd destroy it that God would destroy him." Mr. Olivier thought it a little unmanly to take religion so seriously, but not so his wife, and in this, as in other details, Chester followed her. He prayed hard and bitterly, for instance, after the desertion of his father, hoping evidently in this way to bring him back. In periods of anxiety and defeat he also turned to prayer. It seems likely that his greater feelings of weakness and helplessness gave a special urgency to religious behavior in his case; what he could not fight for, he could attempt to gain by prayer. It must be noted too that he saw in the church an organization where he could be dominant, for he promptly became a religious worker and Sunday school teacher, thus winning distinction for himself.

If Mrs. Olivier was able to instill a stern conscience into Chester, she was not able to root out his biologically founded sex wishes, nor to keep him from that participation with lower-class boys which gave him an example for expressing them. If he had acted as his mother wanted him to, he would have been quite shy with girls. He has therefore to thank his lower-class clique for the fact that he is not afraid of girls. Somehow, when he was a very small boy, he and this group used to see adult Italians in the neighborhood having intercourse. He found this experience very exciting. When he was nine years old, he had intercourse for the first time with one of his Creole cousins and repeated this occasionally for some years. More recently he has had a young married woman as his mistress; he has had several affairs with girls of his own age. These he describes vividly and fearlessly, and with the obvious attempt to interest the interviewer in cooperation. In connection with his current affairs, he shows a marked aversion to marrying and a wholesome fear of the girls' fathers. There may be some boasting and showing off in his accounts, but his behavior nevertheless clearly reflects the less fearsome attitudes of lower-class boys. He has tried to conceal all this from his mother. It may well be that his behavior reflects the permissive example of his father in going off with "another woman."

Chester seems to be aware in a devious way of the degree to which he has been intimidated; his awareness is devious because he reports himself as being a physical, instead of a moral, weakling. He writes of himself, "During the earliest part of my childhood I was a physical nothing, very weak, puny, and a nervous wreck." According to his mother this is not a statement of fact. It seems instead to be a realization on his part that he was an unhappy and severely intimidated child, suffering under the urgent class training of Mrs. Olivier. He feels, however, that he has built himself up and made himself over, for he writes again, "While in elementary school I was advised by a physician to watch my diet and exercise regularly and I, very eager to build my body, competed and took part in all sorts of athletics, but excelled only in track and swimming. I obeyed every health rule and very soon I began to improve physically." His view is that he got off to a bad start, but through his own efforts and adherence to discipline has improved himself. He feels that he has been "physically mobile" to an unusual degree; it seems truer to stress that he is symbolizing his social mobility, as well as his escape from those oppressive feelings of helplessness and weakness (*vis-à-vis* his scornful father, for instance) which he had in the family.

It seems probable, also, that in the statements above he is gloating over his escape from his first (lower-class) cliques in which he could not have been very comfortable. Because of his fear of combat, he was forced into a subordinate role as a hanger-on to older boys. From their attitudes and those of his father he must have known that he was not regarded as a real man; he must have been glad, therefore, to escape from the social circles where such unattainable manliness was demanded of him.

Chester has also built up a defensive picture of his childhood, which he presented at first to the interviewer. It led to great mystification. He tries to represent himself as an extremely independent, forthright, and determined boy. He tells that when he was a youngster, his mother paid an older boy to take him across a dangerous street intersection on his way to school. He arranged with this boy to go by himself, and meanwhile let the fellow accept the pay. After he had had a year's practice in crossing the street, he finally revealed the plot to his mother. Again, he says he and his brother controlled the block where they were selling papers and "dared any of those boys to sell papers on our corner." The supposition here is that Sidney did the fighting, if any was called for. The function of these defensive beliefs is to gloss over his actual miserable state as an anxious, frightened boy.

According to his mother, Chester is the smartest of the Olivier children. His score on the Stanford-Binet test is 113. Probably his anxiety in the rough-and-tumble life of his play group led him to cultivate skills and talents by which he could in some measure redeem himself. These skills have really made his later mobility possible.

First impressions are often telltale. One of the writers saw Chester at first glance as a "softish person," a sissy. This he is in relation to adults upon whom he is attempting to make a good

CHAPTER VI

*CREOLE MISS**

WHAT EVERY American needs to know about caste is that he could look about as he actually does look and yet "pass for colored." All he would have to do is to associate with Negro people and let himself be taken for one of them. He would then be in a "learning situation" as far as caste regulations go. Depending on his social class and the area in which he lived, he would face a variety of vexing restrictions: in the South he might work as a shovel man in the ditch but might not drive a road machine; he could be the village bootblack but not the county sheriff; his wife could work as a domestic servant but not as a stenographer for whites; he might have trouble getting relief if he needed it, and might have to accept less than whites get; he might not be able to get a Pullman berth and be compelled to sit up all night on a train; he might have soup spilled on him if he went to the most desirable restaurants; if a scholar, he could not be a professor at Johns Hopkins; he would occasionally or frequently hear himself referred to as a "nigger"; he might have white friends, but could not be invited to their homes—certainly not if other white people were present; he would not be asked to join Rotary no matter how representative a businessman he might be; he might often have to depend on favorably disposed white people to protect him from illegal violence; he might have to tolerate having his wife or daughter crudely ogled or saluted

* The word "Creole" has found wide usage to indicate a group of white people in New Orleans who are of French, or mixed French and Spanish, descent. It is denied that they have Negro blood in any case. There is no quarrel with this usage here. It is affirmed as a matter of social fact, however, that in Negro society there is also a group of persons who have a history of French language and custom in their families; these persons also refer to themselves and are referred to by others as Creoles; to be perfectly clear, we shall refer to the latter group as *colored* Creoles. Whenever the word is used here it means the latter group and not the white group. The subject of this history is a colored Creole.

by any passing white man. If a white man did thus "pass for colored" for a while, it is inevitable that he would long for the restoration of his privileges as a white man and would beat a prompt retreat from the hazardous conditions of Negro life. With the Negro, the more "like white" he is in color or in culture, the more he also will see the disadvantages of his status and strive for the most privileged kind of life he can see, that lived by white people.

These considerations will serve to introduce Jeanne Manuel, who is very much "like white." In appearance she is a tanned girl of fifteen with sharp features and wavy brown hair. She is a colored Creole of good lineage. She was interviewed by a young colored man of her own Creole group, to whom she talked without hesitancy. She seemed to feel that she had nothing to hide from him, whereas she would undoubtedly have been cool to a dark "American" colored person.

Jeanne, her mother and father, and three sisters live in a middle-class neighborhood in "downtown" New Orleans, where the colored Creoles have traditionally lived in that city. They have a four-room house which they own, though it is not quite paid for; Mr. Manuel did the plastering work on it himself. The parents sleep in the bedroom, the girls, in two pairs, on a day bed and a sofa in the living room. The house is tidy, though modestly furnished; there is, for example, no radio or piano, for "the girls make their own music when they dance at home." The Manuels go in for the solid things but not for show.

Jeanne, true to her middle-class family type, was able to give good data on her father and his people. Her father's father was a sugar tester in a refinery and also owned some land. He had money, but "his children just ran through it." He was a darkish man, married to a "very light" woman. His wife could speak French, though it was not the language of her daily life. Jeanne said about her, "She was a sharp old woman. If she was a man she could have been president." As evidence for this view the fact was cited that she tried to get Jeanne's father to sign away his share of the paternal estate without proper recompense. This grandmother had ambitions for her three children; she

refused to let them work on the farm and "tried to make princes out of them."

Mr. Manuel is now forty-four years old. His mother's success in training him is evidenced by the fact that "he was a farm boy and yet he don't know a thing about it." He finished seventh grade and speaks both vigorously and expressively. His first job was as a Pullman porter, a middle-class job among Negroes. His wife made him stop this work and take up plastering. Later he joined the union; he has made as much as $60 a week in good times. When Mr. Manuel was young, he was a "socialite." He says that he was a great dancer and went to a party every night, though, to be sure, he came home at ten-thirty and did not do those violent dances the younger people do nowadays. He used to go to the "Jeunes Amis" hall to dance; he states that he was the "darkest person" at this Creole institution of high status. He is still the darkest person in his immediate family, and is said to have been getting sadly darker as the years go on; his daughter describes him as "that big ole Turkish-looking man." He is a loyal husband and devoted father.

Mrs. Manuel has told Jeanne that her maternal great-great grandfather was a white man and a member of New Orleans' swankiest club at that. Was the great-great grandmother one of those tawny Creole girls who fascinated the legendary beaux of their day? It is certain at any rate that memories of distinguished ancestry float down to the present Manuels from the mother's side of the house. The family used to own property, "the very property where the Hotel Chateau now stands." The mother's father was a plasterer also, but one child refers to him as a "contractor," thereby jumping his occupational status a notch. Mrs. Manuel's mother did not know how to speak English and never learned it to the end of her days; she spoke only French and could communicate only with those members of the family who also spoke that language. One of Mrs. Manuel's sisters lives in New Orleans and is a friend of Mrs. Nobile, an upper-class woman. This linkage of the Manuel family to upper-class people is of vital importance because it stresses the fact that they do not come from a lower-middle-class group; nor do they have inti-

mate participation with upper-middle-class people; they seem actually to belong to a well-defined group in between, which will be referred to here as middle-middle class. Two characteristics seem most obvious in distinguishing this group from the lower-middle class; one, just mentioned, is that they will be acquainted with a few persons who are in the upper-middle and upper classes; the other is that their lineage has "cleared up." This means that there is no record of relatives or immediate ancestors who were members of the lower class. With lower-middle-class people, the converse is likely to be the case, and the family record will be "spotty"; there is always "poor uncle so-and-so" who is "making cotton" somewhere for a white man. The Manuel history, as is shown, is solid middle class, with no unfortunate lapses.

Mrs. Manuel herself is thirty-eight years old, and in addition to her main occupation as housewife, calls herself a practical nurse. She wanted to be a trained nurse, but finished only the eighth grade and could not qualify. She apparently is more energetic and mobile than her husband. Jeanne says, "My mother is ambitious and have a get-up about herself." It seems that her family-status platform within middle-middle class is slightly higher than that of Mr. Manuel and that she sets a higher standard of performance for her family and children than he does. Mrs. Manuel is very light, like Jeanne. As a girl, she went to a white school, but she was uncomfortable there and never again attempted to "pass for white." She worked in a clothing factory both before her marriage and later to help the family budget; she seems to be an extremely competent house-keeper.

Mrs. Manuel named six women as members of her intimate group, all but one between the ages of thirty and thirty-nine. Two of these women are housewives and four are employed; of the latter, one is a nurse, one is a cigar-maker, and two work in insurance offices. None, it will be noticed, are domestic servants of the upper-lower class type. The wages of the workers are all above $15 a week. Two have finished high school, and the others have all completed sixth grade or better. Five of the

six are married. Three of the women have children who are in college or hold college degrees. Mrs. Manuel has known these friends all her life, and they live in the Creole section of the city. Five of the six are Catholics, and half of them own their homes. These facts about Mrs. Manuel's friends confirm her place as a middle-middle-class person.

Mrs. Manuel also has the proper organizational traits for a middle-class person. She belongs to a benevolent association and is its secretary. She is a church member of lifelong standing and takes a vital part in church activities. Apparently she is more "religious" than her husband; at least she is said to be a much more regular attendant at church.

She and her husband belonged also to an organization facetiously called the "Us Club." It was "just our bunch, not a club," meaning that there was no election to membership as in a formal club. "It was just married couples; but it's broke up now." The members went to different houses, played cards, danced, and drank beer. The men in the group all seem to have been firmly placed in middle class from the occupational standpoint; one was a baker, one a contractor, one a painter, one a plasterer, one a cigar-maker, and another "worked for the railroad." The Manuel parents show in all their associations the strong middle-middle-class orientation of the family.

The dominant type of family organization in America is the patriarchal; its influence is felt all through the Negro class structure and is not missing from lower-class Negro life. It is especially visible, however, in middle-class and higher groups. Jeanne is quite clear on this point with regard to her own family; she says, "Daddy hardly ever gets mad but when he does, I'm telling you, we don't fool with him. My mother is not like that, though; she talks plenty before she does anything." Here is seen the stern but indulgent father, and the mother who does not discipline in her own right but in that of her husband. It comes out in family joking also, as when Jeanne and her father wanted to go to a movie but the mother demurred and said she would not cook for them if they came home late; but "my Dad said it was all right and that she would cook if he wanted her to, because she knew who was the boss."

The parents seem to agree, however, on the kind of children they want. The children are taught to "obey and respect their parents" and to learn to do things around the house. Mrs. Manuel says, "I want to see my children brought up right," by which she means, of course, according to middle-middle-class standards. The parents also present a united front to their children; father does not interfere when mother "is showing them right from wrong." Said he, "When my wife corrects them and they come to me, I just tell them their mother is right." In the usual middle-class family the parents do not compete for the favor of the children but put first their joint duty of training them correctly.

Mrs. Manuel feels, however, that her husband has an easier role than she with the children. On her falls the daily duty of administering discipline, even though it be done in his name. She says, "I know I love my children, but they love their daddy more. They say I whop 'em and he don't." This is the mother's dilemma in every family of this kind, but she forgets that she administers the primary rewards to the children, also, and so has a chance to gain their love.

In the Manuel family one sees the compact, relatively isolated middle-class family; perhaps it can be so because the Manuels have not needed the immediate support of relatives as a lower-class family would; in the lower class the extended family is undoubtedly a kind of insurance system against the bad chances of life. Father's uncle is tolerated in the house because the pinch may come where he will be the only one earning. When they were first married, Mr. and Mrs. Manuel lived with his mother and sister, but Mrs. Manuel soon tired of waiting on these women, and the young couple moved to a separate house. Mrs. Manuel feels that she and her husband have brought up their children with little "interference" from relatives; they do not "go out very much" but devote their evenings to home and children. The mother says she "made" her husband give up his job as a porter because she "wanted him to be home with her and the children in the evenings."

The parents have few close friends and rely little on outside associations for companionship.

Noteworthy, too, are the strong positive ties in the Manuel family group. Apparently it is a really loving family. An evidence of this is the behavior of the father, who has recently been incapacitated for work; the mother says to him, "And what about you? There's nothing much you can do now but go to the show for your pleasure. And what do you do? You're always giving your show fare to the girls." Constant sacrifice on the part of the parents is typical of the middle-class way of rearing children.

The reliable middle-class conscience is no social accident; it is built up by a continuity of discipline not found in lower-class life. If the mother has delegated authority to an aunt or teacher, she stands solidly behind the surrogate and against the child. Jeanne's sister said, "Mother always took auntie's word for anything we did. She wouldn't ask me nothing, nor none of us. She'd just whip us. She thinks no grown person would lie." The child must remain strictly under parental control, directly or indirectly, and other influences are strongly resisted. Jeanne said, apropos of this, "When I was five years old I remember catching a whipping because I stopped on the way home to talk, and my mother was waiting for me. When I got home she whipped me." To this day, all the Manuel children are suspicious of any association not sanctioned by the parents. Jeanne does not now go swimming unless her mother is there with her. If other children come to play with the Manuels they all must play in the Manuel yard or the house itself; neighborhood wandering is taboo. If the visiting children create disorder, Jeanne herself has to clean up after them. She has to be in the house by ten-thirty at night, and promptly too, "though five or ten minutes late won't hurt."

In the course of reciting what she did on a sample day, Jeanne said she took a bath in the afternoon before she went to a picnic, and another that night before she went to bed. (A sense of kinship between people is probably more solidly founded on the number of baths they take than on the language they speak!)

Jeanne has been taught to cook, sew, and do housework, but this is not considered as training for working for "white folks," as it might be in upper-lower class; it is a preparation for marriage, the all-important destiny of a middle-class girl. Jeanne has learned her class-ways from her parents, and is thus prepared for effortless association with other middle-middle-class people. Without the excellent Manuel parents to aid her, she might have learned the same class-ways, but she would have had to face another process, and a longer one, called *mobility*. She would have had to uproot old habits before the new ones could be perfectly learned.

Colored Creoles, no less than the parallel white group, are proud of their lineage, though they do not seem to have given Creole society the aura of romantic pathos which many white writers have. Approximately twenty adult Creoles testified on the history of the Creole group in New Orleans. Most of them stressed the point that, in their youth, class stratification had not been as sharp as it has lately become within Creole society. It seems that the Creoles from the beginning have felt themselves to be an "in-group," or rather an in-between-group between white society and "American Negro" society. Membership in the Creole group was based on French-speaking ancestry, on lighter skin, and particularly on "good," that is, nonkinky, hair. Creoles of "low" (class) habits were excluded from this society, and all "dark Americans" were excluded. But there were undoubtedly differences in social position within the early Creole group. Frequent mention was made of exclusive clubs and parties and of wealthy and prominent Creole citizens; some were "free people of color" before the Civil War, and even plantation and slave owners. Quite a number were government employees after the war and established high social position in this way. Apparently the bulk of Creole persons until recent days were artisans, carpenters, plasterers, cigar-makers, slaters, and the like and as such they had good rank in their group. Whereas in white society the artisan group was mainly composed of upper-lower-class persons, in colored Creole society artisans were lower-middle class and above. It is to be recalled in this connection that there is no sacred number of classes in any social group, nor any inevitable rank of specific occupations; there are as many classes as the community recognizes, and occupations are ranked by the participants themselves.

Creole informants said with regret that they were formerly "classed" with whites in many ways and allowed to go to white schools. For example, Mrs. Manuel's father attended school with whites, but then "they separated them" and forced the colored Creoles to go to colored schools. One informant said that the Creoles refused to go to school with colored people, and "that's why there are so many dumb Creoles." There is this much truth in the statement: Creoles in general did not send their children beyond the sixth year of parochial school, but instead sent them to work in the trades traditional in the group.

In more recent years, however, the colored Creoles have been identifying themselves more and more with Negro society. They send their children to colored schools, and, as educated dark Negroes have risen in social status, there has been increasing social participation between them and the Creole group. Because young Creole men who have entered professions have found themselves excluded from business contacts with whites and therefore dependent for their support on the mass of American Negroes, they have come increasingly to accept status in Negro society and to make the most of it. Many colored Creoles have, of course, "passed" over into white society; it is said, "When one brother could pass in olden times, he did; the other one, who could not, remained a Negro." In both the alleys and the avenues of New Orleans, rumors of this kind are heard, and the "touch of the tarbrush" has been whispered even about well-placed whites.

Today, the separation between Creole and American Negroes is a live matter in the Negro group. The areal division has already been mentioned. People say that the "uptown" (that is, American) Negroes are much tougher than the "downtown" or Creole people. "Uptown" Negroes are said to be harder on

white people, more defiant, and less considerate. A Creole
woman of refinement said that "they will take over a streetcar,
and the conductor is afraid to tell them anything." Undoubtedly
she was referring to lower-class Negroes, but apparently she
looks at all American Negroes as lower class. The Creoles
remain an in-group, predominantly middle class, artisan, and
Catholic, with nostalgic memories of a lost status; but they are
definitely of the lower caste.

Many Creole children still learn French, either the local
patois, or "Paris French," depending on their class. Jeanne's
older sister had to learn it in order to communicate with her
doting grandmother. Jeanne herself did not wish to learn it and
has not done so, but her life is nevertheless profoundly shaped
by her heritage from the Creole group.

Making the inevitable middle-class criticism of lower-class
people, Jeanne says, "There are some nice dark people but
most of them are low-down, mean, and rough." She disavows
prejudice, of course, just as most white people do, but shows it
nevertheless at every turn; the "nice" dark people are those of
her own class. Her attitudes toward color and hair come from
her mother, who instructed her girls "not to play with the little
black ones." Jeanne makes the class point against them by
saying that the little "dark ones" were always fighting and
"didn't want to play right." Even now, she does not associate
with dark people and said that in her "bunch" even the brown-
skinned girls would not go with very dark people. She said in
explanation, "I might walk in the street with them, but I feel
funny. The light people criticize you. When I was little, I
sometimes played with them at school, but when I'd meet 'em
on the street, I'd turn my head from them and didn't speak."
Jeanne is a "Y" girl, and the interviewer noticed that almost all
the girls in this group were light; Jeanne said, "There are some
dark girls, but they were in the club when it started, and they
haven't taken in any more since." The "Y" authorities probably
forced some dark girls in at the start, but once the girls got
control of the club, they stopped that. Asked if she played with
a certain girl who lives fairly near her, Jeanne said, "No, indeed,

you don't have to go that far to find black people to go around with. I really don't have prejudice, but the kids we play with just happen to be mostly our color."

Skin color is a matter of teasing in the family. Jeanne's next younger sister is brown-skinned, and the grandmother would sometimes call her "black." The other children, however, would "fix" the grandmother; they would say, "Look at your husband, how black he was." Jeanne says, "We'd tell her she had had a black husband and then we'd tell her about her daughter, about that knotty-headed daughter she had. She'd want to die." But the old lady knew they were exaggerating to tease her, much truth as there was to what they said. They also said that the grandmother did not really discriminate against the dark child.

Jeanne is the lightest one among the children, and the only one who can pass. Her mother is light also but does not pass; "she'd be all uneasy if she went to a white place," though nobody would know the difference. What is really crucial behind the color point is class; the implication that light color goes with higher status, and Negroid appearance with lower status, is what makes these characteristics so important. Caste feelings of solidarity are weak compared to the strength of considerations of rank within Negro society. Jeanne's behavior illustrates nicely the great satisfaction that middle-class people take in their superior rank and prestige; they inevitably behave so as to maximize these prestige satisfactions, since in many other ways they must forego impulse gratification.

Analysis of Jeanne's clique yields the same information as that gleaned from the discussion of her mother's intimate associates. The clique is strictly middle-middle class. Jeanne named thirteen boys and girls with whom she associates. In many cases she does not know their parents' occupations, although her parents know or know of their parents, but she did name such occupations as carpenter, factory worker, Pullman porter, and officer in an insurance company. Most of the children are in high school, and comparison of their ages and school grades indicates that there is little retardation in school among them—unlike Mary Hopkins' clique, for instance. Most of the children's names are obviously those of colored Creoles. Jeanne would be expected to marry someone from a group like this, thus maintaining class and Creole status.

Jeanne tells quite a story about her club participation. She belongs to a social club and used to be president of it, but the club has deteriorated lately, and she is getting out. For one thing, she does not like the boys in it very well, saying, "Them ole stupid boys don't know how to act." She further objects to the fact that a committee appointed to buy flowers for the funeral of a dead member misapplied part of the funds. The dissolution of the club seems to have been designed to dispose of the unreliable committee. Jeanne's crowd has a newspaper called the "Gossip Times." She says, "It's a little paper. Every time we know something about somebody we put it in the paper. For instance, if a boy goes out with somebody else's girl friend, we put that in the paper." The boys in the clique are not allowed to read this paper, and the girls seem to feel a slight hostility toward them in the group.

The purpose of Jeanne's club is to have parties and dances; "we ain't got no special aim, except to have fun." But she does not share fully even in this aim; she seems to value the club because it gives her a chance for leadership rather than for the "fun" it provides. It gives her, she says, "a chance to do the work and the planning, the serving, and all the other work," and apparently she excels in these activities. Perhaps Mrs. Manuel has done too good a job of bringing Jeanne up "right and decent." The important rule in her group is that the girls are not to steal each other's boy friends; and a boy is not allowed "to try to make all the girls fall in love with him," because, apparently, this would arouse feminine jealousies which would be fatal to the existence of the clique. Jeanne does not like Theresa Noël, for example, because the latter is a stealer of boy friends. The boys and girls often gather at Jeanne's house, where they dance or play cards, but Jeanne sees to it that they do not come on week nights because then she must do her homework. The girls in the clique talk about the boys when they are not around, especially about "how foolish and silly they act." These mysterious actions on the part of boys are at once fascinating and ridiculous, but the latter description is the official dogma of the group. Jeanne belongs to a very orderly group, in sum, in which there is no cursing, hair-pulling, or unexpected babies.

It is a proud boast of middle-class Negro people that they and their relatives "have never been in any sort of trouble," meaning, of course, with the law. This is a claim that few lower-class families can make. This "lack of trouble" is a result of the firm family and community controls on aggression, controls which are rigidly internalized in the personalities of middle-class people. For this reason, lower-class people often regard middle-class individuals, both white and colored, as pale and mousey, and lacking in proper spirit in the face of injury or affront. Jeanne's younger sister testifies to the strength of aggression control in the Manuel family by saying, "None of us fights much. My mother got that out of us early." Mrs. Manuel remarks similarly, "One thing I can say; all of my children get along good. We don't never have any fussing or fighting." She stresses the point that no one curses in her home, and that the children have never heard bad language there. Jeanne's sister insists that they are not a spineless lot, however; she says that none of them fights at school, although "if somebody do me something, I'm not going to stand still and take it; but just to be always fighting, I don't like that." She states that her parents will let her fight in self-defense only and are determined that she will not be "always fighting" like the lower-class children.

Control of aggression in middle-class children does not seem to call for daily beatings. As the Manuel children tell the story, the beatings, though some are bitterly remembered, all seem to be of early date and are no longer likely to occur. It seems probable that there are more powerful coercions upon children than the threat of infliction of pain. For one thing, the constant supervision of the parents over the children often prevents the occurrence of rebellious acts, thus diminishing the actual need for punishment. Also, parents are powerful figures to middle-class adolescents; the children still expect their parents to assist them materially in reaching and consolidating full status as middle-class adults. Parental admonitions therefore always carry the implied threat of withdrawing important support if they are not heeded. "If you go gallivanting around at night this way, I don't see any use in sending *you* to college."

The middle-class girl is headed for marriage and must be fitted for the kind of career that is expected of her. Her training begins early, is rigorous and consistent. Control of the girl's contacts with boys is one important aspect of this training, and the teaching of housekeeping duties another. Mrs. Manuel has been assiduous in both. By constant association with her mother, Jeanne has learned the skills and duties of a good wife. Her contacts with boys are carefully scrutinized. In the middle class, girls are respected and well treated and are not to be married off to get rid of them. Jeanne says, "My mother don't believe in giving her children away. She says we have to finish school first." "Finish school," in the middle class, means at least high school, and preferably college or professional school as well.

Neither parent likes to have Jeanne go out with boys, but she goes occasionally when "they know the boys and their families are good friends of ours." In this case, the boys are apparently responsible to their own parents for proper behavior toward Jeanne. Jeanne refuses to associate with girls of shady reputation, for instance with Theresa Noël who "goes around with a married man." Jeanne looks forward to marriage, though somewhat vaguely; the boy, when he comes along, has "got to be olive or white, with pretty hair, square shoulders, and sharp features." This is the colored Creole girl's ideal man, and, one may suppose, quite close to the general American ideal as well. Jeanne hopes to marry a professional man; she might or might not have a profession herself, but she is sure that her husband ought to have one. On a class basis, this is a conceivable marriage for her to make, although perhaps giving some evidence of aspirations toward mobility. Mrs. Manuel says that the girls shouldn't marry "until they are able to take care of a home."

It is further held in this family that children should not live with their parents after marriage but should "have a home of their own," where, of course, they can set up the isolated, middle-class type of family life.

Jeanne is a good student. On the first day she was interviewed, she had come to school early to study geometry, a subject with which she has difficulty. The family urgency is heavy upon her to do her school work well; should she fail, she will have to go to summer school, and she hates walking through that hot sun. Her general average in school is around 89, and her I.Q. is 116. Although her father is sick and out of a job at present, he and his wife would not "think" of making the children leave school and go to work. "They said we got to go to school. Mother says we are going to school even if we end up going barefoot." This evaluation of school as the door to higher status is part of the middle-class mores of this family; even sickness has never been a very good excuse for missing school. Jeanne says, "We got to have a mighty high fever for Mother to let us stay home." Jeanne has great aspirations so far as school is concerned; she says she is going to finish college "because you haven't done nothing if you've just finished high school." Even college does not seem enough to her, for she asked the interviewer how long it took to get a master's degree.

Jeanne's forms of recreation are conventional for a girl of her status. She likes to swim, play tennis, go to shows and pictures, read, play cards, and sew. Moving pictures, though much appreciated, play no such role in her life as they do in that of Edward Dodge. The whole Manuel family seems to love food and to lavish great care on its preparation. Mealtime for them is a ritual attended with great pleasure; eating is one of the delightful and innocent things that a whole family can do together. How different from the lower-lower-class family, each member eating when he likes, and often out of a can at that!

It has already been suggested that middle-class Negroes take their religion seriously, and Jeanne is no exception. For her it is both a ceremonial and a guide in her personal life. She is a Catholic, like her parents, and goes to church two or three times a week. Her parents do not have to make her go; rather, she says, "I got to make them go." Jeanne cannot remember when church did not have the same importance for her that it has now. "When I was small, Mother used to take me with her and carry me in her arms, so you see I just grew up in church." She has made her first communion and been confirmed. She never skips her prayers at night, and, according to her sister, sometimes prays so long that she falls asleep at it. She always puts money, even her own money, into the collection box on Sunday. She stresses the church's ethical value to her: "It helps you live right. I don't see how some people can live without going to church." "Church" is not a mere ritual to Jeanne as it is to so many upper-lower-class girls. She likes particularly "that silence in church" and likes to pray in it. Asked what she prayed for, she said, "You ask for different things or favors in your prayers," and she states that she gets everything she asks for. She also prays for dead people and believes that her prayers help them out "because they can't pray for their own selves."

Jeanne is an earnest Catholic and lives by the precepts of the church. She does imply, however, that priests often make caste points against Negroes, saying, "When some are in the confession box, they talk just as loud and fuss with you. And some of them try to be just as snubby. They talk with you in church, and when you see them in the street they hold their head high up and don't tell you nothing." It is undoubtedly difficult for the church to evade the pressure of the caste mores of the area and to provide a type of treatment for Negroes within the religious institution which is not conventional for them outside it.

The Manuel family has had a comfortable and successful career in its middle-middle-class position until the present time; it has now been plunged into a perilous situation by the illness of Mr. Manuel. The doctor says that he may never be able to work again. Jeanne is very protective about the situation and does not like to admit the existence of any threat to the family status. Twice she refused to tell the interviewer how the family is getting along since her father became sick. Finally she said, "Well, my mother sews for out, but she does it at home." Mrs.

Manuel makes barely enough to get along in this way; Jeanne says, "We live about half the way we should live since father has been sick." If economic support adequate for the maintenance of a middle-class mode of life disappears, downward mobility is inevitable in the long run; the Manuels are now facing this disaster. Mrs. Manuel already feels the shock and says, "You know, where a person has been used to have what she wanted and now don't have it, that's hard, I'm telling you." She has had to swallow her pride and try to get a job as a domestic servant, but she was offered only five dollars a week and refused to take it on the ground that she could make more at home sewing. She hated to apply for relief, but did, in desperation; she was refused, since some of the grandmother's insurance is apparently left. If she could get enough work as a seamstress, she could manage, but she cannot, and her earnings are uncertain as to time and amount.

The reaction of the family has been to tighten its bonds and pull in its belt. The members are trying in every way not to alter their mode of life. Some people criticize them for keeping up this front. Jeanne says, "There are some people around my house who think we dress too nice since our daddy wasn't working. My daddy had on a nice new shirt yesterday . . . and people talked." It must be understood that the quality and neatness of the clothes one wears are important class marks, and to change them may be an admission of defeat.

Mrs. Manuel is trying to protect the children from the knowledge of how tight matters actually are; she thinks it might break their spirit. She says, "The children have always got what they wanted, and now I feel that it would be like cutting something out of them if I told them the real situation and that we don't have much." She will not hear of the children going to work—it would "kill" her, and she does not want them to marry young. Either course of action would be an admission of the family's fall in status. The usual expectation in the Manuel family has always been to the contrary effect, that the children would *raise* the family status in their generation. The mother says fiercely, "I want to see my children finish school, and I'll do it if

I have to beg on the corner. They must be prepared for what'll happen in the years to come." Jeanne herself reacts proudly and stubbornly to the idea that she might have to leave school, saying that she would not object to working if she had to, would not feel inferior to her friends, and would not "mind" what they would say. She is deceiving herself, though bravely, and it is to be hoped she will not have a chance to learn how she would actually feel.

Mrs. Manuel is candid in her mobility strivings for the children. She states, "We are trying to bring all our girls up to be nice and decent and get 'em a good education so they can be somebody." This can be interpreted as meaning "somebody better than the parents." The father has no plans for the children and leaves the whole matter to his wife with the statement, "Of course, I know she wants them to be something and whatever she do is all right with me." He knows that Jeanne wants to go to college but doubts that he will be able to send her now that he cannot work. Jeanne wants to be a bacteriologist or maybe a druggist. She believes that education will help her to advance and points out, "If my mother would have been advanced, then I'd be better off now." She is not afraid that she would not be able to go to school if her daddy should die, for "My mother will send us to school if she'll have to work all her life." It is plainly the mother who is determined to advance the family status, and who stoutheartedly faces the world, needle in hand, to sew her daughters' way into a brighter future.

Without a backlog of capital, such a fall in status as threatens the Manuel family is always possible; it is for this reason that the fever of mobility strivings is bound to run in the blood of middle-middle-class families. They have seen friends disappear into obscurity, from a middle-class standpoint, and grasped the lesson which is implied for them. It is only in the absence of ordinary bad luck that the middle-middle-class family can run a secure course and succeed in projecting its children into the greater security of upper-middle class. It is probably because of this chronic insecurity that every sign of success or lack of it from a mobility standpoint is perceived and evaluated in a child.

A dark skin or a slow mind may be a calamity; a fair face or an energetic character will win parental approval as a sign of success to come.

If the frame of life in which Jeanne lives and moves is now clear, it will be possible to have a more intimate look at her as an individual. Her clear-cut personality is of a kind which might not be suspected from examining her social role alone. She is described by her friends as an "old-timey girl," that is, as being very conventional. It is further said that she has "a dry disposition" and does not know how to take a joke. She shows that the latter is not altogether true by saying, "Yes, I had a too dry disposition but my daddy didn't like it; he likes laughing and joking, and now he's sick, I guess I'll have to change my disposition so he would like me, huh, sis?" Her father says that Jeanne is more settled and serious than his other daughters. Her mother puts it this way, "I tell you, Jeanne, she acts just right. She ain't backward; she ain't forward; she gets her lessons fine. I don't have to tell her what to do. If she wants something and I say 'No' she don't beg or fuss. She's got a wonderful disposition." It can be judged from this that Jeanne is a highly satisfactory child to her mother, which may or may not be a good omen of her later adjustment. Mrs. Manuel adds somewhat guiltily that Jeanne "is my best child. I've never had a bit of trouble with Jeanne." Both parents agree that she is a model worker; she needs to be told only once what to do, and often not even that once, for she sees a need and meets it. With people outside the family, Jeanne is not as popular as her two nearest sisters; people say she is "too settled" and feel she is a little severe. She probably makes them uncomfortable by setting too high a standard of dutiful behavior. Jeanne, for instance, often sits up at night doing her homework while the other children are playing. She is the most religious of the children, so much so that the others joke about it. But she is right on the spot when trouble comes; she does not lose her head or indulge in hysterics. When her mother fainted (from "high blood pressure") Jeanne was the only one of the children who stayed on the scene, rubbing her mother's arms and legs, trying to make her come to. They all say, "You can count on Jeanne when there's trouble."

She has her fears, however, like everyone else. She once fainted after witnessing a blood test in a hospital. Now she avoids the sight of blood but feels that she might conquer this fear by becoming a bacteriologist. She does not like to think of cutting up cats and dogs in a laboratory, but she is not afraid of germs. She is afraid of a mouse "if he is alive." She is afraid to "pass," though she knows she could and would like to "go as white." Apparently her conscience is so strong that it does not permit her to resist any kind of authority, not even that of caste, which she feels to be an unfair kind. If she resists authority, she becomes "uneasy," that is, anxious, and has to give it up. She is afraid to go bathing unless her mother is there because in the latter case her mother is responsible; if she went alone, she would be responsible herself. It can be seen from this that she is still quite dependent on her mother; this prolonged dependence is an important characteristic of middle-class children; sometimes it is lifelong.

Socially as well as biologically, the young Manuels are their mother's children. Being a middle-class mother, she was able to do more than simply bring them into the world, which is sometimes what lower-class motherhood amounts to. The lower-class mother bears the child, but then must go back to her "job" outside the home, so that she cares for the child only at night. Relatives and friends pinch-hit for her during the day. The middle-class mother, on the other hand, spends most of her time with her children. A child is more likely to develop a stable and consistent character when it is subject to just one kind of discipline and is cared for by only one individual.

It is therefore characteristic of Jeanne's class that she was taken care of exclusively by her mother up to the age of six years. Apparently she had a singularly placid nursing period. There was no pain (colic) following eating, and the transfer from the breast to solid food was begun at ten months and uneventfully concluded. She was "a fine, fat baby" and never cried much. She seems to have come out of the nursing period with the serene faith that she would always "get enough." The only painful spot in her early childhood seems to have been her teething; "she gave a yell in bed one morning," the teething cry, and was uncomfortable for about three days. Her mother says that she accepted frustration without much protest; even today "if she can't have what she wants, she acts just the same." This lack of protest in Jeanne has already been noticed and requires special attention.

Jeanne was, in fact, so fat a baby that she could not walk until "almost two." It seems that she was dependent on her mother to bring things to her for an unusually long period, and this may have been the beginning of the unusual attachment to her mother which she now has. Such an attachment can be important in compelling the child to smother its protests; it fears that if it does "anything against mamma" her cooperation may be withdrawn. This threat of withdrawal of favor is a "punishment" as effective as or perhaps more effective than infliction of pain.

Nor did Jeanne altogether miss spanking when she was a child. It was one of the reinforcements used in cleanliness training. This training was begun "early" by her mother with the use of reward to persuade Jeanne to use the pot. The mother said she did not have "much trouble" with her. The high value which she now places on her mother may already have been functioning and have persuaded her to accept cleanliness discipline. When the training was finally being consolidated, Jeanne was not only rewarded but occasionally spanked, especially by her grandmother who had ideas of her own on how children should be trained. It is to be remembered here that spanking must have meant not only pain to her but also the threatened loss of support from her invaluable mother.

Mrs. Manuel had the standard middle-class (and every-class) attitude toward sex play in small children.[1] She "smacked the

[1] There is a serious question whether early punishment of sex responses is necessary and whether it may not do more harm than good; it is perhaps too

children's hands" if she found them handling themselves. At about eighteen months, the children were put into tight panties with the idea that this would make the practice more difficult. From this time on she had little difficulty with masturbation, but she adds, with good practical sense, "Of course, that's only what I could see, but I don't know what they did when I couldn't see." The chances are that they didn't do much, especially Jeanne, who was so very anxious to please her mother. Jeanne's conventional character emerges from these early phases and changes little in later life; it seems to be based on a very satisfactory early relation to her mother, for which she was willing to give up various types of impulse gratification.

Jeanne's way of adaptation has been to do exactly what her parents want; by this means the circular reinforcement mechanism goes into action. She does what they want, and they in return give her an unusual measure of love, approval, and service. She was already a "little mother" at five. She used to insist on going to market with her mother and learned how to evaluate and buy different kinds of meat, "so they could send her by herself." She was very proud of this feat, especially because her older sister didn't learn it and "she can't buy meat now." Jeanne recognizes that she is very much like her mother today and says, "If she had a twin it wouldn't be able to think like her as much as I do. Our minds run together." If her mother went away, Jeanne is proud to say, "She would leave the house in my hands because she's got confidence in me." Her mother asks her opinion about articles to be bought but does not ask the other sisters, a fact which Jeanne enjoys. She has made a specialty of being just like her mother and never expressing any impulse contrary to the mother's wishes.

She likes her father too and always has, but makes no open

---

early to say with absolute finality since the argument stands that every item of culture training must at some time have been functional and may still be. The important thing to remember is that masturbation training is training not of an isolated act but of the sex impulse itself; it is therefore also to be thought of as training for marriage and family life. It is this consideration which prompts toward caution, because no one wants to make the latter adjustment more difficult than it is.

claims on him which would interfere with her mother's rights. She remembers a whipping that her father gave her as a small child and says, "I was so brokenhearted because I thought he shouldn't have whipped me. I felt some sad." The whipping carried with it the threat of loss of her father's protection, and she could not endure this. But she says that she did not get slapped much by her father because, "I always listened when they spoke to me the first time." She learned early how to avoid trouble by a willing and wholehearted obedience, and she is proud of being a good, obedient girl, thus following her class ideal. She says she likes her "daddy a little the best" but likes her mother very much too; "I am like parts of both of them." And she is right; she is dependent upon and identified with both parents.

Parents of any class are not supposed to have favorites, and one hears over and over again, "I treat 'em all the same." Jeanne has become so adept in her role as model child that she cannot help being her parents' favorite, and she knows it. She admits it very reluctantly, however, because she knows it is a bad position to be in, since it draws resentment and contempt from other people, especially from her sisters. She denies that she is the favorite in that she gets more clothes or privileges than the others; it is just that the parents "like" her better. The mother says that Jeanne has always been her father's favorite and that she always liked him too; "when she was small she always wanted him to pick her up." Jeanne denies that there is any "baby" in the family and has tried to abolish the custom of calling the youngest child by that name. She is known also to have expressed the wish that she were the only child in the family. Her sisters are quite aware of the situation and twit her sharply with such remarks as, "Don't hurt her," and "Daddy's precious."

There is little doubt that under the smooth conformity of Jeanne's character is a profound streak of jealousy. She would like to be the only child. Failing that, she wants to be so good that her mother and father will consider her, as they do, their "best child." She was very jealous at the birth of her next youngest sister, when Jeanne was two and a half. She did not fight with her, since that was forbidden; but she did think that her mother ought to hold her instead of the baby. She "hung around watching all the time" as the mother performed services for the younger child. Later she used to fight with this sister, who was a spirited child, "a little pepper." It was more usual, however, for her to take her grievance to a parent and thus show her obedience to the rule against in-family fighting. "My younger and older sister used to whip me, but I used to get my revenge when I tell my daddy on 'em. He used to make 'em leave me alone, and if they didn't he'd fix 'em. My mother used to say, 'You are always telling your daddy when they hit you.' My mother used to take up for all of us, but my daddy used to take up for me."

At present, Jeanne is resentful and even spiteful toward her sisters. The youngest one may not have her role as "baby." The next one, just younger than Jeanne, is nice, but Jeanne doesn't want her to "get feeling too big." The older one is babyish, "acts just like a child," and Jeanne considers herself much older than this older sister. Jeanne is dominant over her younger sisters and says, "I boss 'em around." She wants to be able to give them orders and feels that this wish arises because she is like her mother. If the children do not obey her, she often succeeds in getting her father to make them obey. She wishes she had a big brother but not a little one. "That's out"; no more rivals for Jeanne, she has enough to cope with. She does not want her little sisters to go everywhere with her, explaining cryptically, "They're too disgusting, that's why." Her sisters are jealous when she goes to the movies with her father, but she defends herself by saying that they go out with the mother at the same time; that's fair because each has a parent to go with. Jeanne has won by obedience and efficiency the central position in the family. The parents, struggle as they will to be even-handed in their dealings with the children, cannot resist the rewards which Jeanne offers them. They see in her the model child of their class and hope that she will be as successful in dealing with people outside the family as she has been with those inside.

Jeanne has learned to achieve dominance in the family group by subordinating herself to the regime. Like every other achievement, this has its price. The price, in this case, is a relatively extreme suppression of her natural biological tendencies. It has already been recorded that her disposition is considered to be "dry," a word which her family seems to use to indicate a lack of spontaneity. In no aspect of her life is this lack more evident than in her attitude toward sexual matters.

Just how this training was stamped in is fairly explicitly stated in the record. It was begun with the punishments for childish sex play. Similar pressures were probably exerted against any other spontaneous interest and curiosity which she had in early years. Accidental factors may have figured, such as the experience she had at the age of five. On her way home, she saw a crowd in front of a house, and stopped. She was told that a man had chopped up his wife and put her in a trunk because she had been going around with another man. He had also done away with his wife's sister because she had known about the affair and had not told him. The man further stated that he was going to put his rival through a meat grinder if he could find him. Jeanne does not remember being frightened by this event, but it is hard to see why it did not frighten her. It was a situation in which she could easily have established the idea that men were dangerous. Certainly she had learned by this time that her sex impulses were in conflict with her devotion to her mother.

Mrs. Manuel states that the children never slept with their parents when they were small. It seems probable therefore that Jeanne never had opportunity to witness parental intercourse or to be disturbed by its implications. Still, the house is small and the walls are thin. The mother has never given any of the girls sex information, and feels that she has been remiss in her duty, but she thinks that the girls all "know" now. Until she was twelve, however, Jeanne thought that babies came by the boat or stork, or that the nurse brought them. This kind of ignorance, or this pretense of ignorance, is again class-typed and would not be expected in a lower-class child. Jeanne thinks that sexual intercourse is dirty and revolting, either before or after marriage. She says, "That's how children are born. My sister told me that's how they were born. She said it was nasty." Jeanne, of course, always accepts the official view—especially if it is on the side of impulse renunciation. She adds, "My grandfather said he would not touch a baby right after it was born. Right there I thought children were awful and dirty." Perhaps that is why she does not want another child in the family; she may not be able to stand the thought of her parents having sexual relations. Her views on sex may have been further complicated by the fact that her initial menstruation at twelve was painful and protracted; "I kept on losing blood."

The sex controls exerted by the family have continued and have produced a condition of ignorance and fear in Jeanne. For example, when the three girls went to a party recently with their beaux, the mother and father came after them, and they walked home in a column, first the girls and their boy friends, then the parents, bringing up a watchful rear. This big parade is typical of middle-class family training with regard to sex. Nor can Jeanne accept the idea of sexual relations even after marriage; if she is to have children, she expects to adopt them. She thinks of the whole matter as immodest and obscene, and says, "The night I get married I'm going to have some keys, and I'm going to lock myself in my room. I ain't going to sleep with him."

Some of her sex fears are expressed in the record, but undoubtedly many are not. She looks on the sex act as one with no possibility of pleasure for her, but rather as submission to a kind of assault. She thinks if you get a baby started and anything stops it, you will die. Of premarital intercourse, in addition, she says, "People would talk about you if it got around. They'd say you were indecent." This is a strictly social control of the middle-class group; she is afraid of being obnoxiously conspicuous and isolated by gossip. She and her girl friends have spoken critically of a girl who had a baby before she was married. To perceive how different it may be in the lower class, one must remember Mary Hopkins and her group, with their very mild notice of the same kind of case.

Jeanne has had various boy friends but holds them all at arm's length. She never gives them "too many liberties." Her sister remarks about Jeanne, "She doesn't know how to talk to boys, and when she dances with them she always dances a mile away." This testimony would be expected. Through fear of her own impulses, she is actually awkward with boys. This fear goes further and inhibits her from behavior which might arouse her impulses and make them an uncomfortable problem for her. She is rather opposed to dancing, apparently seeing in it, unlike less inhibited people, a strong latent sexual meaning. She "does dance," but not very much. If she were to go to a ball, she is afraid that she would make mistakes. Another detail is that she does not wear lipstick and rouge, calls it "all that trash"; these vanities would serve to make her more attractive to boys and this is just what she is afraid of. She says that she does not like the "noise and excitement" of being with people and would rather be by herself and do a little sewing; this self-isolating behavior is again a defense against the arousal of sex impulses in the mixed clique.

Where there is so much avoidance, there is certainly something to avoid. Jeanne is strongly suppressing her womanly feelings, but they are there none the less, otherwise she would not be afraid of them. It is surely no accident that her dreams show a marked preoccupation with sexual themes, and seem to illustrate quite clearly the punishments for sexual actions. Granted that Jeanne's parents want her to be a virtuous girl, they probably do not want her to shun marriage and parenthood altogether, and perhaps they have trained her too well.

By American society as a whole, Jeanne is considered a Negro despite her fair skin. She says that she learned she was colored when she played with some white children in the country; "I was darker than them, so I could see I was different." But her mother would not let her play with darker Negro children, saying, "There are enough of your own kind of children to play with, and you don't have to play with them little black niggers." In this simple way she expressed the dilemma of the colored Creole group; too dark for whites, too light for "niggers"!

Mrs. Manuel denies that she tried to bring the children up so that they would want to be white; she knew the hopelessness of that. Jeanne says her mother would turn them loose on the beach to get tanned when they were children, saying that she did not want them to be too white—"white is too rough and stringy. I want you a rich looking color." She is expressing, perhaps defensively, a pride in the Creole physical type. Jeanne would like to have it that way too. She says, "You know, there should be three classes (castes) of people: white, Creole, and colored. It wouldn't matter if they had some dark ones in the Creole group, so long as they were nice, but I wouldn't go around with them." The dark ones must, of course, be "nice," that is, of Jeanne's class or better; no lower-class dark people could be admitted. One thing that caste has done to Jeanne is to plunge her into this conflict between allegiance to the white and the Negro groups; she can never be quite sure where she belongs. She must aspire to a position in the white group which she knows she cannot have and must reject the status of the Negro group which is assigned to her. Another Creole, a boy of about Jeanne's status, reports the dilemma in this form: he is called a "nigger" by the whites and a "peck" by the colored. Mrs. Manuel says pathetically that there are some nice white people and that she has some friends who are passing for white, but "they can't entertain if they got anybody else around and that's bound to make you feel bad, that they have to keep being a friend to you a secret." That's what Jeanne will meet, at the best, if she moves toward the white side.

Yet Jeanne knows well enough how social bread is buttered. She knows that by being assigned to the Negro caste her opportunity for full participation in American social life is sharply limited. In a sense it is true to say that she does not want to be "white"; she wants just to be human, with full human privileges and no uncertainty about it. Her "wish to be white" must be understood in that way. She says, "Sure I wish to be white. They have everything." The parents point out to her that Negroes have poor schools and facilities. "It's a wonder these poor kids learn anything, as crowded and bad as these schools are." Poor schools are especially damaging to people who count chiefly on them to launch their children into higher status positions. In another mood Jeanne says that she does not like white people; "They got too many conveniences. They got pools to swim in, parks to play in, nice theaters." She thinks that if she were "away" where there were no segregation she would like white people because then "we would be all alike." For lower-class white people (pecks), she has the same scorn that she has for lower-class Negroes; "There is plenty ole cheap pecks around our neighborhood, but there is only one in our block. My mamma says keep away from them." She could like "nice" white people, those of the class parallel to hers, if they would not discriminate against her, but cannot think of liking any kind of lower-class people.

So near, but yet so far, seems to epitomize the dilemma of the Creoles. And to make matters worse, Jeanne knows that she could "pass" and enjoy many of the privileges which she envies the white group. She knows some girls who have passed and liked it—"They say it is much better than being colored." She feels the pull of superior privilege, but she is afraid; afraid of being exposed by whites, afraid of having colored people see her and say the branding words, *passé blanc.* It is explained by a brown girl that *"passé blanc* is for those people who are so dumb they decide to pass for white, and then think they can't speak to any colored people." But if they do speak, they endanger their status as "passers"; and if they do not, they experience the stinging envy of the excluded Negroes. It seems as if all the suppressed hostility of Negroes toward whites comes out in their condemnation of "passers" in their own group.

Jeanne should at least make a good middle-class marriage; it is too late for downward mobility to check that. She will continue her orderly and conservative life and always be a joy to conventional people. She will probably be a rather stern mother, if she becomes one. She will probably not "pass," great as the temptation is, because her anxiety spreads promptly to any situation of challenging authority. She will yearn to be white and suffer being colored, making the most of the consolations of her Creole citizenship and her middle-middle-class status.

CHAPTER VII

ELLEN HILL, THE WINNER

IT HAS been shown in the cases of Chester Olivier and of Jeanne Manuel how strenuously the Negro middle-class child is trained by his parents in those goal responses and modes of interpersonal relations which will enable him to maintain his middle-class position within Negro society. When these habits of the child lose support of the parents, however, as a result of a decline in his family's class position, he faces an urgent learning dilemma. Either he must attempt to maintain his old habits, without the reinforcements which his former status secured for him from his friends and teachers, or he must begin to accept lower-class relationships and modes of behavior which *are* reinforced.

A family's loss of status may begin with (1) a sharp decline in income or occupational status; (2) desertion by the father; (3) drunkenness or promiscuous sexual behavior by the parents; or (4) family involvement in lottery-selling, bootlegging, or other "shady" enterprises. The child, as well as his parents, experiences his decline in status as a series of punishments. In the case of loss of income, the downward pressure becomes especially acute through the blocking of the roads to status, such as higher education, skilled or professional occupation, and the status symbols of "good" clothes, food, and housing.

The psychological impact of downward mobility upon our students, as measured by the anxiety which they experience in this dilemma, appears to differ to some degree according to their basic personality tendencies. Ellen Hill is a person whose anxiety was very high in this situation, and who developed an incipient neurosis. Ellen's case suggests that there are types of mental illness and character disturbance which develop in a configuration of "status anxiety," and which, in the lives of persons who have experienced rapid change in status, either upward or downward, may be viewed as a form of "status shock."

Ellen Hill is a light-skinned girl of fourteen, whose family is in great danger of losing its lower-middle-class position in New Orleans. She was interviewed by a light-skinned Negro woman of upper-class position. In order to understand Ellen's behavior in a situation of acute social punishment and derogation, it is first necessary to know the main lines of her personality structure. The central question raised by her case may then be thrown into sharper relief.

Ellen's own statement that, at the age of five, she was the first child in her class to learn her A B C's is typical of her desire for dominance. Her mother recognizes this passion in Ellen; she states that Ellen torments her two older sisters, and that this behavior can be allayed only by granting Ellen privileges which make her "seem more important" than the sisters. Ellen herself consistently emphasizes the fact that she is impatient of control; she does not like anyone to be "over" her, and she would not accept any work, she says, not even that of a teacher, in which she would have a "boss." For this reason, she wants to be either a physician who is the *head* of a hospital, or a lawyer, or the principal of a school. She dearly loves little babies, whom she can completely dominate, but she torments her sisters, and imperiously rules her school friends. In the interviewer's presence, Ellen compelled her closest friends to run errands for her, and forced them to agree that she was "smarter" than they. In her clubs, she is the most aggressive member, and usually becomes president. She deeply envies children who are above her in class position and denies at every point her inferior status. She even resists the restrictions of her sex. She wishes she were a boy, she says, because boys have greater freedom, and she has chosen as her goal two professions, medicine and law, which are limited almost entirely to men in colored New Orleans. A tremendous drive for dominance is symbolized by her heartfelt statement, "I want to be *bigger* than Booker T. Washington." Ellen's first and usual reaction, therefore, is to resist all the major forms of control which individuals in our society must bear, namely, those governing their privileges as members of age groups, sex groups, and social classes.

In her battle against systems of privilege which she considers unjust, Ellen is inwardly supported by a stubborn, tenacious quality. Both she and her mother insist that she never cries, not even when whipped or cruelly teased. "My tears come hard." When her mother or grandmother spanks her, she always laughs. She confides in no man, tells no one her troubles, "neither my mother nor my grandmother." "Nobody knows me," she says. When her sisters or friends try to tease her, she always agrees with them. She has learned to make herself invulnerable, in the sense that she will not reveal weakness or hurt to an opponent. "I wouldn't want them to know they hurt me none." Her protectiveness was a constant obstacle during the early months of interviewing, and to the very end, she was slow to confide, even when she had come to place high value upon the interviewer.

Ellen's relations with adults, while not intimate, are notably easy and pleasant, however. Until recently, her mother, her grandmother, and her teachers had found her an especially agreeable girl, "sweet" in her disposition, and eager to comply with normal requests. Her mother and grandmother agree that Ellen is the "best" of the seven children; she never "gets mad or ugly," and is never sassy, impudent, or troublesome. She "smiles off" her difficulties, the grandmother says, and the mother remarks that Ellen does not complain about poor clothes or food.

In spite of her ability to win people, however, Ellen is not a hard worker, nor is she conscientious about her duties at home or in school. Her mother points out that since Ellen is a very "smart" child, she has been able to "take things easy-like in school"; at home she is more happy-go-lucky than the other children. Her teachers agree that she has a very quick mind, so that she does not have to study as hard as her classmates.

Her winning behavior toward adults contrasts sharply with her aggressive behavior toward her sisters and schoolmates; but it achieves the same ends. "Ellen was always a child who could get other people to do things for her. She keeps all her little friends waiting on her," her mother says. "She got good marks in school without working, because the teachers all liked her."

Toward powerful adults whose aid and approval she wants, Ellen is not openly aggressive. She has learned to win their indulgence by compliance, by good manners, and by exhibiting a quick, eager interest in them. To her parents, she appears to be a girl of remarkably even temper who never fusses or cries, and who grins off hard words and even blows. In graded school, her teachers were genuinely fond of her, for she was quick to adapt her behavior to their wishes, to learn by their example, and to show her gratitude for favors. At the same time, she was not an "apple-polisher"; she had a stubborn but likeable self-respect.

According to her parents, teachers, and friends, then, Ellen was a very tractable girl in her relations with them before the abrupt change in her behavior which we shall now describe. Their testimony agrees, moreover, with the observations of the interviewer, who found Ellen a pleasant and effective individual in her relations with teachers, parents, and the interviewer, after her incipient neurosis disappeared.

The history of the change in her manifest behavior begins with her transfer from grammar school to junior high school in September 1937 at the age of fourteen. In this new school, Ellen very soon became markedly aggressive toward her teachers. She complained to her mother that the teachers had "pets" and were hostile to the other children, particularly to her. The teachers on the other hand described her as "impudent," "malicious," and "sly." The girl who had always been a favorite with her instructors in grammar school was regarded by one of her new teachers as "the most troublesome child in her class—always disagreeing and very belligerent." Ellen admits that she called another teacher "an educated fool" to his face, and was sent home from school for the first time in her life. Before the end of the first semester, she became a leader of student aggression toward teachers, and developed a sullen, resentful attitude toward her instructors. Her attitudes of hostility were generalized to her family who, she claimed, disliked her because she was ugly.

Her mental state at this time is indicated by her crying in school when one of her teachers refused to give her a test with the other children, because her mother had not paid her dues in the Parent-Teacher Association. In January, she failed her grade. When we remember that Ellen had always obtained ratings of 80 or above in school, and that she had never been a girl to cry, even for spankings, we understand that matters had now reached a critical point with her. But worse things were to follow. After being "kept back" in her old grade, Ellen was put in a section composed chiefly of "repeaters" and lower-class children. Her behavior toward instructors became definitely abnormal at this time. She would not look at them when they addressed her, but turned her head to one side. She answered only in monosyllables, "Yes" or "No."

In March 1938, when Ellen was behaving in this way, her principal asked the interviewer to talk with her. He said that Ellen was the "problem child" of the school, the most troublesome, the most disliked by her teachers. He was especially concerned over such behavior as turning her head when addressed, and answering only in monosyllables.

Ellen acted in the same manner at first with the interviewer but soon agreed to abandon this behavior, and did so in the second interview. During the first three interviews, nevertheless, she lied about the time of her father's desertion, the occupation and income of her mother and oldest sister, and the number of rooms in her house; she also concealed the fact that a baby had just been born to her mother.

From almost the very beginning, however, her overt behavior toward the interviewer was compliant and winning. She kept her appointments for interviews and asked to come more often. She at once brought her closest friends in, and soon invited the interviewer to visit her grandmother's home. Within a month, Ellen had easy and mutually satisfactory relations with the upperclass interviewer, and was a regular visitor at her home. During the two months remaining in the spring term of school, moreover, she improved her classroom work markedly, obtaining grades of 80 or above from all of her teachers except the one who had sent her home from school. The principal agreed to let her pass the grade she had failed on condition that she continue her excellent work. In the fall term, Ellen's grades rose to 90, and she was elected president of one of the leading girls' clubs in the school. The same woman instructor, who a few months previously had called her the most belligerent and impudent girl in her class, now said that she was the most cooperative and pleasant.

The problem, then, is to understand why Ellen's behavior changed abruptly after she entered the junior high school, and why the incipient neurotic traits which she developed there disappeared during the period of the interview relation. To seek an answer to this question, we must retrace our steps carefully and rephrase our questions in more specific terms, as follows: (1) What are the basic motivations underlying Ellen's personality? (2) What were the *social punishments* to which Ellen was subjected during the period of her delinquent behavior in school, and what were the *social rewards* to which she responded in the interview relation? (3) Why should a girl with a personality like Ellen's be extremely responsive to the punishments and rewards connected with status?

Remembering the basic importance of a child's first learning, we must look into Ellen's early life for the social background in which she learned her dominance behavior toward weaker individuals and her pliant, engaging behavior toward adults. Mrs. Hill reports that Ellen was a healthy, happy infant, her "best baby" out of seven. She was breast-fed, had an easy and gradual weaning, with only one or two attacks of colic. Her mother applied the cleanliness training with severity, however, whipping the child for soiling herself after the age of thirteen or fourteen months. "I can't stand nasty children," says Mrs. Hill; she claims that all of her children had completed their cleanliness training by the age of eighteen months. "That's one thing I've really worked hard on, bringing 'em up to be clean." Today, Ellen is a very clean girl who lays great stress upon taking baths, cleaning her teeth, and washing her underwear. It may be that her stubborn, retentive, acquisitive qualities were learned in the battle over stool-training.

As in our other cases, the mother reports that the child began to play with herself as early as the age of one year. To break this habit, which she says all the children exhibited, the mother whipped Ellen's hands and frightened her. At present, Ellen has no courting relations with boys and repulses them. It is possible that her intimidation on this score is a result of her mother's early threats; the only whippings she remembers receiving were for playing "mamma and papa" and "having a baby" with her older sisters.

The family into which Ellen was born was really a clan headed by the maternal grandmother, whose house is still the gathering place for six daughters and twenty-three grandchildren. Ellen's immediate family was an unhappy setting for a child, because her father was a drunkard, although he made good money as a waiter and a baker. He was eighteen years older than his wife. Ellen remembers that when she was four years old, her mother, her two older sisters, and she would bring her father home from a beer parlor, "my papa drunk, my mother tired, and us crying." When she was nine, her father lost his job. The family went to live with the grandmother until the father obtained a WPA job for $38.50 a month, most of which was consumed by his drinking. The family barely had food, clothes, and shelter. After four years of this life, the father deserted, just two weeks after Ellen had entered junior high school.

What marks did Ellen's relations with her family grind into her personality? Ellen now says that she does not want to be like either of her parents, because her mother cries too easily and her father has disgraced them. But she has not always been hostile to her father. Her most pleasant early memories concern him, his frequent gifts to her, her excursions with him to fish and to shop, his stories of his own early life. Mrs. Hill reports that all the children were "crazy about their father." He bought their

love, she says. "He'd be drunk, an' he'd stop an' buy more candy
and toys and junk for the children, and right natural, they'd
fall for that." He was especially fond of babies, and "made a
big fuss" over each new baby until the next one superseded it in
his favor.

When she was very young, Ellen responded positively to her
father's gifts and to his petting. Her daddy was a "good-time"
person, whereas her mother was necessarily the disciplinarian
of the family. Ellen also identified with her father upon the basis
of color. They were the only light members of the family, and
the others teased them at times about their "redness" and "ugli-
ness." She got along better with her father than did either of
her older sisters, who "sassed" and teased him, and who were
severely whipped by him. "He'd just as soon see the oldest girl
as a snake," the mother says. "He was always beating on her,
and he kep' slapping on the next girl till I thought he'd knock
her out. It got to the point where I was scared to leave them in
the house, even to go to work." But he never whipped Ellen,
and she never set herself against him, nor spoke to him impu-
dently, nor took the family's side against his. In her relationship
with this chronically drunken father, whose aggression was as
unpredictable as his generosity, Ellen learned to be pliant, to
win him by anticipating and yielding to his wishes. She was the
smartest of the children; her I.Q. on the basis of the Stanford-
Binet test is 129. Under the continual threat of punishment, she
learned to protect herself by her wit, to parry her father's aggression with her "sweetness." She learned readily because she was
continually in a dangerous position. "It ain't no wonder all my
children are nervous," the mother says, "that man aroun',
fightin' an' drunk, jes' kep' 'em scared all the time." When we
understand, with the mother's help, what it meant to a child to
be constantly subordinated by a drunken and therefore chronically aggressive father, we begin to realize the long and effective
training in meeting powerful aggression which Ellen underwent.
She learned to avoid her sisters' model of impudence and coun-
ter-aggression which were punished, and to adopt the opposite
role of compliance. She learned to be winning and friendly, thus

escaping punishments which would otherwise have been certain.

When she began to realize that her father's drunkenness was a social disgrace, and to see the episodic nature of his affection, her feeling toward him changed. She seems even to have learned to exploit him during his drunken fits of indulgence. At the age of eight, when she saw him reeling on the streets, she "felt awful." "I'd be so 'shamed when he come home like that." After she came to realize that her father's drunkenness was actually a rejection of his family, and a class stigma, she often wished that "he'd break his neck, or get put in jail, or that he'd die. I was always wishing something like that." After his desertion of the family, her attitude toward him changed to open dislike. She said bitterly that he had been drunk when she was born and that he was just like his drunken brother, whose children "all hated him." She showed no desire to have him return to the family, and when a relief agency offered to force him to return, Ellen opposed the idea. It seems clear that she has rejected her father, because he disgraced his family, and stigmatized them as lower-class people by his drunkenness and desertion, and by leaving them poverty stricken.

Between the cross-fires of her father's spasmodic rage and her mother's strict middle-class discipline, Ellen cleverly learned to win both parents. Her mother finds only one fault in her. She has always tormented her older sisters. Moreover, she teased and even pinched the younger children when they were babies. We seem now to be on the track which may lead to the origin of Ellen's marked striving and dominance behavior. Ellen's relations with her two older sisters and with her next younger sister have been extremely competitive. She remembers fighting with her older sisters at a very early age, and crying because she could not go out with them and do the things they did. Her mother remembers that Ellen strove against her older sisters and "fussed and fought" with them constantly in spite of the fact that neither of the older sisters was aggressive toward her nor seemed to resent her coming.

Ellen has always tormented and attacked her sister Rose, who is one year older than she. One of her few whippings was received for striking Rose. Her mother states that Ellen has always "fought most" with Rose, and Ellen volunteers the information that she is continually "teasing" and fighting with Rose at present. Rose is a harder worker than Ellen, the mother says. She is an extremely conscientious girl and an excellent student; she does better work than Ellen both at home and in school. Against this strong competitor, Ellen has again called upon her wit, her "smartness." She is cleverer than Rose, and so can torment and outwit her. She escapes her chores at home, and throws them upon Rose's shoulders. When Rose is doing the work which Ellen should have done, Ellen boasts, "Why should I work, when I got my servant?"

In the same intense fashion, Ellen strove against her next younger sister, Vera, who replaced her in the father's favor, and has been his "pet" ever since. Ellen asserts that Vera is mean and spiteful. She claims that the father made this younger sister mean by his indulgence and protection. When Vera was a baby and Ellen was three, Ellen poured scalding water upon the baby, and a little later Vera pushed Ellen so hard that the latter fell and broke her arm. The mother remembers that Ellen frequently pinched the baby, Vera, and made her cry.

It seems likely, therefore, that Ellen's desire for dominance arose in her battle with her sisters. She competed with them for the favor of the parents, but she also competed directly with them for the superior privileges which they enjoyed, either through age, as in the case of the older ones, or through favor, as in the case of Vera. It is clear from the record of both the mother and Ellen that Ellen fought and tried to dominate the older sisters. She never learned to accept her subordination on an age basis. Just as we later find her throwing herself against the stubborn barriers of class status, which were almost hopelessly steep for her, so we discover her in her earliest days lunging fiercely against the ramparts of age privilege.

Her behavior in this respect is extreme. Most individuals in our society accept the restrictions which are placed upon them as members of an age group. Movement from one age grade to the next higher one is a process of status evolution through which all persons in our society must pass. Most children, adolescents, and young men and women learn to accept subordination in certain fundamental respects to the members of higher age groups. As a little girl, Ellen refused to accept this form of social subordination. She tried to "beat the game" of age privilege and to secure not only the rights of her older sisters, but even higher privileges. Her native wit helped her succeed in this endeavor. In brief, she learned to overcome her sisters not by being older, but by adeptly winning the personal favor and indulgence of her parents. In this game of her early years, she was a remarkably effective and "mobile" child—that indisputable conqueror of whom she dreamed later during the interview period, "Ellen Hill, the Winner!"

As Ellen grew older and went to school, however, she met children from other families. She characteristically made her goal the very top of the middle class, and strove vigorously and for a time successfully to identify herself with the children and families of the upper-middle class. But she soon found that the hierarchy of social classes was even more rigid than that of age grading; her little friends were constantly being referred to and measured (by themselves, their teachers, and their parents) in terms of their *families'* status. By the time Ellen was nine, both they and their families knew that her father was a drunkard, and that her family was "on relief."

Here was a battle for status and privileges which could not be won on personal merit or wit. Ellen quickly sensed this truth; her remarkably adaptive behavior was to spend most of her time at her grandmother's home, and to invite her friends there. She was trying in this way to detach herself from her drunken father and poverty-stricken family, and to identify herself socially with her maternal grandmother.

Why with her grandmother? The grandmother and her large, well-furnished house, which she owned, provided an anchor for Ellen in strong lower-middle-class position. This woman had not only bought an eight-room house, but she had enabled all of her daughters to go to high school and had sent two of them through college. Her own class position was unshakable despite the fact that most of her daughters, including Ellen's mother, had been downward mobile.

Ellen's mother married a man who came from a "nice family" and whose sister is now a school principal. Until Ellen was eight, Mr. Hill made as much as $15 a day as a waiter during the resort season, and his wife saved enough to enable them to live well during the off-season. They rented a seven-room house, and Mrs. Hill seldom had to "work out." Even her cooking and washing were done for her at the hotel where her husband worked, so that she had none of the stigmas of lower-class position. But when Ellen was nine, her father lost his job. At that time, four years prior to our study of Ellen, rapid downward mobility began for the family. As Mrs. Hill says, "We been comin' down in the world ever since."

The process of the Hills' "coming down in the world" began with the steady loss of their middle-class marks of "respectability" and ended in the actual prospect of starvation. Mrs. Hill says that the first step was "when he had to go on WPA. That's what killed us, 'cause with that little bit of money, he kept on drinking jus' like before." Mr. Hill was no longer making enough money to be able to provide the necessities for his family, and also whisky for himself. "Each year," Mrs. Hill says, "he jus' got worse until even when he did go to his WPA job, he'd drink up every cent of it, without bringing me a cent or gettin' a thing for these kids."

The mother had to find work as a domestic servant, while the father usually stayed at home, where he fought the resentful and hostile children. The family of eight now lived in a three-room house. Mrs. Hill had been compelled to give up her intimate associates, her clique. She could not return their favors or entertainment; for this reason, she could no longer participate effectively with her lower-middle-class group. She and her children were in the painful and isolated position of people who are rising or falling from one level of class participation to the next.

While the crisis in this relentless downward pressure was still to come, Ellen was throwing all her courage and intelligence into the battle against her loss of status. She made it her business to win the friendship and patronage of her teachers in grammar school. From the age of eight, she selected her closest associates from the children of upper-middle-class families. Her clique has been a remarkably stable group; for a period of almost seven years, Ellen has kept the same upper-middle-class girls as her best friends. Her mother remarks this fact, boasting that "all of Ellen's friends are from very nice families," but admits that she herself does not visit the parents of these children, nor does she know them well. "They're very nice people." The distinction between "poor but respectable people" and "very nice people" which Mrs. Hill makes is a distinction between people of her own lower-middle-class status and those of upper-middle-class or upper-class position.

Ellen not only maintained her contacts with upper-middle-class children through all these years, but she kept lower-class children at a distance, both at school and in her neighborhood. She avoided the theaters which were preferred by lower-class people, and condemned the schools which had chiefly lower-class pupils. Nor did she associate with the children of lower-class families in her neighborhood. "We wouldn't go aroun' with them," she says. "We don't have nothing to do with them, because they quit school, an' they are dirty; they go to beer parlors, and hang aroun' with ignorant boys."

These people who lived in her own neighborhood were just a step below her in class position, but Ellen set her own goal far above them. She chose the families of her upper-middle-class friends as a model for behavior. By the time she entered junior high school, she was planning to go to college and then to professional school. With scarcely enough food or clothes to enable her to continue in public school, she had already determined to be a physician or a lawyer. Nor was this an idle daydream, for she steadily resisted the efforts of her mother and grandmother to train her in the habits of domestic work. Not only is she firmly set against the caste-way of working as a nurse girl for white people, but she has never learned to do housework at home. Her mother complains of this unrealistic behavior, but Ellen explains to the interviewer, "My mother says to me, 'You better learn how to wash clothes,' or, 'You better learn how to cook. Some day you might have to do it just like me.' But I always say, 'No indeed, not me. I ain't gonnuh cook or wash for nobody.' I don't know what I'll do, but it won't never be that. You can always find something to do."

As Ellen grew toward adolescence, her striving to attain higher status within the Negro group (basically a flight from the social and economic punishments of lower-class life) was increasingly expressed as "racial ambition." Like Chester Olivier and many other lower-middle-class Negroes who are aggressive and socially mobile, she began to express her push for higher class position as a desire to be a "race leader." The usual caste role of Negroes in the lower-middle class is to be a "good Negro," to avoid all conflicts with whites, and to observe the caste taboos in detail. They attempt to compensate for this chronic frustration by maintaining or increasing their superordinate position in relation to the great mass of lower-class Negroes. But Ellen feels the sting of racial subordination too keenly to make this adjustment easily. She resists the middle-class demands of her family for a protective accommodation to caste.

Ellen says that she has always been conscious of the color differences within her family, of the "darkness" of her mother and the "lightness" of her father. Nor was there ever a time, as far back as she can remember, when she did not know that she was colored. She remembers little white children calling her "nigger" when she was about three. Her mother says that none of her children wants to be as light as the father; "they say they might have got his evil ways along with his color." Ellen herself says that she does not prefer her father's and her own "red" color to her mother's "black," and that her darker sisters are "better-looking" than she. But her dreams reveal a wish to be even lighter than she is.

Although Ellen's parents and grandmother approve of "respectable" methods of asking white people, through Negro middle-class organizations, for better schools and playgrounds, they tell her always to try to get along with white people "without trouble," that is, without open aggression. Their own compliant behavior toward white neighbors, clerks, and bus drivers provides an example for her to follow. They try to teach Ellen what they have learned, namely, that by accepting the harder route which the upper caste imposes on Negroes, one can still obtain the basic goal responses. They have been reinforced in taking this longer but safer route and in repressing their tendencies to resist, because by so doing they have gained the responses and avoided severe punishment. But the frustration is certainly there, as Ellen hears the grandmother admit, "The Lord really started something when he fixed up Cain—or Ham—or whoever it was. He really made some kind of a mess! Looks like it's something that will never get straightened out either."

This is an important admission, for the defenses which Negroes build against the admission of their fundamental caste deprivations, even to themselves, are strong. Ellen defended herself against this humiliation by denying it in the first interview. She began by claiming not to object to the necessity for climbing eighty-six steps to the colored gallery at the movies, and by insisting that light Negroes should not "pass for white." She dogmatized, "It ain't right because God didn't make you white."

In Ellen's case, it was easy to get behind these defenses, however. By the second interview, she was telling a deeper story. She relates that she fought even a Negro boy for calling her "nigger." On buses and in stores, she is remarkably aggressive toward white people. She bursts through middle-class restraint, enforced by her parents and teachers, and challenges white superiority. She challenges the white superordinate to his face. She refuses to sit in the back of a shoe store, where the clerks lead all Negroes. At times, she insists upon having another clerk; sometimes she turns from the clerk and leaves. This behavior in New Orleans requires a powerful burst of aggression in an adult, and it is extreme in a small girl of fourteen.

Ellen stops only at the point of physical conflict with whites. When such conflicts occur between lower-class Negroes and whites on the bus or in stores, Ellen leaves at once. Although her aggression stops at this point, deep hostility is repressed beneath her fear of physical punishment by whites. She blames white people for lynching Negroes. "They lynch them for doin' nothin'. That really isn't right. God's supposed to know what He's doing, but it seems an awful sin to me." Later she says that whenever white people try to lynch a Negro, Negroes themselves should "get guns, an' get up in trees, an' just shoot every white person you can. They ought to practice shooting so that they could get at least half a dozen whites, an' then if you die, it won't make no difference; six for one, that's good. That's worth dying for."

At the root of this hostility is the deprivation which Ellen suffers at the hands of whites. She and her sisters constantly point out that the city government did not provide Negroes with the school which they attend. The building was provided by a Negro institution, and is now badly in need of repairs. "Our school is a dump. They won't give Negroes anything but shacks for schools. They won't even give them old white schools, which they ain't usin'." Her mother says that Ellen and Rose "fuss every mornin' about the poor schools for Negroes. They fuss about all sorts of things like that, all the things colored people can't do, an' ain't got, but it's the school 'specially." The deprivation which Ellen experiences in her lower-caste position is made clear to us by her reaction to the great City Auditorium, which Negroes are not allowed to use. "I was standin' in front of the Auditorium. I was thinkin' that some day we will have many beautiful buildings like that. It has a large swimmin' pool, with everything new and modern. It's beautiful. I saw some girls my size diving in it, an' I thought while I was lookin' that colored people shouldn't pay taxes an' not get the benefit."

Ellen's drive for superior class position has been translated into intense manifestations of "race pride" and identification with "race leaders" like Booker T. Washington and Dr. Carver, a nationally known Negro chemist. The fervency and conviction with which she achieves this sublimation is an index both of her dominance responses and of her quick identification with persons of higher status. "I want to be famous and a credit to my

race," she says, and at the same time she names the famous Negroes whom she wishes to imitate.

Unlike Chester Olivier, whose intense hatred of any class subordination drove him to attack upper-class Negroes as violently
as he did whites, Ellen is highly disposed to identify herself
with these Negroes. "If you have Negro history, you are learning about your own people—the ones who are famous—an' maybe
you can be like them." Through her expressed wishes to go
away to the North to school (not, she says, to attend with white
children, but to have better schools and professional training),
or to start a hospital for Negroes, or to be a lawyer to protect
them, Ellen states her fundamental purpose clearly. "I'm gonnuh
be a doctor—I want to be famous—I'm gonnuh be a lawyer—
I'm going away [from her downward mobile family] where I
can be somebody." In her wishes and in her dreams, the actual
situation of her family appears as the background for this desire
to flee upward. She dreams of meals which disappear before she
can eat them, of moving pictures which stop just as she comes
into the theater, of poverty which is even more grinding than
that of her family. The dreams which she prefers, and enjoys as
if they were almost realities, are those of "nice things happening
to me—going nice places, eating nice foods." Among other things,
these dreams certainly indicate the deprivation which she experiences in the downward mobility of her family, and her longing
for the class-ways "above" her.

Until the autumn of 1937, when she entered junior high
school, however, the social stigmas on Ellen's family had not
reached the point where they endangered her relations with
her middle-class teachers and friends. Her father still lived with
his family, and provided them with a face-saving, though nomi-
nal, income. There was the expectancy, at least, that he would
find skilled work again and support his daughters through high
school and perhaps college. His work on the WPA was not
enough to declass his family, for in New Orleans a rather large
number of lower-middle-class people have been forced to accept

"relief." Even the Hills' three-room house was a great step above the houses of most lower-class people, which consisted of one room, or one room and a "lean-to." It is true that things were growing strained and embarrassing, especially with the mother's having to work as a domestic, but no one could yet say that the Hills were not "good respectable people." In her clique relations, furthermore, Ellen was still sailing far above her parents and sisters. And unlike her sisters, she was still popular and winning. Even when conditions at home seemed to be at their worst, Ellen was elected president of her church club and secretary of her community center club.

Then, without warning and without a chance to use her wit or courage to save it, Ellen's world seemed to fall from under her. The hopeless chasm occupied by the "worst class of people" appeared immediately beneath her, and her family suddenly took on the traits and the disgraced position of lower-class people. A few weeks after she entered junior high school, her father deserted the family. The mother and six children were left with no income except the four dollars a week which the mother earned at housecleaning. A month after the father's departure, they were forced to give up their three-room house, and move into one room in a lower-class tenement. The oldest daughter was taken out of high school and apprenticed to a hairdresser, who paid her $1.50 a week. And less than three months after her father's desertion, it became apparent to Ellen that her mother was pregnant.

During the first months of her attendance at the junior high school, therefore, Ellen's family was deprived of the father as well as of other vital symbols of middle-class status. In the middle class, the father is the anchor of social rank. He is the real source of status, although the mother usually expresses the family's class position publicly by her clique, club, and church participation. Upon the father's acceptance of his economic and social responsibility to his family depends the successful orientation of the child to middle-class society. Without her father, drunkard though he was, Ellen's chances for an education, a middle-class home and clothes, and for the other status symbols necessary for a "good" occupation and a "good" marriage, were greatly lessened.

The father's desertion, therefore, meant the loss not only of the family's income but also of the status symbols into which his wages could be translated. It meant the loss of middle-class "respectability" to a large degree, for desertion and illegitimacy are the two forms of familial behavior most abhorred by the middle class. With her father gone and a new baby coming, Ellen foresaw the loss of her clique, her teachers, and her "career."

In this new situation at home, the disabilities of lower-class life were at once experienced by Ellen. We can visualize the deprivations through her mother's eyes. "This is the worst year we've ever had. When we moved into that one room, the children liked to died. They were all so ashamed, they didn't want no one to know where they lived. Then there was plenty of days those kids were jus' plain hungry, an' I jus' didn't have no money to buy food. Ellen's had plenty to worry about, all right." The mother pictures the filth of the tenement, the lack of sewerage, the inadequate heating, the smells, and the noise and fighting of the lower-class neighbors. "I'm telling you, it's really hard to live like this when you've known better. We're worse off now than we've ever been before."

The girls were so ashamed of the bare one room that the mother promised them she would try to buy curtains and a linoleum rug, but the money was not to be found. "My girls all got nice friends an' it ain't right for them not to have no home they can bring them to. They oughtn't to have to be ashamed of their own home." For the first time in their lives, the children had no bathtub. They had to go to their grandmother's house to bathe. Clothes were few, and washing had to be done in the room with six other people. "They'll stay up at night washin' an' ironin' a dress to go to school in, an' they set up till twelve o'clock at night tryin' to get out their school work, with this one room full of people, an' the baby hollerin'. You can't live like that." Ellen and her two older sisters had to share one bed, and the mother and the three younger children slept in the other bed.

In its physical aspects, Ellen's life was now like that of the people at the very bottom of the lower class.

But her habits were not. Ellen and her family had the deeply fixed habits and goals of middle-class people. When they could no longer obtain the goal responses to which their habits were directed, they still refused to adjust their behavior to lower-class modes, with regard to aggression, sex, care of the house, study, and personal relations. For this reason, they experienced continual and basic frustration in their lower-class environment.

Under the drive of her powerful dominance strivings, Ellen reacted excessively to this blocking of her habits. She resented and feared the loss of middle-class status, and therefore lied to the upper-class interviewer about the size of her house, the occupation of her mother, and the wages of her sister. She concealed the facts that her father had deserted and that her mother had borne a baby seven months after his leaving. When the interviewer visited the mother after her third talk with Ellen, she learned the truth on all these points. Mrs. Hill said that Ellen had lied because she was ashamed of their present situation. The mother said, "When Ellen found out you was here that last time, I'm telling you she nearly had a fit. She liked to died. 'Mamma, you oughtn't to let her in—you could have talked to her out front.' Then she said she wasn't going to school the next day; she couldn't see you. I told her that wasn't no way to feel—that you was a friend to her, and then she wanted to know, 'Well, what will I tell her, Mamma?' "

When confronted by these facts, Ellen told the interviewer that she had lied because she was ashamed to tell the truth about her house and her family's poverty. She further admitted that she had been worried by the signs of her mother's pregnancy, and that she and Rose had counted the months between her father's desertion and the baby's birth. The mother said that she believed Ellen's delinquency in school was the result of their moving to the one-room house, their lack of food, and the birth of the baby after the father's desertion. The grandmother likewise stated that the older girls thought the birth of the baby "wuzn't right with the father away." She also immediately put forward the middle-class defense, which lower-class people do not advance, "But the mother was that way before he left her."

Ellen's anxiety over the downward mobility of her family was expressed in her marked interest in stories of other people who had met reverses of status, as well as in her dreams. She became morbidly devoted to the pulp magazines, and identified herself with the stigmatized persons in the "true stories." "While my mamma was pregnant, I used to worry about the people in those stories. One girl had run away from home; some man stole some money—all sorts of troubles people had. I'd just be thinking about them all the time, so I wouldn't do no work at school." She dreamt constantly of loss of food and household comforts, and of humiliation in social participation. In her dream-fears, the situation at home was even worse than in actuality. Vivid and typical is her dream that the family was so destitute that her mother had to cook their food in "a little ol' tin wash-basin" and sleep on a cot instead of on the bed which she actually used, and that there was no light or even a match in the house. "That was what was worryin' me most—that the house was dark, an' I never did find a match."

It was during this period of seven months, when Ellen and her family faced the critical danger of being ranked and treated as lower-class people, of being lower class, that she became delinquent in her school behavior. Why at school, and not at home? We are now in a position to solve this central problem.

Two weeks before her father's desertion, Ellen entered one of the three Negro schools in New Orleans where the class level of students is generally recognized as high. Ellen's new school was not a private school like the one where Chester Olivier fought his battle for status, but its student body included the largest proportion of colored Creoles of any school in the city. The class position of Creoles is high in the Negro society, the great majority of them being of middle-middle-class or upper-middle-class status. Most of them are light-brown or yellow in color, with types of hair closely approaching the white type. For these reasons, they are quick to make social distinctions against the more Negroid types, whom they divide into two groups, *les petits négres* and *les grands négres,* upon the basis of occupation, income, education, and other status symbols.

The teachers at this school are predominantly of the upper-middle class and upper class. They are proud of the high class level of their students, especially of the Creoles. Distinctions of a class nature between teachers or between pupils are definitely expressed in the schoolroom, whether it be among colored or white children. The teacher's high class position is concretely presented to the public school child by her dress, her language, and her behavior toward lower-class, as compared with middle-class and upper-class pupils. As we have had ample occasion to see in our other cases, the child is well aware of the preferences shown by the teacher in giving prominence to upper-class students in recitations and public programs, and in relations with the teacher herself.

In fact, Ellen was intimidated by the class distinctions at this new school even before she enrolled in September. Her next older sister, Rose, had attended the school for a year and had constantly made the charge at home that the teachers gave preference to children of Creole parents and of the "big shot" Negroes. Ellen says that Rose often cried over this discrimination, and that before she entered the school, Rose warned her against two teachers who were especially unfair to students of low or unknown status. Ellen studied under these teachers and felt that she was not preferred. Since we know that she is ordinarily compliant with adults, was well liked by her instructors in grammar school, and even placated her drunken father, we agree that she must have met discrimination. Ellen says that one of her teachers would allow only one girl, her "pet," to use necessary equipment, and that another embarrassed her publicly because she could not pay her Parent-Teacher Association dues. This incident was the crisis in Ellen's battle to maintain her lower-middle-class position with teachers and students. Ellen fled from the humiliation of admitting her family's extreme poverty. When the teacher charged that Ellen had spent the money, Ellen would not tell him the true state of affairs at home. The teacher refused to allow her to take the test upon which successful completion of her work depended, and Ellen, who always laughed when she was spanked, cried.

Her basic habits are not like those of Chester Olivier, or of her sister Rose. When these two met a similar discrimination based on social class, they intensified their work habits and thus won approval and status in their new school situation. Ellen, however, had learned to win the approval of adults by being pliant and friendly, rather than by working conscientiously, and she found her techniques ineffective in a situation where social class was a more important criterion than personality.

She responded to this situation with violent aggression toward her teachers, and this maladaptive behavior was generalized to all the students who were "teacher's pets." Ellen names these students bitterly and charges repeatedly that they are "stuck-up" and "think they are cute. I hate them, and I be mean to 'em every chance I get." She points out that when she and her sister applied for NYA jobs, they were refused, while all the leading "pets" received jobs. Instead of winning the friendship of students of higher status, as she had always done previously, she now made enemies of them. She did keep her original small clique of three upper-middle-class girls, but she lived in constant fear that they would discover her one-room home and abandon her.

The character disturbance which appeared at this time in the physical manifestations of turning her head away from her teachers, and refusing to talk, is clearly apparent in her phantasies. She often thought of going away, of leaving her family, of being adopted by well-to-do persons. "I thought," she remembers, "about a story I had read, 'titled *Mildred, the Child of Adoption,* wonderin' an' wishin' I would have been left on someone's doorstep." She wished to go to school in another city, and frequently had the desire to go away from her home. She dreamed of a "pretty little yellow bird in a cage, and it flew away." (She is nearly as light as yellow.)

In January, Ellen's delinquency reached its climax in her failure to be promoted. In addition to this punishment, which was extremely severe for a middle-class child who had always received "good marks" and been a favorite with her teachers, Ellen suffered social degradation by being placed in a room with retarded, disorderly, and chiefly lower-class pupils. Her aggression toward teachers, her head turning, and her trouble making among the students continued during the first two months of the second semester. In late March, Ellen met the upper-class female interviewer, and agreed to talk with her regularly. At this time, she said that all the teachers in the school were "down on" her, a statement which the teachers confirmed. But the interviewer had higher status than most of Ellen's teachers and she did not make class points against Ellen. This was the kind of relationship for which Ellen had been searching. Her behavior with the interviewer improved rapidly. The only points of concealment were class stigmas, which Ellen had good reason to know might be a threat to her acceptance by persons of high status.

During the first interview, she agreed to look the interviewer in the face, and pointed out that she turned her head away from teachers only, not from students. After the first interview, she asked if she might come back the same day for another talk. At the beginning of the second interview, Ellen looked and acted quite unlike the "mean," "sly," and "malicious" girl whom the teachers regarded as the "worst child in the school." She was extraordinarily friendly, easy, and winning in her manners. She began this second interview by saying, "All right. I'm gonnuh look right at you an' talk. What do you want to talk about?" Her head turning disappeared in her talks with the interviewer, and soon was abandoned with her teachers.

From the beginning, the interviewer reinforced Ellen's friendly behavior by allowing her to express her hostility toward her teachers and their "pets." "I worse than hate them," she said in the first interview, "always hangin' aroun' the principal's office. I sure hate 'em." When she saw that she was not rejected by the upper-class woman for showing these repressed hostilities, Ellen soon dropped this type of verbalization.

Ellen was further reinforced in regaining her former winning behavior by being allowed free social participation with the interviewer. The interviewer brought Ellen to her home, had her to dinner, took her for automobile rides, and invited her to a Negro college to a sorority party for children. Ellen's behavior on all these occasions was uniformly pleasant and successful, and she responded positively at once by inviting the interviewer to her grandmother's home.

On discovering the poverty-stricken condition of Ellen's own family, the interviewer had succeeded in having the mother placed on relief, so that the family had an assured, though small, income. They at once moved into a three-room house. The mother gave up her $4-a-week job, and devoted herself to the care of her family. Ellen soon began to invite friends to her home, and admitted to the interviewer that she had been ashamed of her former house and of her mother's domestic work. She also admitted that she had concealed the fact of the baby's birth, because she was ashamed of its apparent illegitimacy.

With the approval and encouragement of the interviewer, Ellen now began to work effectively in school. The principal and teachers were astonished by the change in her behavior, and began to praise her as one of the "nicest" and most cooperative girls in the school. Ellen became quite satisfied with her teachers, and even said of the teacher who had called her the "most troublesome girl" in her class, "I like her lots. She knows how to teach, too."

We should miss the whole point of the status barriers which Ellen faces, and of her basic dominance drive, however, if we assumed that her problem were solved. The class system is a stubborn reality. Like the caste system, it cannot be reasoned away. There are, it is true, techniques for rising in the ladder of social rank and for increasing one's privileges. Education, profession, and forms of talent may secure upward mobility for an individual from the lower levels. Even with these qualifications, however, the "rise" is slow; to "rise" one subclass in a person's lifetime is to have a high degree of mobility. Ellen's unhappy conflict resulted from her inability to conform to the demands of a deeply laid system of privilege, and she still has many obstacles to contend with. Her family is on relief, and will undoubtedly remain there. Her father is gone. Her one chance is that her grandmother may pay for her college education.

But Ellen wants nothing less than the very top. She cannot bear *any* final subordination. We may say with truth that during the period of her delinquency she suffered from "status shock" as the result of her family's downward mobility, and her consequent rejection on class grounds at school. People who are upward mobile constantly must fight off attacks of status anxiety. Ellen, therefore, must make the realistic adjustment of setting her class goal, her "ceiling," not very far above the lower-middle class, and of integrating her habits on this level.

Although she can now admit to the interviewer that she tried to conceal her status weaknesses, and that she is actually unable to participate with the girls she likes, because of lack of money for the theater, the beach, and picnics, she nevertheless insists that her house, which has leaks and no bathroom, is as good as her friend's house, which has a landscaped garden and huge tiled bath, and is worth $6,000. Nor has she stopped making envious criticisms of people "below" her, on a class basis, and of those "above" her, on a personality basis.

Her eyes are set on the future. She knows that she must get an education and make a good marriage. Her own and her family's middle-class habits and goals are a powerful incentive in this direction. But economic deprivation is a handicap which even "the moral poor," as George Bernard Shaw calls lower-middle-class people, can scarcely be expected to overcome when there is no wage earner in the family. When Ellen told the interviewer that her mother was unable to have the baby christened until they "got on relief," the interviewer asked her if the relief payment of $31.25 a month was adequate. "It's a lot to my mamma since we didn't have nothing. I hope it won't be a lot to me, though. I want to make some money when I get big. I'm goin' to be a doctor; then I'd like to marry a doctor, too."

This straining toward the future is Ellen's unrealistic escape from her present class position, and it may lead to more serious mental difficulties than those she developed in meeting the class barriers at school. She told the interviewer a story in which the phantasied happy solution of her own dilemma was projected. She had read of a little Italian boy who was kidnapped by an old woman whose own baby had died. The old woman brought him up in loneliness, with only a cat for a companion and the cat always slept. They were very poor, so the little boy finally persuaded her to let him go to the city to sell vegetables and flowers. One day a beautiful lady bought some of his flowers. She looked into his face and asked him his story, and discovered that he was her own sister's child. So the rich lady took them all—the little boy, the old lady, and the cat—to live with her.

"It was really a good story," Ellen said.

It is important for Ellen to understand, however, that it is a fairy story.

THE UPPER CLASS

The Upper Class

The upper class in Negro society in New Orleans and Natchez constitutes less than one per cent of the Negro population. As in white societies, the rate of upward mobility into this class is smaller and the time required for the change in position longer than for any other status rise. Moreover, owing to the overwhelming preponderance of lower-class individuals in Negro society (a result of the caste disabilities fixed upon Negroes), parents face an added difficulty in teaching their children upper-class behavior. The following case illustrates the problems involved in the training of a child for upper-class position in the Negro caste in Natchez.

CHAPTER VIII

THE BLACK SHEEP

PEOPLE like Ellen Hill, whose lives are largely organized around their efforts for upward social mobility, must be constantly on the march. The sanctions of class position are continually pressing to keep them down in the class of their parents. In order to escape from the status to which they were born, such individuals must wage a powerful campaign for higher education, money, "well-placed" friends, and an opportunity to learn the behavior of the social class above them.

This effort is most difficult in the upper-middle class. The struggle to rise from this position into upper class is especially long and feverish because the upper class is the smallest and most closely knit class in the social hierarchy. The family of Martin Neal, our next student, is attempting this difficult maneuver; but Martin, unlike Ellen Hill, is not interested in rising socially. Provided by his family with the social and economic privileges which Ellen Hill sorely misses, Martin refuses to use them as his class and family demand. In fact, if he were left to his own devices, he would be content to slide down the class ladder.

Nevertheless Martin is a very dynamic boy. Action is in his blood and things move swiftly when he is around, though seldom smoothly. His mother says, for instance, that there is no peace in the house when Martin is at home, and his father complains that "Martin don't want to do nothin' but lay down under that tree in the back yard, and holler at his brother, and worry his mamma." Martin is the black sheep of his family; his brother and sister agree with his parents and friends that he is mean, hardheaded, bossy, careless, stupid, lazy, and "ignorant." Daily his parents are tortured by the fear that they have not brought Martin up successfully; indeed their neighbors are already saying that the older Neal boy "has turned out bad."

Martin Neal is the second child and older son of upper-middle-class parents in Natchez, Mississippi. His family is upward mobile into the tiny Negro upper class of that city. He is sixteen years old, has medium skin and straight hair, and a strong, well-made body. He has completed the local high school, and his parents intend to send him away to a Negro college next year in the fervent hope that association with "nice people" will change his behavior. His father mumbles angrily that he "can't seem able to drive no sense into Martin's head," with regard either to his studies or to his chores at home. His mother agrees that Martin is irresponsible and "don't-careyfied." She says, "He doesn't do anything right you tell him, and he doesn't think of anything a minute after you tell him."

Martin replies that he cannot stand to be told what to do. "You see, it is like this. Whenever I get it in my head that I am going to do something, I am going to do it regardless of what anybody says. I will go on and do it when I know that I am going to get a whipping for doing it; but I really can't help myself." He often wishes to run away from home, "and go away some place where I can do like I want to do." His mother says that he has always been "bull-headed" and self-willed, and attributes this behavior to the fact that he was "spoiled" by an indulgent nurse, "Aunt" Lily. Martin actually did run away from home once, and has told his father that he will do so again if the father whips him. He resents any instruction from his parents, and forgets it immediately. He "sasses" both his mother and his father, and in return he is frequently whipped and continually threatened and condemned by them. In order to escape this conflict at home, he regularly goes off on his bicycle and stays until late at night.

Martin's aggressiveness toward his parents goes no further than impudence and refusal to work, but he beats his brother Phil, his sister Helen, and all of his clique members. His father says Martin has always tried to make Helen and Phil obey him, and that he is quick to grow angry and break things when crossed. In his gang his will is law; he enforces his bidding with his fists. While he is quick to repent and to make amends to his friends, he is apparently unable to control his fits of rage. "I

don't know what happens to me when I get mad. It seems like
something goes all through me, an' I don't know exactly what
I'm doing. I am sorry afterwards, an' I give them things an' be
nice to them to show them I didn't really mean to hurt them."

Martin's stubbornness and wild aggressiveness would not lead
one to expect the softer side of his personality which the record
shows. He needs company, he loves to invite his friends into his
workshop, to yell and laugh with his gang, and "to tell a lot of
funny tales, to have excitements, and things like that." He cannot bear to have his parents refuse to talk to him. "That hurts
me more than any other kind of punishment. I feel worried and
lonesome for their company. You see, I have always been use' to
talkin' a lot." Nor does he take his whippings like a "tough" boy;
he "begs and pleads mightily," his mother reports. Recently
when his father scolded him for being disorderly at school,
Martin made such a clamor that his mother turned on the radio
to drown his cries. When he came into the living room, she was
astounded to learn that he had not been whipped at all.

Martin is extremely vulnerable, furthermore, on the score of
his girl, Thelma. He is unusually jealous of her and flies into a
rage when his brother and clique members dance with her or
tease him about her. These, he repeatedly says, are the only dis-
agreements which are lasting and bitter between him and his
friends. At the same time, he admits that he has been afraid to
make sexual approaches to Thelma himself because her mother
might find him out.

Phil attributes Martin's sexual intimidation to "dumbness,"
and adds with brotherly vindictiveness that Martin "ain't got no
sense about nothin'." The parents agree that Martin is stupid,
and quickly point out that he is "one of the laziest boys God ever
made." These charges refer to Martin's inefficiency at housework
and his consistent refusal to run errands for his mother. In spite
of his inadequacy in tasks set for him by his parents, however,
Martin does well enough at his studies and is talented in several
ways. He is a rather good mechanic, electrician, and photog-
rapher, as well as a musician; he enjoys himself more fully in
these roles than in any other, and he feels that they carry more

prestige than that of a "good boy." He says, "I don't get any en-
joyment out of runnin' to town to pay a bill, or runnin' across
the street to a store. Anybody can do that, but can't anybody
fix up things, fix the electric light wire, make fences, develop
pictures, and do other things like I can."

To his parents' charge that he is stupid, Martin responds, as he
does to all their efforts to control him, with impudence and
with stubborn persistence in his negative behavior. It seems that
no punishment can now stop him from being a poor errand boy,
or a reckless dishwasher, and that no reward can make him obey
his parents. He is hardened in his ways. And yet he cannot bear
adverse criticism; he flies into a rage at any suggestion of inferiority by his clique members or his brother and sister; and he
claims too much on his strong points. The problem is to find
the source of Martin's stubborn and aggressive behavior, and at
the same time, of his deep sense of inferiority.

Martin began life as a "fine, fat, healthy baby," his mother
says, but at the age of six months he developed severe colitis. He
cried a great deal during the period of his weaning, and was so ill
afterward that his physician expected him to die. By the time he
was a year and a half old, he used the stool regularly, and never
relapsed in this behavior. Cleanliness and masturbation training
were enforced early and rigidly by his mother during the first
two years of life, when Martin was ill with colitis. His mother
says he exhibited no marked defiant or aggressive behavior toward her during the first two years, but that "he cried a good
deal while he was sick both times" (before and after weaning).

His brother Phil was born when Martin was eighteen months
old, during the period when Martin was a sick baby and when he
was therefore especially dependent upon his mother. The
mother states repeatedly that a marked change in Martin's personality appeared at this time. "He completely rebelled against
me and Phil. He wouldn't come to me, nor would he have anything to do with Phil. He wouldn't even look at the baby. For a
very long time, he wouldn't allow Phil to play with anything

which belonged to him. I would have to watch him all the time, for fear he would do something to Phil. He resented his presence just that much."

At the time of Phil's birth, it is to be remembered, the mother had already begun masturbation training with Martin, and was threatening and punishing him on this score. At a time when Martin was being systematically punished for masturbation, the shift of the mother's care to the new baby may well have appeared to him as a rejection by his mother. He was still sick, he still needed her protection against the nameless and irrational fears of masturbation which she was instilling; but suddenly her care and, as it probably seemed to him, her love were withdrawn.

At first he tried to force her to return to him, by sulking and by openly attacking the baby. When these actions were unsuccessful, he abandoned his mother, but evidently nourished his bitter resentment. In the mother's place, he adopted a lower-class woman who had come to live and work at the Neals' at the time of Phil's birth. Aunt Lily, as the Neals called her, although she was not quite thirty years old and was not their kin, soon gained a favored, semifamilial position in the Neal household, like that of a Negro "mammy" in a southern white family. By the time he was two, Martin had taken Aunt Lily for his sociological mother. She responded with equal possessiveness, telling the parents themselves that Phil was the mother's child, Helen the father's, and Martin hers, and consistently reminding Martin that his parents liked him least of the three children.

According to our record on the parents, it appears that this charge was a true one; at any rate, before Aunt Lily came, the deprivation Martin experienced from his mother seems to have convinced him that she loved Phil, not him. Today, the mother admits that she gave most of her time to Phil; yet she is surprised that "Martin is jealous of me right now, just like when he was a baby. He wants me to whip Phil, and tries to get me to do it." The mother obviously prefers Phil, although she weakly claims that it was Martin who chose to have it so, by loving Aunt Lily.

The strength of Martin's emotional attachment to his lower-class nurse is strikingly revealed by the accounts of his behavior

toward her at the age of four. Both his parents remember that
he showed marked character disturbances between four and six,
and particularly that he insisted upon sleeping with Aunt Lily.
Up to that time he had always slept by himself or with Phil. His
mother remembers that "when he was four or five, he wanted to
sleep with Aunt Lily all the time. It seems that she took my place
with him all the way 'round. At the first part of the night we
would have all kinds of trouble to keep him from going to her."
His father states that at five or six, Martin would "run off from
his mamma and try to sleep with Aunt Lily, and cry after her
at night. And he followed her all day."

Since it is exactly at this age, four to six years, that the incest
taboo is imposed upon a child in our society, Martin's parents
had to include Aunt Lily among the persons toward whom all
intimacies were forbidden and with whom he could not sleep. It
is apparent that Martin strongly resisted the restrictions upon
his relations with his adopted mother, and that he had fundamental difficulty in resolving the Oedipus conflict which so often
occurs in children at this age. With the parents and especially
the father insisting that he must regard Aunt Lily just as he did
his mother and sister, however, the incest-ban was extended to
her. Martin himself testifies to its effective internalization in his
character. When asked by the interviewer if he had experienced
any sexual desires toward Aunt Lily after he reached puberty,
Martin replied, "No, I don't. To tell you the truth, she seems
jus' like a member of my family by kin, an' I wouldn't fool
'round with any of my kin people for anything, I don't want
anything like that to happen, because I feel the same toward
all of my kin people; I don't care if they are third cousins."

Aunt Lily was a vital factor in Martin's training; as his mother
puts the case against her, "Whatever is the matter with Martin,
Aunt Lily is behind it somewhere." But in order to visualize
clearly her role in Martin's life, it is first necessary to examine
his relationship with his father. Mr. Neal, who is twelve years

older than his wife, is a man with a tremendous body, a powerful, bull-like roar, and a quick temper. His wife says that he is extremely jealous of her, "just like Martin." Although Mr. Neal has a well-paid, secure position as an industrial employee, both his wife and his brother say that he was "lazy and irresponsible, just like Martin," as a young man, and that he still has no initiative. His wife adds that she handles his money because "he is a man without any ideas; he can't plan and carry out a single thing." In this respect and likewise in his extreme attachment to his mother, concerning whose health he often cries, Mr. Neal is "just like a baby," his wife reports. He is also childlike in his sudden bursts of temper and in his equally unreasonable economies; for example, he has refused to register the family automobile this year, or to purchase furniture for the living room during the whole of his married life.

Martin has always been afraid of his father, who in moments of rage has beaten him "with anything he could get his hands on." Mrs. Neal admits that when he was small, the boy was frightened by his father's "rough talking." She remembers only one violent whipping which Martin received from his father before he was six, but Martin, who has better reason to recall, says that his father whipped him for drinking wine, fighting his sister Helen, and "forgetting" his chores. He was also whipped for running away from home one night. It is clear that Martin experienced great anxiety at home, even as a small boy; home was a punishing situation from which he tried to flee.

Martin remembers that he always felt strong resentment toward his father for whipping him, and that he sought to damage the father in return, either by refusing to obey him or by attacking him physically. "I'd always do the same thing again, or do something to his things that I thought would hurt him. I use' to go on off to myself an' talk about how mean he was. He use' to be good to Helen jes' lak he is now, an' I'd jump on her for tellin' him things an' beat her. I couldn't do nothin' to him, but I use' to tear up my things, an' throw 'em aroun', so he'd hafta buy me more." Martin still attacks his father in this way. When

Mr. Neal bought Helen an expensive coat last year, Martin tore the pockets and lining from his own best suit, so that his father would have to buy him a new one.

Martin seems to have been reinforced in this aggression toward his father by Aunt Lily's protection. When the father sought to punish him or to make him obey, Martin would run to Aunt Lily and she would lift him up and take him away. "She wouldn't let me bother him," the father says, but adds that Martin was afraid of him nevertheless. Mr. Neal seems almost proud of his success in instilling this terror into the boy. Martin, strong and quick-tempered though he is, admits, "I have always been afraid of daddy. I have always been afraid to roll my eyes or talk down in my throat at him. He will get boiling hot."

Martin is not only afraid of his father, but feels that the father, like the mother, has rejected him. He says repeatedly that his father likes Helen but does not like him. The only one who liked him was Aunt Lily. "My daddy don't treat none of the rest of them like he does me. He'll do all he can for Helen, 'cause she is his heart, but he won't do nothin' for me lessen I beg him for ever so long, an' *then* he won't do it 'til mamma ask him."

Now, at sixteen, Martin faces the constant demands of his father for those habits of work, study, saving, and recreation which his class expects. The father says, "Martin had his way all the time when he was small, an' now he wants to go on, but I shore ain't goin' to encourage him in it. I'm goin' to teach him to work, an' make him go to school, an' save." Under the pressure of this belated upper-middle-class training, Martin has become increasingly aggressive toward his parents. He complains, "You can't do nothin' to please my daddy. He always got to be grumblin'. He jus' likes to be hollowin' atchou an' fussin' all the time." Martin responds by criticizing his father for stinginess, for drinking a half-pint of whisky each pay-day, and for being "ignorant." He will not submit to the father's control, even if it means losing a new suit or being denied spending money. "I get tired of worryin' with him, an' go on. If you don't set right up under his nose, an' baby him, or beg him all the time, he ain't satisfied."

Based on pride rather than love, Mr. Neal's demands upon the adolescent Martin have only increased the boy's sense of rejection. The son has good evidence for the charge that his father does not love him, indeed the best, for he says truthfully, "Everything bad my daddy can say about me, he always says it." If his father whips him again, Martin plans to leave home and join a local jazz orchestra. In the meantime, he temporarily escapes from the anxiety-arousing parents by going off on his bicycle and staying out late; but when he returns, he is invariably scolded and threatened. Surrounded with punishment, Martin feels that he can solve his problems only by running off or going away to college.

But he will not take "low bridge" at home, even to escape certain punishment. He is a bull-headed boy, as his mother says, and pressure cannot move him. His mother whips him regularly with a strap; on his last birthday, she whipped him twice. She, the father, Phil, and Helen all punish him with isolation, scorn, threats, and economic penalties. Martin's reaction is to persist in his disobedience and aggression; as he says, "When I get it in my head to do somethin' they don't want, I jus' do it anyway."

In the face of this blind resistance, the family has concluded that Martin is stupid. He has been continually told by all of them that he has no "sense," because he does not follow instructions concerning errands and chores, and does not yield to punishment. But his parents do not face the truth that Martin does not like them; his deep hostility to them leads him to resist their demands and to forget their instructions. Martin says, "I jus' trained myself not to listen to them; I wouldn't hear what they'd be sayin'. They'd all talk about me, an' make me mad. Then I wouldn't care what I'd do. When they'd send me to the store or anywhere, I'd always do the wrong thing." He attacks his parents by this form of sabotage, as well as by making life miserable for Phil and Helen. "I can always do somethin' to make mamma an' daddy mad. If I want to start mamma, all I got to do is to do somethin' to Phil; an' if I want to hurt the ol' man, I do somethin' to Helen. I know both of 'em got their choice." If he runs away, he knows that he will hurt his parents and the family's reputation; "I wouldn't care," he says, "because they would be the cause of it all."

If the loss of his mother to Phil and his fear of his father constituted the original dilemma in which Martin learned his hostile behavior toward his parents, he owes to Aunt Lily the violence and specific forms of his revolt. At the age of two, when Phil was born, Martin transferred to Aunt Lily his already strongly fixed dependence upon, and love for, the mother. As his mother says, "After Phil was born, Aunt Lily was his heart, not me." Martin obtained from his nurse the unconditional protection, care, and love which he seems to have received during the first two years of his life from his mother. He used Aunt Lily as a buffer against all the disagreeable facts of life, including his parents' discipline. She told him that they were wrong, and he was right. Martin reports that "she made my bed, ate my oatmeal for me if I didn't want it, and would even let me pour out my medicine when I was sick." His mother admits that she and the father "never knew much about Martin until after Aunt Lily left us when he was twelve. She put him to bed, and taught him a different prayer from the one I taught him. She was crazy about him, and wouldn't let anybody else do anything for him. If I would go to whip Martin, she would hide him in her apron, and if I did whip him, she would carry on worse than he would." Mr. Neal says that Martin "stuck right to Aunt Lily's coat tail all the time." She did his work for him and supported him in his resistance to the father's demands. "She ruined that boy. She got him to the place where he didn't want to mind nobody."

Of the three "parents" in the family, one for each child, Martin had the nonpreferred one, in the sense that Aunt Lily had the least power, money, and prestige. From the child's standpoint, however, she was probably the most valuable because she was more indulgent and protective. Aunt Lily rewarded his aggression and taught him to be domineering. In ruling her, he was "spoiled," as his parents say; that is, he was reinforced in attempting to impose his will on the parents, and on everyone else. Martin says that when Aunt Lily left the home he "jus' felt lonesome an' lazy, an' jus' all alone."

Martin's aggression may now be viewed in a new light. He was deeply attached to a woman who filled the position of mother to him. In spite of his present virile and tyrannical front, he clung to this woman's apron strings and was constantly defended by her from the normal controls and dangers incident to growing up. At the same time, his adopted mother had to deprive him erotically and was therefore herself continually frustrating him; we remember that the most troublesome period in his life, according to his parents, was from four to six, when he fought persistently for the privilege of sleeping with Aunt Lily. Years later at the age of thirteen, he says, he had his worst experience in the form of an hallucination of a terrible man about to attack him. He was alone with his mother and Phil that night, and it is possible that the horrible figure represented a punishment for his emergent sex phantasies toward Aunt Lily, or his mother, or both. Immediately after this experience, Martin said, he "felt like running away." It is even possible that his sex wishes toward the tabooed women in the family and his resultant anxiety before the father reinforced this desire for flight.

Whatever degree of truth these conjectures may hold, it is remarkable that Martin exhibits extreme jealousy and sexual intimidation concerning his girl, Thelma. Martin is identified chiefly with a woman, Aunt Lily; the violent type of jealousy which he shows is often found in men who are strongly identified with a woman. When another man approaches his sexual partner or talks about having intercourse with her, as Martin's brother and clique members do with regard to Thelma, such an individual responds as if the act were really to be performed toward himself. From this standpoint, his jealousy may be therefore a kind of self-defense, resulting from his deep-set identification with a tabooed woman.

In view of Martin's hostility toward both his parents, it is probable that his chronic aggression toward his brother and sister is displaced from the parents. He was supported in his attacks upon Phil and Helen, moreover, by the omnipresent Aunt Lily. She made them both obey Martin whenever the parents were not present, gave Martin the choice foods, and even allowed him to beat Helen and to tear up her dolls. As a result, Martin's brother and sister are thoroughly vindictive toward him today and join in the solid front of abuse and rejection which the family has reared against the older son.

As upper-middle-class people, rising gradually into upper class, the Neals cannot understand how such a rowdy and unambitious boy as Martin came into their family. Unless they can quickly remake him, by whipping him into upper-middle-class form, they will be disgraced. They are working feverishly to forestall this calamity. Throughout his life, a great deal of the punishment and abuse which Martin has received from his family has been directed at his anomalous class habits. But he remains a suspiciously lower-class "ugly duckling" in a very respectable and status-proud family. He has clung tenaciously to his habits of fighting, cursing, and being disorderly at school, as well as of resisting the house chores and the professional career toward which his parents seek to drive him. There can be no doubt that Martin's ingrained negativism and unending aggression were strengthened by the chronically frustrating class controls which his parents sought to apply.

Mr. and Mrs. Neal were almost diametrically opposed to Aunt Lily in their class background and therefore in their ideas of how a boy should behave. Mrs. Neal was born into a farm-owning, upper-middle-class family in Mississippi. After completing the graded school in a near-by town, she was sent to Natchez to high school and then to a Negro college in Jackson, Mississippi. All of her brothers—she had no sisters—are interior decorators in Cleveland. Like all middle-class Negroes in the Deep South, Mrs. Neal is quick to distinguish her family from lower-class people by pointing out that none of her brothers has ever been "in jail." She makes several other important class claims. Her father and mother are very light people with straight hair. They were among the six "oldest and most influential" Negro families in the county, Mrs. Neal states. They had a relatively high income, so that when Mrs. Neal returned from college and was appointed as a school teacher, her mother would not allow her to work for the small salary paid a Negro teacher. Even more diagnostic of her class position is the fact that her mother gave her a "very strict" rearing; she was allowed to associate with only one girl in the county, who was from the "best" family, and she was never permitted to go to a dance or a frolic. "I was brought up," she says, "right under my mamma's dress-tail."

Mr. Neal was born and reared in the same county as his wife, but he came from a lower-middle-class family. In naming the "oldest and most influential" Negro families in the county, Mrs. Neal did not mention her husband's family; when asked, she stated that Mr. Neal's father was an uneducated Baptist preacher, and that though his relatives were "nice people," they did not associate with her family and her family's friends. In fact, she pointed out, her husband was a rather "ignorant" man, and her mother had refused her consent to the marriage. Upon questioning, she added that Mr. Neal's father owned only ten or fifteen acres of land, that neither he nor any of his sons had completed graded school, and that all the boys were "bad men," who drank and were involved in shooting scrapes. Except for the fact that Mr. Neal's father was a minister, his family would probably not have held even lower-middle-class status.

After his marriage to an upper-middle-class woman, however, Mr. Neal secured an excellent position in Natchez at a salary of $250 a month and he has held it for thirty years. He soon bought a ten-room house in a Negro neighborhood where his neighbors were physicians, dentists, teachers, and businessmen. His wife became one of the four most prominent leaders of the Episcopal church, which upper-class and upper-middle-class colored people attend in Natchez, and a member of an upper-class clique of married women. As the final step in the family's upward social mobility, Mr. Neal took a course which only the most rapid "climbers" take. He changed his religion from the low-status Baptist faith of his father to the Episcopalian, and thus became a member of the congregation which had the highest social rank among Negroes in the city.

By the time Martin was born, the Neals were regarded by both lower-class and lower-middle-class people in Natchez as "big shots," with a position just on the verge of upper class. Today they lack full participation in the top group only because Mr. Neal works at a semiskilled occupation, and because he has not been able to erase the marks in speech and etiquette of his lower-middle-class training. But in another decade when Helen and Phil, who now associate with upper-class adolescents, have established their position, the Neals will be in the upper class, a far cry from the illiterate Baptist preacher who was their grandfather.

For this rapid mobility, they have their mother to thank; with the father's large income and her own upper-middle-class behavior, she has been able to orient the family toward upper-class position. Like all rapidly mobile people, however, she is extremely anxious concerning her social rank. Economic symbols are not enough, and except for this point, the father's position is weak. Now the problem of Martin's "laziness" and "stupidity" has arisen. It is not to be wondered at, therefore, that throughout the interviews Mrs. Neal, who is the real backbone of the upward mobile drive in the family, was fearful lest "anything embarrassing to the family" should be discovered.

Martin was born, therefore, into a family where the parents were striving for a higher class position. In certain respects he follows the behavior of his class; he has a bedroom of his own, a well-equipped workshop, an allowance of fifty cents a week, and an expensive bicycle. He says proudly that his parents have had an automobile "ever since two weeks before I was born"; that they have their dinner at half-past two in the afternoon, as do upper-class people in Natchez; and that they make a practice of having guests to meals, a luxury which only a few Negroes in the city can afford. When he invited the interviewer to dinner, two firmly established upper-middle-class guests were also present. The meal consisted of two fried chickens, three vegetables, gravy, lettuce and tomato salad, hot buttered rolls, iced tea, ice cream, and cake. In his economic privileges, Martin would appear to be an upper-class Negro boy. He also exhibits the specific class antagonisms of upper-middle-class people. He is hostile to the lower-class Spiritualist congregation whose preacher tried to persuade his family to be "converted"; and to the upper-class Negro men who, he claims, have subordinated him on class grounds in the Boy Scout organization.

In his basic habits and motivations, however, Martin is in revolt against his class. The fight which he is now waging against the upper-class leaders of the Boy Scouts is typical of this revolt. His mother insisted that he join the Boy Scouts, just as she also forced her daughter to become a leader in the Episcopal church. As soon as Martin joined the troop, however, he at once began to act in a very un-Boy-Scout-like manner. He cursed, stole the troop's sardines on a camping trip, beat the other boys, and resisted the discipline of the adult leaders.

This is exactly the type of behavior which Martin exhibits at home. The clock-like discipline of his upper-middle-class family has had little or no effect upon his behavior. His mother says, "We strive to teach him the right thing now while he is young, so it can grow up in him to think something of himself, and mind out who he goes around with. If he can learn these things while he is young, they will be a part of him when he grows up and he will naturally be with the right people." Martin's reply is a ruffianly guffaw. "Yeah man, they beat on me so many times I can't count 'em, but I go on and do jus' like I want." His father tried to teach him to save by paying him a cent for every dime he put in his bank, but Martin spends freely, tears up his clothes, and wants more money for "good-timing." His father says, "I want my boy to go with the better class of people," and his mother tries to make him "associate with nice girls and nice people." She admits, however, that "he is just dirty and don't-careyfied, and not interested in nice girls." Until his father stopped him recently, Martin associated with a clique of boys who were gun-toters, thieves, and "bad men." His best friend was sentenced to the penitentiary.

This is strange behavior for an upper-middle-class adolescent, but it is not unexpected conduct for a child of the lower-class Aunt Lily. She was Martin's sociological mother and his trainer. He is identified with her in his habits. Aunt Lily was a poor woman who lived in a shanty until she came to the Neals'. She did not sit on the Neals' large front verandah in the evenings, but on a box in their back yard. She wore a gingham apron and a bandanna on her head, and she did not speak to the upper-class and upper-middle-class neighbors of the Neals. As we know, she had almost complete control of Martin; she did not demand work and renunciation of him, but rewarded him for habits which were like those of her class. The men with whom she had been reared, and among whom she had lived, were fighters, cutters, and shooters. They had little education and no interest in study; they were "loud" and rowdy, and the least of their concerns was social mobility. They were her idea of what a male should be.

In rewarding Martin's aggressive tendencies, in encouraging him not to study, not to obey his parents, not to meet their demands for the hard work and postponement of gratification which upper-middle-class habits require, Aunt Lily was following her own inescapable lower-class training. Martin was "her" child, she said, and she made him her kind of child—in the image of herself and her menfolk. In only one respect is he unlike the lower-class man, and that is in his sexual intimidation. It is probable that he owes this personality trait to Aunt Lily also, for they loved each other excessively in his early years, and yet he found she was tabooed.

The severe maladjustment which Martin now experiences is chiefly attributable to the conflict between his established lower-class habits and the increased demands of his parents upon him for upper-middle-class behavior. Martin's recalcitrance has aroused anxiety in the parents concerning their own status; it is urgent that at the age of sixteen their son should begin to accept his adult responsibilities for the family's mobility. Following Aunt Lily's departure, Martin was subjected at the age of twelve to the authority of a highly status-conscious family, with its strict demands for work, study, and impulse control. In all fundamental aspects, Martin's situation is like that of a boy who has been adopted by a family of a different class from that in which he received his basic training. He does not accept their ways, and they do not understand his.

Martin conforms to the demands upon him as a Negro, however, much more readily than he accepts his class role. He yields because he must; a Negro in Natchez cannot rebel against the caste restrictions without endangering his life. Not only is Natchez the center of a plantation area where Negroes are economically and physically subordinated by white landlords to a degree approximating that experienced by their slave ancestors, but it is also a very small city. Half of its 14,000 inhabitants are colored, and it is scarcely an exaggeration to say that the white half of the population spends a large proportion of its time watching the Negro half in order to keep the Negroes in their "place." In a plantation city so small that highly elaborate policing of Negro areas can be maintained and each Negro can be tabbed and observed by whites, the caste sanctions are found in their most rigorous form. Each of the thirty-eight Negro boys and girls interviewed in Natchez showed a deep and immediate fear of punishment and attack by whites. As compared with the 159 colored adolescents interviewed in the metropolis of New Orleans, the Natchez boys and girls exhibited a far more constant realization of the downward pressure of the whites upon them. Even at their age, caste is a grim and inescapable reality.

The impact of the all-powerful white society upon Martin's family was dramatized for him in terrifying circumstances when he was eight years old. At this time, when the economic "depression" was most severe, an organized group of white men sought to take by violence the industrial jobs held by Martin's father and a few other Negro men. According to Martin six of the colored workers were murdered by a hired gang of whites. During the year when these murders were carried out, Martin's father was continually threatened, and his family lived in constant fear of his death. As each of his six co-workers was killed, Mr. Neal was again warned. (During the period he lost fifty pounds but he did not yield his job!) Martin learned from this experience that the subordinate position of Negroes was enforced not only by social and economic punishment, but ultimately by physical force. The police and the judge were not his protectors, but his enemies. "It was bad," he remembers, "the way they were killing up all them poor colored men. You know, they killed one right there on St. Catherine Street and they never did a single thing about it. They claimed that they didn't know who was killing them men, but they didn't try to know. I bet one thing, if they had been colored men killing white men, they would have found out who did it. The laws and things don't care a single bit about colored people."

Following the dogmas of the upper-middle class, Martin's parents look toward an eventual solidarity of the Negro group as a means of their winning full human participation in southern life. They are "race conscious"; they are agitators for Negro rights. Mr. Neal is continually "inventing" hackneyed schemes for "Negro business" which, in view of the poverty-stricken condition of lower-class Negroes who constitute 90 per cent of all colored people in Natchez, can be merely wishful thinking. When he faces the actual situation in Natchez, Mr. Neal is less hopeful. He makes a habit of warning Martin and anyone else who will listen that the white man does not want any Negro to make a decent living, or to "rise" in the world. "The trouble here is that the white people want to keep us down. I am old enough to know that these white people don't think nothing about Negroes and the Negroes have got to look out for themselves." In this apparently hopeless dilemma, Mr. Neal attacks the lower-class Negroes for not cooperating "to try to do something for our own race."

Martin's mother is more aggressive on caste lines than his father, as one would expect from her early upper-middle-class training. She feels that Negroes should steadily resist the caste system and condemns those Negro leaders who try to accommodate Negro society to its lower-caste restrictions. "If you know anything about the life of Booker T. Washington, you know that he was an Uncle Tom. If there is anything I hate, it is a white man's Negro and Booker T. was a real Uncle Tom type of Negro if there ever was one. I don't think much of men like some Negro politicians either. They will come down South and white-mouth. They will give their white audience just what it wants to hear while they are in the South, and when they get back to the North they will put on the works, and break down on the white people. I can't stand that type of Negro. I want a person to be a man, and stand up for what is right." In the effort to prepare her children for occupations which will establish them in upper-class position, she has felt keenly the caste differentials in schools. The Negro schools, as she rightly points out, have inadequate teaching staffs (one teacher having as many as 120 pupils) and very inferior equipment. "There's nothing to the colored schools here. They only cripple the children, and we know it, but we can't do anything about it."

Nor can Martin's characteristic aggression effect any change in the schools, in the police and courts, or in the whole network of restrictions which the caste system enforces. When he was a small boy, he cut one of a group of white boys who beat him and took his bicycle; now that he is sixteen, he is a man according to the white law and would be sent to the penitentiary for protecting himself in this way. When he is called "nigger," he consoles himself with his mother's class doctrine that this epithet is not a color stigma, but refers to any "low-down bad person." "She told me that I was not a nigger, but the white boy was a nigger for using that word!" Trained to the dogma of paternalism which the caste system sponsors, Martin believes it is not the "better class" of white people who subordinate Negroes, but the lower-class whites. "I wouldn't want to have nothing to do with no poor-white children because they are too nasty and low."

Martin is not the type of personality to accept caste, like most Negroes, as an inevitable frustration, and to "forget" it; nor is he the kind of effectively aggressive individual who can compensate by moving upward within the Negro class structure; nor is he the "Uncle Tom" type, who is externally highly accommodated and has built a reaction formula of deference out of excessive fear of whites, and as a defense against smouldering hostility within. Martin shows escapist phantasies as a reaction to his lower-caste role in Natchez, and it seems quite probable that he will go "North," as all of his mother's upper-middle-class family have done. If he does, he will have fled from his anxiety-laden family situation and from some of the rigors of life as a Negro in the South. But unfortunately he will find that personality and color-caste will travel with him.

PRACTICE IN ANALYSIS

CHAPTER IX

A CASE FOR THE READER TO TRY

ONE OF the premises of this book has been that human beings learn well only when their efforts are quickly reinforced. In the preceding life histories, the authors have sought to encourage the reader to learn how to interpret certain kinds of data on personality. To be a good judge of human nature is an intellectually and socially rewarding experience; it is expected that the reader will now be motivated to attempt an analysis of the following practice case. If he finds that his interpretation agrees with that of the authors,[1] he then will be reinforced in trying the same techniques upon his enemies or friends. If he misses the point, however, it is to be hoped that he will be reinforced in rereading the book!

Judy Tolliver is a Negro boy, fourteen years of age, and dark-brown in color. He has been in the fifth grade for three years. Judy's teacher says that he has a good mind, but is impudent and disorderly. He lives in Natchez, Mississippi, with his parents and eight brothers and sisters. His oldest brother is married and has a home of his own in Natchez. Judy's family is lower-lower class. He was interviewed by an upper-middle-class man, aged twenty, who is a resident of Natchez.

Judy's father is fifty-three years old, and his mother, forty-six. The names and ages of all the children are as follows: Henry, 26; John, 23; Joseph, 21; Sara, 18; Lillie, 16; Judy, 14; Mary, 11; Belle, 8; Eddie, 5; Lester, 3.

Because the interviews with Judy, and with his parents, brothers, sisters, neighbors, teachers, principal, and clique members, cover more than 100 typewritten pages, it is not possible to reproduce the entire record here. The following excerpts, how-

[1] See Appendix, page 293.

ever, which have been placed in simple categories for the reader's use, cover all of the essential points.

PERSONALITY

Teacher—Judy has been in my room for three years now, not because he is dumb, because he has a very good ability and could have passed the first year, but because he is just so bad and rude that I have been forced to send him to the principal.

Second teacher—I hate to say this, but Judy is sure headed for something bad if he don't change mighty soon. He is the criminal type and is always doing something under cover. He has always got to have the last word, and it is usually something smart. I really don't see how you got along with him as well as you have. I have been looking for just everything to happen.

Judy (Asked about his studying)—I don't ever study much. I tries to study sometimes at night but jes as soon as I picks up the book I goes on to sleep. I be's settin' up asleep an' makin' out lak I'm stud'in' an' when my papa hits me to wake me up, I makes out lak I ain't been 'sleep. I jes can't study. He tries to make me study, but I jes can't for sleepin'. Mary can set down wid her head in a book half the night. Shucks, I wants to spend my time talkin' 'bout ghosts an' things to my sisters.

Interviewer—Has Judy always been bad about teasing the children?

Father—Yas, sir, every since I knowed him. He has been bad about gettin' in somethin' he ain't had no business.

Interviewer—Do you think he was jealous of them?

Father—No sir, I don't think he was. He was jis dev'lish an' mischievous an' lak'd to annoy me an' his mamma. When I was so sick, I couldn' stand to hear the chullun hollowin' an' runnin' 'cause it'd jis run all over me an' he'd jis wanna bother me. That's the way he is now. I kin git atta him lak I'm going to whip him an' he'll be jis as submissive, an' plead. In a few minutes, he is out here dancin' or got some of the chullun hollowin'.

Interviewer—What kind of fellow is Judy around the house?

Lillie—Just as fussy and mean as he kin be. He sasses everybody out. He sassed daddy the other mornin' and daddy chunked the water bucket at him. My daddy is mean too.

Judy—You know one thing, I has always been bad. I don' know why but I has always got in trouble all the time. I been sent home from school two or three times 'bout bein' bad an' gettin' in things wid the teacher. (Thinking) I don't know what it is, but people seem to be imposin' on me all the time an' they seems to be pickin' on me.

Interviewer—Why is it that you act as you do toward these light children?

Judy (Thinking)—I don' know other than that's the way my papa is. I gits mad jes lak him an' I can't help myself. I jes can't stan' fo' nobody to be imposin' on me 'cause somethin' seem to jes come over me. I gits mad an' can't help myself. I worries 'bout that a lot 'cause I wants to come to school if I kin.

Judy—Now, jes lak I be's out gettin' slop fo' the hogs an' somebody axes me who I'm gettin' it fo' an' I'll tell 'em quick, fo' their big black mamma. I be's mad an' I tells 'em that fo' a fight.

That's somethin' I can' seem to help—my temper. I kin git mad jes so quick it's a shame an' I shore nuff be's mad an' if anybody fools 'roun' wid me, I'm ready fo' a fight. I reckon I been in more fights an' fusses than anybody out to the park. Things jes don' go lak I want 'em sometimes, an' I jes gits ready to fight when somebody mistreats me. I been put off'n the park three times fo' fightin' or somethin'.

NOTE: Judy beat a girl. Also beat another girl who ganged his sister. Mother tells him not to fight girls unless they pull a knife.

Judy—I was way out on Homochitto goin' from school an' a big girl kept on pushin' me off'n the sidewalk an' I hit her. I hit her in the mouth an' cut it, an' we started fightin'. Wouldn't bothered her, but she was a big girl in the eighth grade an' she meddled me.

NOTE: Judy started to run away to grandmother after his father whipped him recently.

NOTE: Clique member says Judy is very aggressive with girls.

Lillie (Saying Judy doesn't do his chores)—He be's gone off some place the biggest of the other times and don't nobody know where he is or nothin'. He don't come to school a lotta times. Last week he was out one or two days off some place, I don't know jes where he was.

NOTE: Judy hides his money from his mother.

NOTE: His mother and his brothers whip Judy for gambling, but he plays horses, dice, lottery. Began when very young.

NOTE: Lillie says Judy is a confirmed gambler, and that he bets regularly on horses and lottery.

NOTE: Clique member says Judy is inveterate gambler; can't stop.

Interviewer—Whenever I am at Judy's home and he comes in, he will drop his head and say little or nothing around his parents. When they leave or whenever we are alone, he is very active and aggressive. He will ask me questions and talk.

Interviewer—I watched Judy at the golf course with his clique of caddies. Eight or ten boys approach each car from both sides and beg the player or players for the chance to caddy. Judy was unusually slow in approaching the cars. When he would run to meet a car, about eight or ten boys would be in front of him. I would watch his face and he would not be enthusiastic over his chance, neither would he plead like the other boys until the person would make his choice. He would just ask and would not persist.

NOTE: Judy says he is afraid to walk home at night alone because the road is dark.

Judy—Got a whippin' the other day for talkin' back. It was the other night. Mamma tolt me to go to the store, an' it was dark an' I said I was scared. She tolt me I better go on an' I went outta the yard raisin' sand an' fussin' back, an' when I comed back papa got the strap an' gived me three or four licks wid it.

NOTE: Judy says he doesn't want to stay out at night with his clique because they steal, and he is very much afraid of policemen.

Judy—I was scared when my mamma said "policeman" 'cause

I thought he might put me in jail for sassin' my mamma. I heard they treats yo' mean an' I don' want 'em to bother me. When you is done done somethin', they beats you an' puts you in jail too.

Judy—One time I did run away. I was thirteen an' mamma wanted to whip me 'cause I wouldn' do somethin' she wanted me to do. I got mad an' ran away an' she said all right, she was goin' to git the policeman an' I got scared an' stood up in the road right down from my house 'most all day. I left 'bout nine in the mornin' an' stood in the road 'til 'bout two that evenin'.

NOTE: Judy does not want to have a common-law wife, because it would get him in trouble with the police.

Judy—I wants a wife an' house of my own so no woman can' never put me out in the streets in the cold an' I won' have nowhere to go. I wants to have my own house so I can put her out an' she be out in the cold 'stead of me.

NOTE: Judy says he is afraid of a drunken white man who runs a lottery.

NOTE: Judy is afraid the movie ticket-seller will have him arrested for disguising his size and age in order to buy a child's admission ticket.

NOTE: Judy admits that he is a "big talker" and that he runs from good fighters.

Judy—I ain't never tolt you 'bout the time I had a fit, has I? Well, I was in the bed an' I seen a great big man jes comin' toward me wid somethin'. He was jes comin' right on straight at me an' I jes hollered an' done ever'thin'. I was 'bout nine years ol' an' I was sleepin' wid my mamma then. It musta been in the winter-time 'cause my mamma jumped up an' put all my clo'es in the fire an' it wasn' long 'fore the fit went off'na me. That was the wors' feelin' I has ever had in my whole life, I b'lieve. I was shore scared an' it seemed to me lak he was goin' to catch up wid me every minute. That was really the biggest man I ever seen an' it seemed to me lak he was comin' after me to hurt me.

Clique member—He's a good kid, but he shore hate fo' anybody to say anything to him to hurt his feelin'. He is so easy to hurt and when you says somethin' that he don't lak, he will jump on you if you is his size and he think that he kin whip you. He ain't goin' to bother you if you is bigger or older than him. He is all the time talkin' 'bout somebody bein' bigger than him. Shucks, I don' think 'bout that when I gits mad and wants to fight.

Judy—You know one thing, I shore don' lak fo' nobody to be joanin'[2] me when they is tryin' to make fun of me. That jes hurts me all over an' I feels so bad I don' know jes what to do. A lotta times when people says I'm bad an' mean, I jes be actin' lak that 'cause they has said somethin' or done somethin' which has hurt my feelin'. I ain' really bad, but I do's bad things sometimes an' I don' know jes why I do's 'em other than I don' want people to do or say 'em to me, so I do's it to them so they won' have a chance.

Judy—Now, you kin take bright people. I be's mean an' treats 'em mean an' be's bad wid 'em jes 'cause it would hurt me if they was to treat me thata way.

Interviewer—Judy asked me a lot of questions about poison, hitting a person behind the head, and shooting a person while alone with him. He was interested to know how the law would discover a guilty person. I asked why he asked about poison.

Judy—I been thinkin' 'bout it. I don' never eat at nobody's house 'cause they might poison me, maybe I did somethin' to some of their chullun.

NOTE: He visits his friends sometimes at their houses, but seldom when they are eating. If he should come while they were eating, he wouldn't eat for fear of poison. He usually meets the boys up on the street and plays.

Interviewer—What about the pistol?

Judy—I felt lak if me an' a boy was together by ourself, I could shoot him an' nobody would know. Or I could hit 'im back of the head. (He knew this would kill the person, and in all cases figured the person would die at once.)

Interviewer—Why have you been thinking about hurting someone?

[2] To "joan" is to tease another person with the intention of starting a fight.

Judy—The boys joans me all the time. Over to the park every day they be joanin' an' pickin' at me. It makes me mad an' I say I'm goin' to hurt some of 'em an' hurt 'em if they don' stop foolin' wid me. I gits very tired an' very mad when boys say bad things 'bout my folks. (Asked what they said) Yo paw don' do nothin' but stay home an' lay on yo' mamma all the time. An' my papa is playin' crazy, but is jes lazy. An' my sisters ain' nothin' but whores, 'specially Lillie. That all jes hurts me an' makes me mad too. I know all of it ain't the truth, but I gits mad jes the same an' wants to kill 'em. I would joan 'em back, but I don' know much 'bout joanin' an' what I say don' seem to hurt 'em lak what they be sayin' to me hurt me. I been tryin' to learn to joan jes lak them but jes can't git 'roun' to it.

INFANCY AND EARLY TRAINING

As a young child, Judy had rickets, a children's disease resulting from defective nutrition and characterized by alterations in the bones. His legs were unusually small and weak, and his head extremely large. His nursing was stopped at three months by a breast ailment of his mother's. Between the ages of six months and three years, he had several attacks of diarrhoea.

Mother—He was a very sickly baby. You see him now big and strong, but we thought he'd die. Everybody said he was goin' to die. He was very small wid little bitta limbs and a big head. When he was six months ol', he got sick wid loose bowels an' he stayed sick 'til he was 'bout three. He never did learn to walk 'til he was 'most four. I tell you, Mr. Jones, we done had some trouble wid him.

Interviewer—How did you give him milk—from breast or bottle?

Mother—From a bottle. When he was 'bout three months ol', I had a disease in my breast. It make your breast swell, an' he wouldn' take my milk. I had another terr'ble time then. He was so small an' delicate-like, an' the doctor tolt me to give him milk from jus' one cow. I couldn' hardly find nobody would furnish me wid jus' one cow's milk. But a ol' white woman who live jus' over yonder in the next house furnished us.

Interviewer—Did Judy have much trouble teething?

Mother—Yes sir, he had a lotta trouble, mo' than any the rest of the chullun. The doctor said it's on 'count of his weak system. You see he had trouble wid his bowels and the doctor said this had somethin' to do wid his teethin' trouble. Dat was when we had a good bit of trouble wid him. We were kinna scared to give him anythin' to keep in his mouth 'cause of his weak stomach.

Mother—He was 'bout four 'fore I could give him anythin' much to eat. When he was 'bout three, I gived him jes some kinna liquors and soup 'cause that was all he could take. We had all kinna doctors wid him an' none of 'em done him no good. A ol' woman gived me a rem'dy an' that done him mo' good than all the doctors' medicine. That was the only thing that done him any good. He was 'bout four years ol' then an' was a real sight.

Mother—He was 'bout four when he started walkin'. His head was so big an' his limbs was so small that ever'body said he wasn't goin' to never walk. Course, I jes think that his limbs was too weak for him to hold himself up.

Interviewer—Was he ever a cry-baby?

Mother—No, he was very good, 'til he firs' took sick, then he would fret some. Mos' of the time it would be when he dirtied himself. I shore wish he was thata way now.

Interviewer—Did any other woman help you with him?

Mother—No, didn' nobody help me wid him excep' my two daughters. I tended to him by myself. You see, he was so sick that I had to stay right wid him all the time. Really we thought shore we was goin' to lose him.

Interviewer—Did he ever soil himself after he had been trained not to?

Mother—Never did after he got well. He ain' never been no

dumb child an' always been quick 'bout learnin' things. Course we have always had a lotta trouble wid him when he was little an' now since he is big we got trouble wid him too.

Interviewer—How did you stop him from playing with himself?

Mother—Ain' never had no trouble with him lak some of the others. I reckon he stayed sick so long 'til he was too big fo' that. Course after he got up some size we never was roun' him much 'cause me an' his papa was workin' out an' the chullun done mos' of the tendin' to him.

Mother—I reckon that must be the reason he is so much trouble. He had such a hard time. He keeps a cold now all the time an' won't keep his nose clean.

Neighbor—He was shore a funny baby. He really wasn' nuthin' but head. He had a great big watermelon head an' a little bitta body. He had a big head clean until he was a big boy. I usta pass there and hollow at him and he would point at his head and say "Head." I'd say, "What you say, buddie?" or "What you know?" and he'd say "Head." I think he had such a big head that everybody would carry on so over it until he got where he couldn't think about anything else when you spoke to him but head.

FAMILY

Judy's father has been a recluse for fifteen years. During Judy's whole lifetime, his father has claimed to be sick; he does not visit his former friends or go to church, nor does he allow his wife to do so. He is extremely jealous of any man who comes to the house and whipped his wife because she talked with the male interviewer. He insists that his younger children be in the house by dark, and always sends one of the smaller children to watch the adolescent daughters when they go out. Judy is sent to watch Lillie, aged sixteen, when she goes downtown, and to report on her actions and conversations. He makes a habit of whipping his children, regardless of their sex or age. Two of his adolescent daughters told the interviewer that all of his children hated him, and wished he were dead.

Neighbor—The father has just shut himself in from the rest of the world. The mother is the same way. I haven't never seen her off of that hill by the park. She never goes no place or associates with anybody. She ain't been to church in fifteen years.

Interviewer—Mr. Tolliver rules his house by a reign of terror over each member of his family. He demands that the children be in the house before dark. At night the mother and father retire very early; whenever the children are out, the house is closed and the parents must let them in. The striking thing about the behavior of the father in the home was that everybody else kept quiet and he completely dominated the conversation. I got the feeling that he was the real boss of the family.

Father—Judy is jes bad. I tries to go sometimes widout beatin' him, but that don't do no good 'cause he gits worser an' worser. Sometimes I tries him for a week widout beatin' him, but then he starts stayin' out 'til two o'clock at night an' tell me he been to the show. Now ain't no show in the world stay open 'til that time of night. Course whenever I goes to whip him, he gits jes as humble an' pleads, but he is jes tryin' to git by an' don't mean to do no better. He is jes as bad as he kin be an' can't nobody do nothin' wid him.

Interviewer—Which parent did Judy like better?

Mother—They all say they lak me the best. Their father is kinna rough on 'em an' whips 'em all the time. They don' like that. I whips Mary, Lester, an' Belle, but the rest is too strong for me an' I leaves 'em to their papa.

Lillie—My papa bosses everybody at home. My mamma works all the time an' don't go to see her mamma hardly 'cause he fusses so when she leaves.

Lillie—My mamma done worked herself almost to death washin' an' raisin' all of us an' my daddy ain't doin' nothin' but fussin' all day ever' day. I has said, an' I mean it, if they git another baby I'm goin' to leave. They got ten livin' an' four dead, an' you know that's enough for anybody.

Lillie—That's a terrible hole out there where we live. Joe Fletcher been tryin' to git me to come an' live wid him, but I don't want nothin' to do wid livin' wid no man. They is too mean. My papa don't 'low my mamma to go nowhere an' don't want us to go much. We kin axe him something an' he won't give you a straight answer for nothin'—jes lak we kin axe him if we kin go to the dance an' he'll say "You is dancin' now." If we slip off an' go, he'll fuss 'bout it a week, an' I hates to hear anybody fussin' all the time lak he does. He don't 'low my mamma to boss nothin'. He jes sets there an' lays 'roun' an' fusses. I reckon that's why all of us is fussy an' disagreeable; he is so mean.

Interviewer—Has your father always been mean?

Judy—Yes, he always been bad 'bout fussin'. He was pretty good 'til he took sick when I was little. He been mean an' fussy every since. Always fuss an' be mean to ever'body 'roun' home. I would feel sorry fo' him an' think he done it 'cause he was sick.

Judy—Papa is mean, but I don' hate him really. I b'lieves my sisters hate him, 'cause they is always sayin' it. I laks mamma best 'cause she is always doin' fo' me an' lets me go places if papa say "Yes." Papa is mean a lotta times an' say "No," an' then I say I don' lak him neither, but I be's all right in a little while.

NOTE: Father and mother punished Judy for being out after dark.

Judy—Sometimes my mamma tells me I can't go an' play. When she tells me I can't go, I gits very mad an' jes fusses. Sometimes I fusses out loud, but mos' times I jes mumbles to myself an' say she jes want somebody to set 'roun' here an' work all the time an' never go no place. (Thinking) I be's mad wid her too 'cause if I wanted to go off somewhar to work an' be makin' money fo' her she wouldn' mind me goin', an' I sets 'roun' an' jes fusses to myself.

Judy—I gits a whippin' sometimes jes lak when she want me to do somethin' an' I don' feel lak doin' it. I don' git up an' go do it when she tell me an' she whips me to it. If I still sets 'roun' an' pouts, she whip me again an' then I gits so mad I could jes run off somewhar.

Interviewer—Do you still whip them?

Mother—Yes, their papa whips 'em most of the time. I would've got holt to Lillie though, but her papa wasn' here an' I thought I'd git the wors' of it. Then she said I ought'na whip her on her birthday. She is seventeen years ol' today, but I wasn' thinkin' 'bout that.

Interviewer—Do you ever talk with your parents?

Judy—Never talks wid 'em much. I be's really ashame' wid 'em. I can't look at 'em in the face while they is talkin'. I don' know why, but I jes feels funny an' don' never wanna. I feels too funny.

NOTE: Judy feels that parents exist for the purpose of punishing you when you do wrong. His parents don't play with him, and don't allow him to play with them. They always tell him not to play with them because he is a man now.

NOTE: Judy "sasses" his grandmother, and won't let her whip him.

Interviewer—Which one of your parents do you love the best?

Judy—I loves 'em both 'bout the same. Both of 'em whipped me 'bout the same an' I laks 'em 'bout the same. I gits mad wid both of 'em but I wouldn' hit 'em lak I do's my brothers when they tries to meddle me, I'd jes git outa their way.

BROTHERS AND SISTERS

Mother—He ain't never been jealous of none of 'em. Lillie, jes older than him, is the jealous one. He never was jealous of her or the baby jes younger than him neither. He never did seem to mind 'bout us takin' up time wid the other baby when he was small, but he would drink her milk. He would drink all of his bottle an' reach an' git her'n.

Interviewer—How did he act toward his sisters when he was small?

Mother—They took care of him while I'd be workin' an' they never had no trouble wid him. He was real good when he was small, but he usta fight them when he got bigger. He wants to fight all of them now excep'n Lillie. He is crazy 'bout her 'cause she help him. She'll put things in his pants now when he is goin' to git a whippin', so it won't hurt. Next to her he laks his brother John. Course he sizes up to him to fight sometimes.

Interviewer—Who are your real friends in your family?

Judy—'Mongst my brothers an' sisters, I got four. My mamma an' papa is my best friend, I reckon, but John is next. Now my sister Lillie is next to him 'cause she be's nice to me too. My other brothers an' sisters don't care nuthin' 'bout me an' I don't worry 'bout them. I works out to the park an' do's enough cadd'in' to buy my things what I wears an' gives mamma some change, an' that's all I cares anythin' about. Don't none of 'em do nothin' fo' me much worth noticin' an' I be's the same way 'bout them.

Interviewer—Which one of your brothers do you like the best?

Judy—My brother John, I laks him the best, 'cause he is the goodest of them all to me.

Judy—John ain't lak my other brothers, they wants to be beatin' me all the time or bossin' me in some kinna way. I can't do nothin' I wants to do fo' them tryin' to meddle wid me all the time. They usta wanna be beatin' me all the time when I was smaller, but they ain't been botherin' wid me since I got to be big 'cause I don't do some of the things I usta do, an' then I ain't quite as bad as I usta be. An' I is too big fo' 'em to be beatin' me now, an' they knows it. I ain't goin' to let none of 'em be beatin' on me all the time lak I is some kinna dog or somethin' lak that. I jes ain't goin' to be standin' fo' it any more.

Judy—The rest of my brothers don't care nothin' 'bout me an' they don't do nothin' fo' me. Now John always acted lak he cared fo' me. He always been good to me an' when he was workin' he'd be givin' me things an' don't never be fussin' at me 'cause I is bad.

NOTE: Judy says his brothers and his father are mad all the time.

Judy—I ain't never lak'd to be havin' nobody meddlin' wid

me, an' I jes gits mad whenever anybody tries to be bossin' me lak my brothers tries to do. They is jes lak my papa, I reckon. He is thata way. He laks to be bossin' you 'roun' an' things lak that all the time.

Judy—Now Lillie has always been good to me. When I was little, she usta let me play wid her things an' be always givin' me somethin'. She usta play wid me a lot too when I was a little boy. Usta have a good time playin' then an' wouldn't hafta do nothin' 'fore I started to school 'cept eat an' play.

Judy—Now my sisters ain't lak my brothers. They is much better'n they is; they treats me nice most all the time. My sister Lillie is the best to me though an' I loves her the best. The rest is all right, but she is good to me. She lets me have a few nickels an' things lak when I is broke. She shore is good to me.

Judy—Jes as long as Lillie don't do nothin' too bad or git in nothin', it is all right wid me. I ain't lak some people who don't want their sisters to be foolin' 'roun' wid boys. She can fool 'roun' wid anybody she want to fool 'roun' wid now 'cause she is ol' enough to take care of herself now.

NOTE: Judy and Lillie go to the movies together and take turns paying for tickets.

Judy—I don't fool 'roun' wid none of the rest of my brothers or my other folks other than the ones I has jes tolt you 'bout 'cause they don't care nothin' 'bout me an' don't give me nothin' neither, so it don't make me no difference 'bout 'em. Most kinfolks don't mean you mucha good noway.

Lillie—Oh, I love Judy all right 'cause he is my brother, but I ain't crazy 'bout him. I takes up a lotta time with him 'cause I kin kinna make my ends meet thata way, you know. I kin get out of the house, if I take him with me, an' he gives me show fare.

Sara—Judy don't like nobody 'round home much, but John and Lillie. He'll do most anything for them but he really seem to almost hate the rest of us.

Judy—Lillie is real mean to everybody but me. Shore b'lieve what people say 'bout dark people studdin' evil. She an' Henry an' papa is kinna dark an' they is the meanest ones in the family.

They is always fussin' an' doin' somethin' mean to somebody. Papa is almost real dark an' mamma is light-brown. Now she is all right, but the others is jes as mean an' especially them dark ones. They is all jes as mean an' grouchy as they kin be.

CLASS

Mr. Tolliver has always lived close to town. His father died when he was a baby, and his mother when he was fifteen. Mr. Tolliver's mother, father, and stepfather never went to school. He is illiterate. The family lived on a place furnished by white people. Mr. Tolliver says, "I was raised right up wid white folks."

Mrs. Tolliver came from the country to live and work in town. Her father died when she was quite young, and from all indications her mother "got around" a good deal with men. Her mother went to school very little, and could barely read. Mrs. Tolliver herself has had almost no education, and cannot read or write. Her family owned no real estate and rented their house both in the country and in town. They attended church in the country, but belonged to no associations. The family has always lived in alleys and other lower-class neighborhoods while they have been in town.

The Tollivers now own no real estate. They are members of no church and no associations, but they do have small policies in a Negro insurance company. Mrs. Tolliver has no intimate friends and Mr. Tolliver only one, a man who has almost no education and who owns no property, but rents in the mill quarter.

Interviewer—Why do you think the father never goes out? Who were his former friends?

Neighbor—I think he wanted to do something in life, but got married and started having children so fast until he couldn't. I know that at one time he took music (jazz). He used to class with a fast bunch who were free spenders at that time. Then after he got married and start having childrun so fast, he quit coming out. I don't know why he married this woman neither. I don't know whether he had to marry her or not.

Neighbor—The father still has that desire for high class. You see, he is very intelligent himself, but his wife is dumb. I often wonder why he married her, but I suppose he had to or something like that.

Interviewer—The father seems to be very proud of the fact that "white folks" raised him and provided his mother and stepfather with a place to live in, rent free. He told me that his mother, father, and stepfather had no education, and that the "white folks" had tried to get him to go to school or study his books, but he never could do either.

Interviewer—For many years after he was married, Mr. Tolliver cleaned houses and made very good money, but wasted it on whisky and gambling. As a young man, he was very bad about drinking, gambling, dancing, and fighting, he said.

Neighbor—When they lived over by the Park, they didn't have but two little bitta rooms and a kitchen. All the boys slept in one room and all the girls in another, with the mother and father. They had two beds in each room and chillun would be throwed in them all kinds of ways. A row at the head and one at the foot.

Interviewer—The grandmother lives in an alley. One uncle is "real tough" and lives with a woman to whom he is not married.

NOTE: The mother works as a domestic and takes in washing. Sara works after school. One brother did work at the box factory, but has been laid off. The father works as a yard man on Saturdays.

Sara—I gives mamma some of my money an' keeps the rest to buy clothes to help mamma 'cause she got to take care of the house an' all the children. Papa don't do nothin' but set 'round home. Mamma has to look out for everything an' if we wouldn't work an' help her, things would be in a terrible fix.

Judy—I be's workin' a lot now. I works every night out to the lottery house. I draws the balls. I draws 'em every night now an' he give me quarters. He say I'm lucky 'cause I don't draw out many hits so they don't hafta be payin' out much money. Jes as long as I kin be doin' that I'll have work wid him. Shore do wish I could draw my number out. I been playin' for a long time an' ain't never hit nothin'. I been playin' kinna heavy lately too 'cause I wants to hit so I kin buy me some clo'es, but I don't seem to be able to do nothin' with it.

NOTE: Judy is always dirty and very poorly dressed in cheap, old clothes. When it is cold, he wears a jumper, as he does not own a coat. He wears his father's old work shoes to school. They are very large, and turned and broken around the tops. His pants are cheap and dirty, and he usually wears a dirty blue cotton shirt. His hair needs combing and cutting. His fingernails are too long and, like everything else about him, dirty.

Judy—I don't hafta git ready to go to work 'cause I jes goes lak I comes to school.

NOTE: The family usually cannot afford milk or meat.

Lillie—I know what a lotta children mean—nothin' but worry, lak that army at my house. I reckon Judy has told you 'bout all them that we has in our house. All them children is too many for any two people to have 'cause it ain't no way fo' 'em to look out for 'em halfway lak they should be looked out for and some of 'em is bound to be hongry and nasty and dirty. (Shaking her head) No, never no children for me.

Judy—I sleeps wid my brother now, but I ain't been doin' that all my life. I ain't been sleepin' wid him long, I know, maybe 'bout two or three years. I usta sleep wid my mamma all the time when I was smaller. I slep' wid her fo' a long time 'til I got to be a real good-size' boy, an' then I quit, anyway she quit lettin' me sleep wid her. (Pause) I reckon I was gettin' too big an' too bad to sleep wid her.

Judy—When I gits grown, I wants to work an' buy things for myself 'cause I ain't never had nothin' much. I needs clo'es an' shoes right now an' ain't makin' no money to buy me none wid. Ain't never had more'an a dollar an' a quarter that I made, an' I ain't never had but one fifty-cents in my pocket at once what was mine to spend. I has always had a very hard time.

Interviewer—What do you want for Christmas?

Judy—Don' know, but I don' want no toys or nothin' lak that 'cause I is too big fo' that. I really wants clo'es an' shoes but I don't think that mamma is goin' to git me anythin'. I wishes all the time fo' clo'es an' shoes an' things lak that to wear.

Lillie—If I has chullun when I gits married, I shore don't want but one. I always has said that 'cause it take too much an' when you has a lot of 'em you shore can't do no kinna providin' for 'em worthwhile.

NOTE: Judy's parents had a big fight last year. His sisters hit the father back when he punishes them.

Lillie—I goes by my boy friend's house all the time. He live by himself an' I goes by there early from school an' stays 'til 'bout four an' goes on home an' tells mamma I been to the show. I cooks for him an' myself sometimes. I knows he is crazy 'bout me now 'cause he fights wid me an' fights 'bout me. When I was small, 'bout thirteen, he didn't care nothin' 'bout me but what he could git out of me. Made a fool out of me, but now he love me an' will do anything he can fo' me.

NOTE: Judy had sexual intercourse at twelve or thirteen, with his best friend's sister. He was ashamed to see her afterward and would not ask her again.

NOTE: Judy's mother objects to a boy's kissing Lillie and punishes her. The same boy once beat Lillie in the street.

Judy—Mamma say she knowed I was havin' a fit, that's why she put my clothes in the fire. Folks say whenever you is havin' anythin' lak that, to put your clo'es in the fire an' the fit goes off'na you, an' that was what she done to run it off'na me that night.

Interviewer—Who are your mother's and father's friends?

Lillie—They ain't got none. It ain't but one man, who live up on Nethervilles Hill, that come down to our house to see my papa sometimes.

Lillie—Mamma ain't got no friends either. Don't either one of them ever go nowhere.

Interviewer—What about church?

Lillie—What church? They don't study 'bout no church.

Interviewer—Do your parents ever say what they want you to be?

Lillie—They don't do nothin' much but fuss an' say they'll be glad when we leave or wish we'd go on off an' git us somebody 'cause they is tired of us. They wants us to git married an' leave.

Interviewer—Do you think Judy will ever finish school and get himself a good job?

Father—No sir, Mr. Jones, I don't think he is ever goin' to do nothin'. He wants to quit right now. He is goin' to be jes lak his brother Eddie. He went to school fo' a long time an' never did do nothin'. He is kinna hard to hear an' he made such bad marks 'til he got 'shame an' quit.

Interviewer—What about the other children?

Father—They ain't never goin' to do nothin' either, I don't reckon, but run aroun' an' drink an' gamble. I never could get 'em to go to school neither.

CLIQUE

Interviewer—Judy's gang not only talk about sex but they go to the bayous with their girl companions. A girl and a boy will leave the group and go off into the woods. Sex knowledge is quite common in the group. The girls and boys discuss sexual intercourse together with little or no feeling of being ashamed. The girls in the group are between the ages of fourteen and sixteen years. They are lower class, as are the boys, and attend school irregularly or not at all.

Interviewer—The members of Judy's clique have little or no work to do at home.

Judy—I shore had a good time when I was a little boy playin' wid them chullun who lived wid us an' aroun'. We was some bad an' used to fight 'mongst ourselves all the time when we couldn't git nobody else to fight. I got plenty of beatin's in my gang then.

Interviewer—Do you ever fight with your gang now?

Judy—We fights a lotta times over joanin' 'bout caddies. Jes lak I goes up an' axes a man if he want me to caddy an' some of the other boys hollows out an' tells the man fo' to don't hire me 'cause I can't see. Well, if I don't git the job, it be's me an' him right then. If I gits the job, I goes on an' makes my roun' an' when I gits through I looks the boy up an' tells him, "You know who *kin see?*" An' he axes me who, an' I tells him his black mamma, an' we starts fightin'. That's what I say it fo', an' if he says somethin' back 'bout my mamma, we will joan each other fo' a while, but it will end up in a fight.

A member of Judy's clique—But Judy don't come up on the street much at night now 'cause his mamma won't let him out. We shore do carry him 'bout that. He ain't man enough to git out at night now. He got to set home 'round his mamma's dress-tail. He gits sore, but he can't whip nobody an' he cools off. He can come out sometimes, but he don't know how to go home when he comes out at night so his mamma has 'bout quit lettin' him come out.

NOTE: Judy's clique "joans" him about his father's staying at home, not working, and giving his mother so many children; and about Lillie's and his other sisters' being "whores."

CLASS PUNISHMENTS AND SCHOOL

Interviewer—Judy says there is no sense in some Negroes' trying to be more than others, because whites regard all the same.

Judy—When colored folks gits hold of a little money, they is right ready to leave the po' colored folks an' go an' class wid the big dogs. They don't wanna have nothin' to do wid the po' folks an' they kin know you too, an' they will walk right by you on the street an' won't say a word to yo' 'cause they thinks they is more'an anybody else. Jes lak I tell you, white folks ain't a bit more studdin' 'bout them than they is me or you.

Judy—I can't do nothin' to the white folks that talks 'bout kickin' me but talk big talk back to 'em, but I shore can handle colored folks who try to ack lak white folks jes 'cause they is bright an' got a little more money than some other colored folks. I shore do drop the wood on 'em an' I don't feel bad over it. (Deep thought) I really don't reckon I could ever learn to lak a bright colored person, I don't care what he'd do for me. I'd always feel funny 'roun' him an' the least li'l thing he do or say to me would make me feel lak jes gettin' somethin' an' try'n to kill him. I reckon white folks feels that same way 'bout colored people.

Judy—What shore nuff gits me though is some niggers jes 'cause they is a little bright tries to ack lak white. That is when I gits my feelin' out on 'em. I tries to kill 'em when I gits on 'em an' see jes what good their color does 'em then. They thinks they is cute jes 'cause they is bright an' got a little more'an the other colored peoples.

Judy—Bright colored people thinks too much of theirselves. They thinks they is more'an anybody else jes 'cause they is bright an' they will pass po' people on the streets lak me an' won't speak. I could jes git somethin' an' knock 'em in the head wid it. That is jes why I be's so hard on 'em when I gits on one.

Interviewer—How long have you felt that way about bright people?

Judy—A long time—all my life, I reckon, every since I has known anythin' 'bout 'em. When I was smaller, the teacher usta treat 'em good—she be better to 'em than she be to anybody else an' that jes made me hate 'em then shore 'nough. She'd always be tryin' to make the dark people feel bad an' wouldn' never call on the bright ones when they didn't know. (Thinking) I'd tell her, too, that she better call on some of them when she'd be axin' me a lotta questions.

Judy—The teachers jes tries to take the bright chillun fo' their pets an' try to make everybody else git their lessons an' don't never call on them fo' nothin' that is hard an' they don't know, but she will be pickin' on the dark people all the time.

NOTE: Judy asked his teacher why she did not call on light children. She took him to the principal.

Judy—I ain't as bad 'bout that as I used to be 'cause I is older an' I has learned better, but it shore seem to me now that the teacher has pets an' they is the bright chullun.

Teacher—Judy is unusually rude to bright children and every chance he gets he really imposes on them. He hits them and shoves them. The other day I saw him purposely spit on one. He just seems to hate them for some reason.

NOTE: The teacher says the trouble with Judy is that his whole family is "really a terrible set"; in the same breath, she admits that his sisters are clean, and we know that two of them are very good students.

Teacher—Of course they send him to school looking like a tramp; last year he came to school for three months wearing the same things. He never even changed his underclothes, and it looked to me like he slept in them. It was really terrible and he was smelling so until one day I just told him he had to change. The next day his things were washed, but that was all. He never combs his hair or shines his shoes at any time. His sisters, even though they all have a record of being very rude, do come to school looking decent. The whole trouble seems to be in the family. I have been told that this whole family is really a terrible set, and the children sure do show it.

Principal—Judy's mother is mean just like him, too. We had some trouble with his sister Lillie and the mother came out to the school to have it out with us. She wouldn't let you say a thing. She just said what she wanted to say. When we would have a chance to say something, we could tell that she wasn't paying any attention at all to what we were saying. She is tough, just like her children.

NOTE: Judy hit a teacher who had hit him for playing in class. He says that he hit her because he felt that she hated him for his dark color.

Lillie—Judy jes hates to come to school an' he usta be playin' hooky all the time before he started comin' in here with you. They ain't never goin' to do nothin' with Judy 'cause he is too bad.

Judy—I always is been bad. I been in the fifth grade fo'—this, lemme see (thinking)—fo', this make the third term. I gits my lessons pretty good, but I gits in trouble wid the teacher a lot.

NOTE: Judy has been expelled from school three times.

NOTE: Judy wishes he were able to keep up with his grade as do his sisters.

Judy—I is too far behind now. I is fourteen years ol' an' I is in the fifth now; by the time I'd git up here I be too ol'. I'd be nineteen years ol' when I'd git in the ninth grade.

Judy—I jes don't lak to be settin' in a schoolroom all day an' doin' nothin'. It jes seem to me that I wants to be doin' somethin'. It look lak it is better to be out in the streets gettin' slop an' waitin' on mamma 'roun' the house than to be sittin' 'roun' in a ol' schoolhouse all day doin' nothin'. I could work 'roun' the park lak my brother do's an' help mamma.

Judy—Ever' time I gits sent home, my papa say I ain't goin' to be nothin' nohow, but he whips me good jes the same. I tells him 'bout how the teacher don' lak me 'cause I is all the time tellin' her 'bout her bright pets, but that don' do no good 'cause he beats me ever' time I been sent home.

CASTE

Mother—The white folks who this house b'longs to raised my husband an' they let him use it widout rent.

Father—Then when you is on these WPA jobs you is always liable to git in a lotta trouble wid these white folks. They is always ready to start somethin' an' these young niggers ain't lak us ol' folks, they ain't gonna stan' back an' let 'em kick an' 'buse 'em lak we ol' folks. Us ol' folks will call 'em "boss" an' "cap'n" an' stan' back fo' 'em, but these young folks ain't.

Father—Well I tell you, this here (holding up a political handbill) ain't for niggers. Ain't none of 'em studdin' 'bout us poor folks. All of 'em is tryin' to git all they kin for their own selves an' ain't studdin' 'bout us poor cullud folks.

NOTE: The mother and father forbid the smaller children to approach or play with white children but they tell them to hit back if attacked.

Judy—My mamma an' papa usta talk wid me (about whites) an' tell me 'bout not to be talkin' back to 'em 'cause I might git in trouble fo' foolin' 'roun' wid 'em, or I might git hurt.

NOTE: Judy had a fuss with a young white man for whom he was caddying. It started with the white's aggression.

NOTE: Judy talks back to white adults, and fights white children.

Judy—I can't do nothin' to 'em, but I shore talks back to 'em though. I always gits outa their way 'cause I knows they is too big fo' me to do anything wid. But when they is my size, I shore will go fo' 'em. The first fight I had wid a white boy was when I was 'bout 'leben years ol'. I was comin' home from school 'long wid some other chillun from my school when some little white boy comed by on a bicycle an' knocked up 'gainst me. I caught up wid him an' pulled him off'na that bicycle an' started fightin' him. I shore did beat him up good. I went on home an' tolt my mamma an' papa 'bout it an' they jes fussed an' tolt me not to be fightin' white folks lessen I jes *had* to fight 'em. I ain't jes had to fight 'em, but I shore did do it, an' I been doin' it every since. I ain't never let none of 'em run over me when I could help myself. I ain't goin' to let 'em do it neither, I don't care what they say.

Judy—If I can't say what I wants to say to 'em out loud, I says it under my breath an' mumbles back at 'em when they say something. Then, when I knows one is mean, I won't work fo' him when there ain't no other boys 'roun'; I don't care how bad I needs money. I jes tells him I don't wanna work. One time I got throwed off'na the park was 'bout talkin' big talk to one of the white mens. He said somethin' 'bout he was goin' to kick me, an' I tolt him if he did, his foot would rot off, an' he started runnin' at me.

Judy—You know there shore is some good white folks in the world jes lak there is some mean ones. Now I broke that man's window one time. I shore was scared when that happened 'cause I shore thought he was goin' to git the policeman an' I runned home an' jumped in the bed. But instead of him puttin' me in jail, he let me pay fo' the glass a little bit at a time. I ben wond'rin' 'bout that fo' a long time. I jes reckon he done that 'cause we buys groceries at his store sometimes.

Judy—I shore was scared that night when I broke the white man's window. I ain't said nothin' to nobody, I jes runned home an' pulled off my pants an' shirt, an' jumped in the bed. When I waked up good, 'cause I was jes dozin' 'bout to go to sleep, my papa waked me up wid a strap. My brother went by the store an' the white man tolt him 'bout it. I was scared 'most to death 'cause I thought the policemen had comed fo' me anyway.

Judy—Now, you talkin' 'bout a good white man, Mr. Moore shore is one. Papa usta work fo' him an' not so long ago he gived papa a house to live in 'dout rent fo' jes as long as he live.

Judy—That's the way white folks do's. They takes the colored mens an' works 'em fo' a little bitta money 'til they gits well fixed an' then they fires 'em 'cause they ain't no more good. They don't care nothin' 'bout you but jes what they kin git outta you. Now, you take my papa, he usta work fo' a white man, Mr. Moore. Now he ain't able to do nothin', an' the man don't want him no more. Course he was better to him than most white folks is, but jes lak I has said, ain't no white folks crazy 'bout a colored person. Now he gived my papa the house that we is livin' in now, but we had to fix it all up an' we is still crowded in a six-room house 'cause there is so many of us. He jes gived him that house 'til he died, then we has gotta start payin' him rent again. An' my papa worked fo' him jes as long as he could, but we ain't got nothin' yet an' that man is rich. They ain't goin' to let no colored person have nothin'.

Judy—I shore don't want no policeman to be runnin' 'roun' lookin' fo' me 'cause they treats you too bad. If there is anythin' I is scared of, it is a policeman. I shore don't want him to be meddlin' wid me an' puttin' me in jail 'cause they treats colored people too bad an' you shore can't do nothin' 'bout it.

Judy—You know, it seem to me lak them polices gotta pick at me anyhow. I tolt you 'bout 'em meddlin' me the other night when I was over at club meetin' standin' 'roun' waitin' fo' my sister. They comed up an' axed me, "Boy, what is you doin'?" I tolt 'em I wasn' doin' nothin' but waitin' fo' my sister to come outta club meetin' an' they tolt me I betta go on home. I didn' go nowhere 'cause they ain't had nothin' to do wid me standin' on the street 'cause I shore wasn' botherin' nobody.

Judy—White folks got all the power an' you can't do nothin' 'gainst 'em 'cause they got you in their han's. They is white. (Long pause—deep thought) It ain't 'cause they is white-color an' yo' is black, 'cause yo' is jes as good as them, but they got money an' they sticks together. I was cadd'in' to' a white man an' lost some of his balls an' he tolt me if I didn't find 'em he was goin' to kick me. I tolt him he might kick at me, but he wasn' goin' to do nothin' to me. A white man who usta be nice to me tolt me to shet up an' don't talk back to that man. He turnt 'gainst me jes that quick.

Judy—Ain't no white folks studdin' 'bout no colored folks, I don't care how good he is to you an' how much he give you. He'll laugh wid you this minute an' turn 'gainst yo' nex' minute to hold up fo' a white man an' he kin know that this man has done treated yo' wrong. They'll shore stick together an' stan' up fo' each other, but colored people shore won't stick together fo' nothin.'

(Judy is a "big talker" but there is no evidence of his having fought whites.) . . . but I shore stan's up to the ones who is my size an' I don't stan' up an' let none of 'em be sayin' things to me widout sayin' somethin' back to 'em. Mamma, now, always tells me some of 'em is goin' to hurt me if I don't quit bein' so hateful an' sassy wid 'em. But I tells 'em they got to catch up wid me firs' 'fore they kin do that. I knows they kin catch me an' beat me an' ain't nothin' goin' to be done 'bout it so I always says if any of 'em ever catch me, I'm goin' to do my bes' to hurt 'em 'cause I ain't got but one time to die noway.

Judy—I don't fool 'roun' wid white folks when I knows they is mean. If they axes me to caddie, I tells 'em no, I don't b'lieve I wants to work, an' goes on 'bout my business. Sometime I tells 'em I can't see so good, or jes anythin' an' goes on an' sets down. Then they has to set 'roun' an' wait 'til some of the other boys gits through wid a roun' 'fore they kin play.

REMEDIAL EFFECT OF INTERVIEW–RELATION

Sara—Judy is always tellin' mamma 'bout you, Mr. Jones, an' talkin' 'bout you. He is crazy 'bout you. That's the only way anybody can get a good conversation out of him is by talkin' 'bout you. He don't never say nothin' else 'roun' there, but fuss and grumble all the time.

Interviewer—His teacher had told me when I first started

working with Judy that he was very bad and the nasty type, and that he was "sassy" with her and very disagreeable with the other children. One of his former teachers, who overheard her, confirmed this statement and said Judy had been the same three years earlier when he was in her room. She said that he comes from a bad family and that all of them are very disagreeable people. When I stopped by today, she praised Judy's improved behavior and asked me to see one of her other bad boys if I had time. She said Judy was doing much better work now, and was being more orderly than he had been for the past three years.

Judy's former teacher—It seems that you have done him a lot of good, Mr. Jones, because his general behavior is better. I only hope he won't relapse when you leave next week.

Interviewer—When I went for Judy, his present teacher called me to the door and explained that he was "sure a changed boy." She said that he was doing better work now than he had done at any other time in the three years that he had been in her room. She said that he always wants to come up and see me, even when I don't send for him or when it is not his time to come.

Teacher—Judy was only permitted to come back to school this term on condition that if he gave any more trouble he would be sent home for good. He has really done so much better this term that I feel he is no longer the impossible boy I used to have, but one who can do, and is doing, first-class work. He is a very good writer, and I tell him all the time that he is one of the best writers in my room. His general deportment is the most outstanding improvement. He behaves better in every way. I used to have a lot of trouble with him about fighting the children and "sassing" me. Now I leave him to take names when I go out of the room, and he keeps very good order. I sure do hope you will take some of the other boys who seem to be impossible, and work with them.

PART II

CLASS AND CASTE AS TRAINING

CHAPTER X

HOW IT FEELS TO BE LOWER CASTE

IT IS difficult for a white person to understand the feelings of Negroes in their lower-caste positions. In the first place, as soon as he begins to live in the South, a white person is taught the social dogma of *his* caste with regard to Negroes. On every hand, he hears that Negroes are inherently childish and primitive. He is taught that they lie and steal impulsively, "like children," that they are unable to control their sexual urges, and that they share none of the complex social and economic ambitions of white people. Since Negroes are primitive and childlike, the story runs, they accept their restricted opportunities as matters of course (although children themselves do not do so), and consequently they feel no pain or deprivation in performing the heaviest, dirtiest work, or in undergoing the severest discriminations. In many essential points, the southern dogma concerning Negroes is the same as that held by the slave-owning classes almost a century ago.

The second difficulty which white people meet in understanding the experience of Negroes as lower-caste people is the *rigidity* which the caste system has attained in the South. Negroes and whites, for example, seldom have face-to-face relationships, except in necessary economic transactions. In those immediate relations which they do have with whites, Negroes must always act deferentially. In life, this means that the colored individual seldom expresses to white people, by word or by action, the frustration or resentment which he may feel toward them. On the contrary, he must dramatize his subservience by using deferential forms of address, and by accepting without open aggression those punishments with which the whites subordinate him. To a white person who observes Negro behavior from his own caste position, therefore, Negroes may appear perfectly accommodated and "happy." Even in Old City, Mississippi, the caste system appears to work very smoothly, except when it has to be oiled at times by a whipping or a lynching.

Yet we know that Negroes in the Deep South are continually expressing to each other the sharpest antagonisms against whites and the deepest sense of frustration over their position in society. They verbalize these tabooed feelings only to their colored friends or to colored interviewers, and to northern white men, that is, to members of those groups which will not *punish* them for such expressions. In order to penetrate the rigid surface of the caste system in our own South, and to get at the human experiences and motivation which are imbedded in the tough, protective layers of custom, we must talk with people on their own terms, therefore, and live in their part of the society. As realists, we wish to pierce the dogma of the "childish Negro" (who at the same time is completely tough-skinned), and to obtain a face-to-face experience with children who have been living as lower-caste persons in America. In order to do so, one must break his own caste bonds—long enough at any rate to enable him to participate in these experiences of Negro children with white people.

In both New Orleans and Natchez, a general form of subordination which Negroes meet from whites is that of being addressed by their first names. In November 1938, a colored school teacher in New Orleans entered one of the leading stores on Canal Street to buy a suit. She is a brown-skinned woman, nineteen years old, of the upper-middle class. A white female clerk showed her one suit and left her. No other clerk returned to wait upon her. The colored woman then left the store and went to a small shop which catered to middle-class whites. There she was waited upon and purchased a rather expensive suit. Finally she gave her name and address so that the suit might be delivered to her.

After writing down the information, the white saleswoman said, "Margaret, what time do you want this purchase delivered?" Neither woman had ever seen the other before that time.

The Negro woman later stated to the interviewer, who was her close friend, "I saw red. I was so mad. But I couldn't say a thing before all those white people. I made up my mind right then, though, that I'd never go there again to be insulted."

An even more frequent use of the caste punishments is in work situations, since most Negroes work directly under whites. The caste system enables the white employer or supervisor to maintain a stricter discipline over Negroes than over white workers because it allows him (1) to use physical violence or the threat of violence against Negroes, and (2) to pay them less. In June 1938, Riley Martin, a dark-skinned boy, sixteen years old, of the upper-lower class in New Orleans, delivered a package for the white drugstore which employed him. He rang the bell of a small, yellow frame house. A white woman, apparently of lower-middle class, opened the door.

"What's this?" she asked. "From Jones' Drug Store?"

"Yes, ma'am. Perfume."

"How much is it?"

"It's seventy-five cents."

"Well, wait till I open it." She untied the package, and drew out a dark green bottle. The stopper was chipped just at the mouth of the bottle. The woman turned red and glared at the boy. "You dropped it and cracked it and tried to slip it over on me. Nigger, I'll fix you! I'll telephone your store, and tell the manager!"

When the boy returned to the store, Mr. Heiner, the manager, yelled at him from the prescription counter, "Come here, nigger!"

He went back to the counter. Mr. Heiner jerked the bottle from him and examined it.

"You broke this. Well, I'm taking this out of your pay, and you'll be a good, long time paying for it. You might *think* you're getting by with this, but you're not. You black bastard!" Then he slapped the boy.

The boy told the colored female interviewer that he "got mad" at this point, but admitted that he took no aggressive action. "I didn't do nothin'. He was a man." When she pointed out that he had been openly aggressive recently toward a colored male teacher, the boy answered, "Yes, ma'am, but Mr. Heiner was a white man. I was scared he might send me to jail."

In the same way, the great majority of our upper-class and middle-class adolescents reported that they "did nothing" when they were called "nigger" or theatened by white people, but insisted at the same time that they "felt mad" or "saw red." A usual response for children of these classes was that of Milton DePuy, a colored Creole boy of thirteen, light-brown in color and of the upper-middle class. Milton said that he hated white people because they thought they were "cute" and because they did not "want you to go places where they go." He then cited an experience he had had with white people on a bus in New Orleans. On buses and streetcars in this city, white and colored people are separated into two groups by a movable sign ("screen"). White people must sit in front of this sign, colored people behind it. One day Milton was sitting on the second seat behind the sign; there was one vacant seat between him and the section for whites, and one vacant seat behind him.

"A lot of white people got on and wanted me to move back, so they could take my seat. I didn' say a word. I kep' my mouth closed. They said I must've been deaf. I just sat there with my mouth closed."

Lower-class Negro children, however, are usually more aggressive in similar caste situations. Lower-class colored boys and girls are trained to fight by their own families, as well as by their neighborhood cliques; they are habituated early to the use of their fists and are consequently much more likely to resist physical aggression by whites than are upper-class and middle-class Negro adolescents. Lower-class children, moreover, have generally had rock and fist fights with white children and they will usually strike out if pushed beyond the normal demands of the local caste system. It is the *lower-class whites,* furthermore, with whom they fight; the parents of these white children do not object to fighting and consider it a test of manhood for white and colored children to fight each other at this age. Such fights were allowed by lower-class white parents in both Natchez and

New Orleans. A lower-class white father in the latter city said to a colored mother who complained to him that his young son had beaten her son in a fight, "Well, I tell yuh. I don' have time to be both'ring with children's mess. Both boys are the same size, an' about the same age. When Waldo (colored) beat hell outtuh A. J. (white), I didn't say nothin' tuh you, an' now that A. J. has beat hell outtuh Waldo, I ain' gonnuh do nothin' about that."

These habit structures learned as a child are sometimes carried over into late adolescence, as in the case of John Simmons, a lower-class Negro male, nineteen years old and reddish-yellow in color, who worked on a bridge construction job. He held the position of foreman of a colored gang.

One day a white man, working with a white gang on the same job, yelled at Simmons, "Hey! You red albinah son of a bitch!"

Simmons cursed back at the white man. The white man picked up a crowbar, and walked toward Simmons. Simmons grabbed a two-by-four piece of wood and yelled, "You tek anuthuh step toward me, an' I'll bus' yo' haid with this boa'd!"

The white man stopped and turned back. Simmons, in reciting the incident to the interviewer, said, "There wuz some othuh white men on the bridge, but they wuz down at the othuh end, an' I knowed they couldn' ketch me. Man, I wuz goin' tuh kill him with that boa'd, an' go on 'bout my business."

On a second occasion, Simmons was struck by a white employer. He knocked the white man down and ran. Other white men threw bottles at him and chased him, but he escaped. That night he was arrested by the sheriff.

Simmons' father told the white sheriff, "Some white man hit my boy."

The sheriff answered, "You mean, yore boy hit a *white* man." Simmons was fined by the court.

As a rule, upper-class and middle-class Negroes who do not work for whites experience little of this kind of direct subordination from white people, except in stores or in public carriers. At times, however, even children of these classes have terrifying experiences with white people.

One of our students, a light-brown, upper-class girl of thirteen, who was exceptionally small for her age, went bicycling with a group of upper-class girls in the spring of 1938. On their way to the home of a friend who lived in a predominantly white middle-class neighborhood, they rode their bicycles on the sidewalk. This practice is common in the city.

The girls had been at their friend's home only a short time when a police patrol wagon drove up to the house, and three white policemen came to the door. Their friend's mother went to the door, and was told that a complaint had been made to the police against some "nigger" girls who had been riding their bicycles on the sidewalk.

The colored mother asked, "Why do you bring a patrol wagon and come with three policemen? They are just little girls."

"Well, we had a complaint. A white lady called up and said a gang of niggers was riding their bicycles all over the sidewalk."

"A gang of niggers? This is a group of nice little girls and they are all from nice families."

The white policemen appeared to be a little ashamed and agreed to drop the matter if the girls would not ride on the sidewalk again. The mother, who had become increasingly angry, closed the dialogue by remarking, "Well, the next time the white girls around here ride on the sidewalk, I'm going to call you up. I'm going to ask for the patrol wagon to come for a bunch of white girls. I hope you'll be sure to come."

More terrifying was the experience of another upper-class girl, Phyllis Logan, with the white police. One night in May 1939, she was riding home from the movies in the family automobile with her father, mother, and sister. Her father is medium-brown in color, her mother white-skinned with light eyes. A car behind them tried to pass but the street was too narrow. The car followed, passed them at an intersection, and then pulled over sharply, forcing Mr. Logan to stop his car.

Two white men in civilian clothes got out of the other car. One of them stuck a pistol into the side of the girls' father. Their mother screamed. One of the white men said, "Why'n hell didn' you get over and let us pass? You're under arrest." Then they made Phyllis' father get into their car.

Since the white men had shown no police badges, and wore no uniforms, Phyllis and her sister and their parents believed the men were thugs. Mrs. Logan began to weep but the girls were too frightened to make any sound. A crowd of white people had gathered but no one interfered when Mr. Logan was taken away by the two white men.

Then, as the women sat helpless, firmly convinced that Mr. Logan was dead, an upper-class white man and his wife got out of their car and came over to the Logans. They expressed their sympathy and offered to drive the women to various police stations to discover whether the two white men had actually been policemen. The Logans went with them.

After a two-hour search, they found Mr. Logan. During this whole time, the mother wept, and Phyllis and her sister sat stunned. They finally discovered him locked up in a distant police station. He was released upon the demand of the white protector. No action was taken against the policemen, however, because no white people would testify against them—not even the upper-class white man and his wife.

In relating the incident to the interviewer, Phyllis concluded, "That was the worst experience of my life. It is like a horrible nightmare. Mother is still a wreck. Nice world, huh?"

In order to understand the caste sanctions as training, we must see them at the moment of their impact upon the individual. In the personal experience of a white person or of a Negro in the South, the caste controls appear as sanctions defining the conditions under which he may reach the basic biological and social goals. They are experienced as privileges and punishments which facilitate or block the road to certain basic goals. These elementary goals may be defined simply. They are:

1. freedom of movement;

2. the acquiring and spending of money, which are necessary instrumental acts to obtaining food, shelter, and clothing;

3. the securing of sexual responses;

4. avoidance of being struck, and of other forms of physical punishment;

5. avoidance of threats which arouse anticipation of punishment (that is, fear);

6. access to instrumental techniques which secure money—namely, education, apprenticeship, and political participation.

If we are to attempt to see the caste system as it appears to the individual living under its controls, we must hereafter think in terms of these fundamental motives which are common to all human beings in our society.

As a result of the physical caste marks with which he is born, the white individual is freed to a large degree from interference in seeking these goals. Indeed, his efforts to make the goal responses are facilitated by the society; his path is eased by powerful legal, economic, educational, and political privileges, as compared with that of the Negro individual.[1]

This finding runs counter to the widespread social dogma which states that the southern Negro does not experience his caste restrictions as punishments. The dogma, popular as it may be, is not borne out by the thousands of pages of interviews which have been recorded for Negroes of all social classes in Old City and its rural background, in Natchez, and in New Orleans. Within their conversation groups these Negroes in the Deep South were often found detailing the instances in which they had been threatened or humiliated by white people and expressing great hostility and resentment toward the local white group. In fact, the antagonism voiced by the local white people toward Negroes, although it was certainly violent and fully supported by group approval, was scarcely more violent than that which Negroes, including the youngest adolescents, expressed to the white group as a whole.

When one gathers detailed accounts of these emotional re-

---

[1] In this caste context, a privilege is the presentation to the individual by society of a more direct and less punished route to certain goals. Furthermore, it is the offering to the white individual of certain goal responses which are completely blocked for Negroes, such as higher technical training or political office.

actions of Negroes to the impact of caste controls, it is not difficult to understand the basis of their frustrations and their consequent verbal aggression. Indeed, it becomes clear that only a
vested societal interest in caste can account for the established
dogma that most Negroes are completely "accommodated" to
their caste status and that they are simple-natured, childlike beings with childish needs. It is necessary for the society to in-
culcate strong defensive teachings of this kind to prevent general
human recognition of the basic deprivations and frustrations
which life in a lower caste involves. But it is certain that the
sting of caste is deep and sharp for most Negroes.

For example, when a skilled Negro worker seeks a job in the
planing mill which employs most of the working population
of Old City, he finds that all of the well-paid positions are closed
to him. If he is hired, he soon learns that he is being paid at a
much lower hourly rate than are white men doing the same
kind of work.[2] The Negro worker, however, must pay the same
price as the white worker for the pound of pork or the bag of
cowpeas which he buys, the same price for his shoes or pair of
overalls (if he is to get the same quality), and the same price for
his children's schoolbooks (which the city does not supply).
Therefore, the imposition of a lower wage scale is experienced
as a basic punishment—as a deprival of food or clothing, or of
access to social techniques for acquiring money. The Negro experiences this punishment as a *caste* deprivation, moreover, because he discovers that it is not administered to white men.

His path to the sexual goal responses is likewise restricted.
The Negro male learns by punishment, or by identifying with
the punishment of other Negroes, that while he is not allowed to
seek sexual relationships with white women, the society does
permit white men to seek such relationships with Negro women.
In actual situations observed in Southerntown and Old City, this
taboo meant that a Negro man could not attack a white man who
sought out his wife or daughter. He must submit and let the

---

[2] If the sociologist analyzes the payroll of this mill, he finds that the few
colored men who are employed as skilled workers receive an hourly wage which
is only one-fourth as large as that paid to white men who perform similar work.

woman go if she wishes. The authors observed several such incidents at firsthand; one interviewer lived in the home of a colored family whose daughter was constantly sought by an important white municipal official. The girl fought her own battle for status successfully (she would have lost rank in the colored group if she had accepted the white man as a lover), but her father and brother could not defend her without risking their lives. The great value which the white man attaches to his cross-caste sexual privileges is indicated by the persistence with which he defends them. In Old City, a Negro minister who protested in his church against the numerous liaisons between white men and colored women was visited the next day by a group of white businessmen who warned him not to mention this subject again, under threat of being made to leave the city. On the other hand, it is certainly a basic deprivation to the Negro man to be unable to protect his daughter, wife, or sweetheart from the white man's sexual advances.

The caste controls likewise withhold from Negroes legal protection against physical attack and the threats of such attack by white persons. By punishment, the Negro individual is trained not to demand certain occupational, sexual, political, and social privileges. This training usually takes place through identification with other Negroes who have received such punishment. The example of a Negro who has been beaten, whipped, or shot by a white planter or by a white mob operates to make all other Negroes in the community *anticipate* that such punishment would come to them if they should violate the caste sanctions. On the other hand, the patronage and the protection which the "good Negro" receives also act to maintain the caste system. By imitating these well-accommodated Negroes, the colored man or woman learns to avoid punishment and to seek only those rewards (substitute goals) which *are* possible within his caste position if he follows the prescribed route.

Both the numerical indices from the census and the observed behavior of Negroes and whites toward each other make it clear that the Negro child in New Orleans or Natchez lives in a caste system which from his birth severely limits his opportunities for economic advancement and for social training. The rewards which the society offers him in the fields of occupational and political status are very few. His opportunities for education, moreover, are greatly inferior to those of the white child, and his incentive to grasp the available opportunities is weak because the society systematically withholds from him the rewards which it offers to the white child.

At an early age, he learns that the economic and social restrictions upon him as a lower-caste person are maintained by powerful threats of the white society, and that any efforts to rise out of his caste position will be severely punished. Both in the city and in the country, the disabilities which his caste suffers are maintained primarily by a system of force. This superior physical and legal power of the white caste is not left to his imagination but is dramatized periodically for the whole society in the form of beatings and lynchings.

The whipping and killing of Negroes by whites as a punishment for resisting caste demands occur in both Natchez and New Orleans. It is not necessary to have a large number of such demonstrations in order to intimidate the Negro population. To be able to understand this fact, we must remember that human beings learn to accept restrictions by means of identifying with other persons within the family or group who *have been punished* for not learning the required behavior.

The study of Old City and its plantation background revealed that the caste taboos were more numerous and the punishments for infractions more severe in the rural areas than in the city itself. The severity of the controls upon Negroes increased in direct proportion to the distance of the rural area from a large town or city. For example, in Rural County, which had no village of more than 1,000 inhabitants, white planters frequently whipped their colored tenants and they considered the Negroes in Old City, just forty miles away, "spoiled" and "sassy." One prominent white planter complained that these urban Negroes did not even know how to act toward a white man; as proof, he cited the attempt of a colored businessman in Old City to shake hands with him.

In Old City itself, however, a colored boy five years old was severely beaten by a white man who accused the child of "making advances" to the white man's equally young daughter. In New Orleans, the largest city in the South, the local white newspapers reported five colored men killed by white policemen between 1936 and 1938. Three of these men were killed in city jails while awaiting trial. The other two were shot while in custody. All were accused of having attacked white men or women. By means of detailed accounts in the newspapers, these symbolic "legal lynchings" were made known to the colored population and served as a means of further intimidation.

As has been stated, mob whippings and lynchings occur in the rural environs of Natchez and New Orleans. It is difficult to write about these matters with scientific objectivity, but the authors will limit themselves to the facts, as given by the New Orleans white radio stations and newspapers, concerning a lynching in Ruston, Louisiana, which occurred while this research study was in progress.

On October 12, 1938, two radio stations in New Orleans began to announce several times daily that an unidentified Negro man who had been accused of murdering a white man was being hunted by a mob of whites at Ruston. Both the radio stations and the white newspapers also announced that a lynching was "feared." On the second day, the radio stations reported that a mob composed of "1,500 armed white men" was searching for the accused, but unidentified, colored man.[3]

On the afternoon of the second day, a Negro man was lynched after reputedly confessing the crime to 1,500 armed white men. Five days later, the parish grand jury, composed of white residents, brought in a verdict that the "evidence is conclusive that W. C. Williams attacked J. W. Breedlove and criminally assaulted his woman companion on the night of September 13,

[3] One may imagine what effect the sight of 1,500 white men, questioning their fathers, mothers, and older brothers, had upon the Negro children in this area. The writers have had eye-witness accounts of such "searches"; they take the form of hunting frolics.

and that since then W. C. Williams (the Negro) has died." After examining fifty-five white "witnesses" of the lynching, the grand jury reported that it had "obtained insufficient evidence to return any indictments."[4]

The judge, after receiving the reports of the grand jury, thanked the jury for "carrying out the instructions of the court," as follows:

Having completed your labors and made your report, the court wishes to thank you for the splendid and unselfish work you have done during the present two-day special session of the grand jury. The court is aware of the difficulties under which you have labored and believes that you have thoroughly and conscientiously investigated the matters submitted to you by the court for investigation. That means that the court feels that you have fully and honorably discharged your duties under your oaths.[5]

This lynching was considered of so little news value by the white conservative newspaper in New Orleans that it was first reported on the thirteenth page.

Another type of physical punishment used by whites to enforce the subordination of Negroes is starvation. The withdrawing of food or the threat of doing so is a technique used to change human behavior in many societies. It has been used recently with great success in Germany, Czechoslovakia, Spain, and England, as well as in America. When a Hungarian prince, for example, wishes to make his Slovak tenant-serfs change their political and national loyalties, he simply refuses them the use of the land.[6] In the same way, a white landlord or employer in the South seldom has to use physical violence to make his Negro employees observe the caste taboos. The threat of legalized force, implicit in his caste position, and his economic power are usually sufficient. Since most Negroes are wage laborers, they depend for food and necessities upon their pay or "advance" from week to week. The white employer can usually enforce any caste demands, therefore, simply by withholding wages or by threaten-

[4] *The Times-Picayune*, October 19, 1938, p. 4.
[5] *Ibid.*
[6] Erskine Caldwell and Margaret Bourke-White, *Beyond the Danube* (New York: Viking Press, 1939).

ing to discharge the Negro. On the plantation, this compliant behavior is reinforced every week or two when the Negro has to go to the landlord for credit for food.

Southern color caste must therefore be viewed as a systematic interference in the efforts of a special group of individuals to follow certain biological and social drives. This interference takes the form of a complex of limitations in addition to the accepted controls of our society upon all individuals.

A white or Negro person in the South learns the behavior demanded of him in his caste position chiefly by experiencing (or anticipating) pain or deprivation if he attempts to reach a goal by any other route than that prescribed by the society. To the Negro child, as our cases show, caste presents a group of arbitrary behavioral demands which he is compelled to learn. He is forced into these learning dilemmas both by his parents and by the white children and adults with whom he has contacts. In following the prescribed behavior, he must (1) accept interference with previously established habits, and (2) substitute new forms of response. All learning, after the first learning of infancy, involves the sacrificing by the individual of some of his earlier goal responses. It consequently entails frustration. When the colored child is learning to behave as a lower-caste person, he is finding a method of acting within the frustrating taboos of caste so that he may reach those limited and substitute goals which the society does allow him.

Both the white and the colored child acquire their caste training in two types of relationships: (1) in their family and from nonfamily members of their own caste, and (2) in contacts with members of the other caste. At the age of five or six, the child learns that he must sit only with his fellow caste members on the bus or in the theater, and that he must attend schools which have only children and teachers of his own caste. Within his family, he receives instruction in the behavior required toward members of the other caste. As he becomes adolescent, both the definiteness and the parental reinforcements of this instruction increase greatly, for it is then that the occupational and sexual taboos become matters of urgency.

In Negro-white situations, a child learns what behavior is permitted, either (1) when he is allowed to achieve the goal response, or (2) when he experiences punishment in attempting to reach it. In general, the Negro child learns from white people that he cannot be a member of their economic, social, or educational groups. He also learns that he must not be aggressive toward them, but must dramatize his subordinate position by various explicit forms of deference. From his own family, he usually learns that white people are extremely powerful and dangerous and that he must therefore not display aggression toward them. If even the powerful adult cannot resist whites, what can the child hope to gain by attack? He is taught, however, that within the bounds of his caste position he may adopt substitute modes of aggression toward whites. For example, certain well-disguised forms of "getting even," such as sabotage in his work for white people (slowness, lack of punctuality, clumsiness), and the use of flattery, humor, secretiveness, "ignorance," and other behavior for outwitting white people, are learned at an early age. We shall have occasion to notice in the next chapter that the type of instruction given a Negro child by his parents varies in some degree according to the social class of the parents.

The actual caste behavior of the parents themselves appears to be more important in determining the child's type of accommodation to white people than does verbal instruction on this point. As in other forms of learning by identifying with a person who has already learned, the child discovers what behavior *will be punished* and what *rewarded* by observing his parents and listening to their accounts of experiences with white people. To be concrete—the child of a Negro domestic servant who hears his mother constantly rehearsing the "injustices" or perhaps the kindness and patronage of her white employer; the boy who hears his father tell angrily of the loss of his job to a white man (and who himself receives less food and heat, and poorer clothes thereafter); the girl whose father is constantly praising his white upper-class patrons and severely criticizing Negroes as a group;

and the little boy who hears his mother express anger and humiliation after experiencing some caste punishment in a store or on a bus—these children learn to expect from whites the same punishments or rewards which their parents have received.

The child whose parents are of unlike class origins usually receives one type of caste instruction from his mother and a different type from his father. For example, if the father is of lower-class origin, he will almost certainly tell his son to submit to all white demands unless he is threatened with violence, in which case he should fight. If the mother has been trained in a middle-class family, she will probably teach the son to avoid whites and not to fight them under any circumstances. A child who lives in such a family, or in a family where one parent has been reared in the South and the other in the North, is placed in a continual and almost insoluble dilemma, which may be expected to increase his anxiety and maladaptive tendencies as compared with the child whose parents have the same class and sectional origin.

A second type of conflict in the caste training of the Negro adolescent is especially prevalent in cities. It is the dilemma of the upward mobile child who is beginning to associate with, and to assume the behavior of, a class which is above that of his parents. The first step in such mobility for the mass of *lower-class* colored children in Natchez or New Orleans is to finish a high school course. In this process of educational mobility, the colored adolescent faces a conflict between the caste instruction and example given him by his teachers, who are usually middle-middle class or upper-middle class, and by his parents, who are lower class. Such differences in caste training apply both to etiquette (whether to be deferential to a white person if he seeks to subordinate you, whether to say "Sir" and "Ma'am") and to the choice of an occupation. The middle-class teacher not only gives the colored child instruction in skills associated with the white caste, but he insists upon being called "Mr." or "Miss" by the student. In spite of caste taboos, moreover, he has gained professional status.

In this situation, the Negro child usually identifies with his teachers in caste behavior; that is, he rejects the training and example of his lower-class parents who must be deferential to their white employers and who must accept domestic or manual labor. When he completes high school such a mobile child faces the basic caste restriction against skilled and clerical work for Negroes. In order to achieve middle-class position he must therefore either go on to a higher school and become a teacher or he must obtain a position as a clerk in some Negro business. If he is unsuccessful and has to accept a menial or domestic job under a white supervisor, he experiences a basic frustration upon both caste and class grounds.

By indirection, the caste sanctions also appear within the Negro family and school in the form of distinctions between children upon the basis of their color, hair-form, and type of facial contour. It must be remembered that the differentiating marks of the white caste are physical. The Negro *class* sanctions, moreover, are in part organized around differences in color, hair-form, and features. It is also true that white people make some distinction in the punishment and patronage of individual Negroes upon the basis of the Negro's approximation to the white physical type. A colored child who is light-skinned with wavy or straight hair therefore has an arbitrary and fortuitous advantage over more Negroid children, both in his own class participation and in his relations with whites.

Colored parents and their children, however, are very reluctant to admit in-family preferences based on color. The lack of evidence from our own informants on this score must be attributed to a general American taboo upon voicing in-family preferences. In America, as is not true in those European societies where the first-born male is given higher privileges than the other offspring, there is a strong social compulsion not to show greater affection for one member of the family than for another. Parents as well as children "cover up" at once when this subject is mentioned, and their subsequent remarks are highly defensive.

In socially withdrawn, light-skinned groups of colored people such as the colored Creoles in New Orleans and the remnants of the "blue vein" cliques in Old City, however, parents make no effort to conceal their preference for light-skinned children, and their desire to obtain equally light mates for them. Until very recently in Old City, a dark child born to a "blue vein" family was sent away to live with dark relatives in another community. The head of the leading family in this group in 1934 said that only a few years before, "if a child turned out black or dark, it was just too bad for him." His own father had used a shotgun to drive off a brown-skinned suitor of his daughter. Even today in New Orleans, some of the light-skinned Creole families who work as white send any dark baby away to a "dark" branch of the family. The grandparents and parents maintain close surveillance, furthermore, upon the courting of the children to prevent the choice of a dark mate. Since these colored Creoles now attend the same churches, schools, and dances as the rest of the Negroes and increasingly intermarry with them, however, such color distinctions are becoming less rigid.

The importance which color and hair-form have for the Negro parent may be most clearly understood from the discussions of colored women or parents concerning a prospective or new-born child. The female interviewers heard several discussions of this kind among upper-class and upper-middle-class Negroes in Old City and in New Orleans. Parents and grandparents were extremely concerned about the color and hair-form of the baby, condoling each other if the child was darker or had "worse" hair than had been expected, and felicitating each other if it was lighter or had "better" hair than had been expected. Even before the birth of a child, some upper-class and upper-middle-class parents surveyed in minute detail all the possibilities with regard to the child's color and hair-form by recalling these traits in each of their parents and grandparents. It is probably safe to assume that such concern is felt by most upper-class and middle-class Negro parents, even when not verbalized. It is a justifiable point of anxiety, certainly, since it is a vital factor in the child's class and caste opportunities.

The basic value of these physical traits is most clearly and bluntly stated by those lower-class Negro women who are dark-brown or black. One such woman in Old City told her colored employer, "I sho' is sorry I didn' git me uh white man, instid uh gittin' me uh black one, 'n havin' a whole lot uv black chil-drun!" The power of light color in aiding the individual to satisfy basic physical and social needs is most clearly seen when the child's father is actually white. Although lower-class colored parents in Old City punish a daughter who has a child by a white man, they nevertheless prefer the child; they prefer it not only for its color but because it attracts vital gifts of money (and therefore of food, shelter, and clothes) from the father. The dark lower-class child in Old City who said mournfully, "Gertrude's father is white, an' she can git ev'ything she wants. Guess I could too, if I had a white daddy!" was expressing the pull of basic biological goals against the weak demands of "respectability."

In New Orleans or Natchez, for a child to come into the world with a dark skin is to have the cards stacked against him from birth. The social and economic world accessible to him is so limited that the chances of his being forced into lower class are about three times as great as those of a white child. It seems clear, furthermore, that the motivation of the Negro child to learn habits of conscientious study, of sexual restraint, of law observance, and of skilled work is necessarily weak, since the upper caste either does not reward his efforts as it does the white child's or it constantly punishes them. We know that effective learning in these fields demands continual impulse-control, and that such learning must therefore be reinforced by rewards which are proportionate to the effort and renunciation demanded of the learner. It is the prime function of the caste system to with-hold these rewards from Negro children.

CHAPTER XI

WHAT IS SOCIAL CLASS?

THE POPULAR belief that "all Negroes are alike" is a caste-encrusted dogma. Although all Negroes have the status of lower-caste people in the South, they differ socially among themselves as far as the poles of the earth. Since white people do not participate in Negro society, they are unable to see its differentiated strata.

In examining the lives of the children dealt with in this book, the reader must long ago have asked himself the question, "Why does their social class appear to have been far more important than their 'racial' status in shaping the habits and goals of these children?" The answer seems to be that social class governs a much wider area of the child's training than do the Negro-white controls.

If we enter the home of an upper-class colored family in New Orleans, we discover that Phillip Randall, the oldest son of fourteen years, has a study of his own; it is equipped with a desk, books, and current issues of *Readers Digest, Life, Photomagazine,* and *Red Book.* Phillip also has a small chemical laboratory and a typewriter on which he and his brothers compose a family newspaper which they sell to their relatives. At his private academy, Phillip reports, he finds keener competition than he did at the public schools, "because the students are more often from the best families." His mother, a college graduate, teaches him French and Spanish, and his aunt gives him music lessons. He is planning to go to college and to professional school and to become a physician, like his father. We are told by his mother that she selects his play group from the children of the "best families," and chiefly from his own relatives. With regard to sexual behavior, she says that she has taught Phillip to postpone the courting of girls until his education is further advanced. "I tell Phillip he doesn't need to fall in love with any of the little girls at the academy. He understands that he still has four years in college, and then professional school. I'm always telling Phillip that he should be able to give his wife a car before he thinks about getting married."

If we visit the home of Sara Mae Johnson, whose family is lower-lower class in New Orleans, we find that the people in her family, neighborhood, and play groups make quite different demands of her. Whereas Phillip Randall knows that his mother will provide him with meals at regular hours, served at a table in their dining room, Sara Mae often is sent out by her mother to beg money for food. The sum of $30 a month which Sara Mae's mother receives "on relief" is not enough to feed the family of eight, so that the biological frustration of getting insufficient food is a recurrent part of Sara Mae's experience. The mother complains, "I don't never git a chanct to git no greens nor corn nor nuthin' good to eat, an' I swear life is bad widout somethin' decent onct in a while. I swear to God I'm sick of eatin' beans an' rice." Phillip would be horrified, moreover, to know that Sara Mae and her brother "sleep on the floor on a quilt," and that sometimes three and sometimes four of her little brothers and sisters sleep in one bed with their mother.

Sara Mae's mother would herself point out the economic element in the class patterning of behavior for us. "What you is depen's on how you wuz borned. Now *you* might a ben borned in a good house where yo' daddy an' mama got some money; my children, they ain't never had nothin' like that." All her children entered school late and have attended very irregularly, she says, because they had "no clothes" and were ashamed to go ragged. The mother vaguely says that she would like to have Sara Mae become a nurse or a "stenography," but she feels there is no chance for her to get the necessary money or for Sara Mae to learn the lessons. Her educational goal for her children is the completion of graded school. "Maybe they too dumb to know they oughta finish school, but I'm gonna try an' beat it into 'em."

When Mrs. Johnson says "beat," she means hit with good solid blows. She and her children frequently fight one another and also their neighbors. Sara Mae casually reports that her sister hit her husband on the head with an axe, and that her brother recently "come to the house drunk an' tore up Ruby's (his wife's) slip, an' it were her onliest one, an' so she was mad an' gonna kill him, an' she runned up to fin' my daddy's pistol, but she couldn't fin' it, so she took his razor an' cut him, an' they taken him to the Charity Hospital." The mother tells the children, "Fight it out, but don't use no gun."

Sara Mae's mother does not demand of her, either by supervision or by example, the long renunciation of sexual goal responses which Phillip's mother requires. She herself was not married to Sara Mae's father. "He was a sweetheart man," with whom she lived for only three weeks. Mrs. Johnson wants her daughters to marry early, between the ages of sixteen and eighteen years, before they have been "spoiled" by a man. She hopes to keep them from having a baby before then, but says that "after they married, they kin be as big whores as they want; it won't be none of my worry." With regard to the relations of her two married daughters with men other than their husbands, she is consoled by the knowledge that such behavior is general in her class. "They ain't no worse than other married girls. You 'spect them to sweetheart aroun'."

In the course of this study, very detailed accounts of the parental demands and methods of training children were obtained for 123 families in New Orleans and Natchez in all the social classes, from upper class to lower-lower class. Upon the basis of the earlier study of Old City by Davis and Gardner, moreover, it was possible to define the adult class-ways of both whites and Negroes in the Deep South. The present research workers were thus in a position to know the specific requirements and expectations of a child's family, of his social clique, and of his teachers, regarding him, and to see the "place" in Negro society for which he was being prepared, and the route which he must pursue in order to secure, or "improve," his social position.

"But what," one may ask, "is the practical use of studying these class patterns of behavior?" Admitting that the sociologist is now able to distinguish characteristic modes of behavior for each of the Negro and white social classes, what good is such knowledge to the student of human nature, and to our society? Is the class analysis of human habits only a novel descriptive catalogue, or is it a valuable tool which will help us to *predict* behavior in any given situation, and in the end to change it?

The writers' studies of the class conditioning of Negro children have convinced them that the second alternative is the more justifiable one, and that when properly understood the sanctions of class position, as enforced by the family, the clique, and the larger class environment, are among the most important controls in the formation of human habits.[1] In order to understand the powerful grip of this class behavior, we must first examine the social environment in which Negro children learn their habits and the specific methods by which this learning is reinforced.

How may one be certain, first of all, that social classes actually exist, and how may one identify their members if they do exist? Social classes were empirically identified by W. Lloyd Warner in Yankee City and by Davis and Gardner in Old City as groups of people who are able to associate intimately together. People always recognize their social class, whereas they seldom know their economic class. In both Yankee City and Old City, individuals recognize their class members by characteristic traits, ranging from dress and speech to education and family connections. Class distinctions are always made on the basis of possible social intimacy, as in the following typical expressions: "They go around with our friends." "We don't go around with those people. They don't fit in with our group." "I know I can't class with the big shots." "They are ignorant people, and we don't have anything to do with them." Social classes are thus operating in our society as groups between which there is no intimate participation.

[1] It necessarily follows, then, that these class controls are an equally important source of *resistance* to efforts by educators, social workers, or politicians to change the motivation and habits of individuals in our society.

The sociologist identifies these groups and describes the forms of behavior which their members have in common. It is the community itself, however, not the sociologist, which classifies the inhabitants into social levels and gives each family its class status in this ranking. Social class is of the society's making. The people of any community ask only one question to determine an individual's class position, namely, *"Whom does he associate with?"* The answer to this question places the individual in the social hierarchy. The reader may determine his class position by applying the same test to his own participation.

In the social class system of our society, therefore, persons are recognized as having equal status and as occupying the same position in the social hierarchy *when they can associate freely together*. In the colored society of New Orleans and Natchez, the best way to identify the members of the various social classes is (1) to attend the large Negro dances, receptions, chili suppers, barbecues, and picnics, and (2) to secure the membership lists of the large social clubs. One soon discovers, in this way, that there are upper-class dances, lower-middle-class dances, upper-lower-class dances, and so on.

Furthermore, in the process of interviewing members of the various classes, the research workers learn that these classes are ranked in the society, and that the members of all classes agree upon the relative status of each class. All people in the society admit that the upper-class families have "higher" status, privileges, and symbols than those of lower-middle class, for example. Usually these evaluations are expressed in the form of deferential or condescending behavior, or in the form of hostile comments upon "the big shots," "the worst class of people," "the nobodies," "the strivers," "the ne'er-do-wells," and by other such phrases.

Members of each class have characteristic designations for people of the other classes. Upper-class people like Phillip Randall's parents, for instance, speak of "the best families" (upper class), the "very nice people" (upper-middle class), "nice people," "good families" (middle-middle class), "poor but respectable people" (lower-middle class), and "loud, ignorant, common people" (lower class). Members of the other social classes make similar distinctions, using slightly different terms. It was found in Old City that the greater the social distance between classes, the less clearly their members saw the subclass distinctions.[2] The upper-class Randalls, for example, think of all lower-class people as one group of "loud, ignorant, common people." The sociologist discovers, however, that lower-class people recognize ranks within the lower class, and that an upper-lower-class person does not associate with a lower-lower-class individual. In the same way, Mrs. Johnson, in lower-lower class, thinks that people in both the upper-middle class and the upper class are one group, "the big Negroes," "the big shots." The sociologist knows, however, that there are important participation barriers between these groups.

The crucial tests of class position are certainly the same all over America, in both white and Negro society. People are of the same class when they may normally (1) eat or drink together as a social ritual, (2) freely visit one another's families, (3) talk together intimately in a social clique, or (4) have cross-sexual access to one another, outside of the kinship group. These relationships are the basic privileges of class equals, and it is to limit the range of such contacts that the class pressures are exerted.

These intimate relationships are made concrete and attainable for the individual by his social clique, which is the smallest class unit. The reader's own clique, which is composed of himself and his most frequent associates, may number less than ten people, but it may contain as many as thirty. Social cliques are the steps in the ladder of social rank. A man's status is judged "by the company he keeps," that is, by the rank of his clique. The rise of an individual in the white or Negro class structure consists in his "getting to know" a very small group of people (a clique) which is just above his own social position.

This smallest class grouping, the clique, which may appear somewhat unimportant at first, nevertheless deserves our closest

[2] The writers are indebted to Dr. and Mrs. Burleigh Gardner for the use of this finding from the Old City research.

examination. For *it is the members of the child's and his family's cliques who actually constitute that "social environment" of which we have talked so loosely, and which, we have said, reinforces the child's habits. Through the demands and pressures of the family and of the clique, class learning is instilled and maintained.*

If, when he comes to adolescence and early manhood, an individual attempts to rise above the class of his family, he must learn new class habits and goals from a *social clique* whose members are already in the higher position. A person cannot learn the behavior necessary for an upper-class individual if he lives in a middle-class family because his parents and their clique will not know the habits and demands of the upper class. It is precisely because the family and its clique can teach the child only the behavior of their own class that most individuals are unable to change their class position even in the course of a lifetime.

The individual who does rise into a class above that of his parents must be willing to take severe social punishments. If he is sufficiently aggressive to put himself in this long and painful learning dilemma and sufficiently skillful to discriminate among class goals, he may become upward mobile. But the people in the position just above him will make persistent efforts to keep him in his "place."

CHAPTER XII

CHILD TRAINING AND CLASS

WHEN WE say that a child has learned to do something, we mean that he has discriminated between a variety of possible actions, performing one of these sequences and avoiding all the others. When he repeats the selected actions regularly, we say that he has formed a habit. A child apparently learns both because he is denied certain satisfying goal responses when he refuses to repeat the action, and because he experiences these desired responses when he does repeat the action. Thus, most babies learn to eat solid food by being starved if they do not eat and by satisfying their hunger if they do eat. In learning to use the stool, a child is reinforced both when he is whipped for soiling himself and also when he is given sweets or approval for the desired behavior.

What is this "approval" which the child apparently regards as rewarding and which therefore reinforces him in repeating those actions which immediately precede the parent's smile, or praise, or caress? If we go back to the infant's habit of crying when he is hungry or in pain, we observe that the baby soon begins to cease crying when the mother appears at the crib or when she picks him up, even though his hunger or pain has not yet been removed. Apparently the sight of the mother's face and figure, the sound of her voice, or the feel of her body, must act as secondary agents to reinforce the child in ceasing to cry; these experiences, he has discovered, always immediately precede feeding or removal of pain.

In the same fashion, it appears, the child learns the more complex habits of class training by being punished for disapproved acts and rewarded for desired ones. In this process, he may be reinforced in new habit formation either by biological pain or gratification, or by the praise or scowls of his parents and other teachers. He also may be motivated to learn new behavior and to

263

maintain his approved habits by anticipating rather than actually experiencing reward or punishment.[1] As he grows older, and is no longer whipped or denied his supper by the parents, the child's behavior is controlled to a great extent by these anticipatory responses to approval or disapproval from his family and teachers. Since punishment is still the most frequently used method of training children, the anticipation of punishment becomes the most constant reinforcement of human behavior. In his relationships with his parents, his clique and his teachers, an adolescent boy or girl, as well as an adult, is motivated by anxiety, that is, by a deeply internalized expectation of punishment, to act in a manner which these groups will approve.

Not only does his anxiety to escape punishment and disapproval impel the child to learn the behavior of his immediate group of class members, but he seems to discover early that he can best avoid punishment by imitating the behavior of his parents and teachers. If he is in the upper-middle class, for instance, he finds that "it pays" to be polite, to go to church "like his father," to be quiet and "refined" like his teacher, to keep sexual impulses hidden and unmentioned like his mother. In the upper-lower class, on the other hand, he finds that it is equally good policy (if he would escape punishment or scorn) to be a hard, steady worker at his chores like his mother, to "be a man" and fight when necessary and carry a knife like his father, and to protect himself from ridicule by beginning sex relations early like his clique.

The most basic differences in habit formation between adjacent social classes are those between *lower class* and *lower-middle class*. The patterns of behavior in these two groups, in either the white or the Negro population, are so widely different

[1] O. H. Mowrer has emphasized the role of anxiety as a reinforcing agent in learning in discussions at the Institute of Human Relations, Yale University. This idea is adumbrated in his paper "Preparatory Set (Expectancy)—Determinant in Motivation and Learning," *Psychology Review*, XLV (January 1928), 72. It will be further developed in forthcoming articles by him.

that it is the common practice, even of sociologists, to speak of the lower class as "unsocialized," from their middle-class point of view. The social expectations and available goal responses of lower-class and lower-middle-class people are separated by a virtual chasm which is maintained by taboos on participation across class lines.

The chasm is a behavioral one. It lies between the stimuli and goals of the "respectable," status-bound lower-middle class and those of the recalcitrant, impulsive, and physically aggressive lower class. The ineffectiveness of the usual middle-class stimuli upon lower-class people and the resultant waste of potential social and economic energy in the lower class are the perpetual concern of middle-class and upper-class legislators, social workers, and educators. More than three-fourths of all Negroes are lower class. It will therefore repay us to look more closely at this social "great divide" as it appears in Negro society, focusing our attention upon the training of children in these class positions.

Among lower-middle-class Negroes in New Orleans and Natchez, the family is based upon legal and continued marriage and sexual fidelity is strictly required of the wife. If the husband has extramarital relations, they must be outside of his normal class relationships and well concealed, or he will be severely punished, both socially and economically. The husband works as an artisan, or as a white-collar employee in the lower income brackets. While the children are small, the wife seldom is employed. She and the husband are usually grammar school graduates, subordinate officers in the church and lodge, and members of social cliques and clubs composed of other lower-middle-class people.

Lower-middle-class parents exert a powerful and continual pressure upon their children to study, to repress aggression at school, to inhibit sexual impulses, to avoid lower-class playmates, to attend Sunday school regularly, and to avoid cabarets, night clubs, pool parlors, and gambling houses. They set before their children the goals of a high school education, a skilled or white-collar occupation, and a "good" marriage.

The child who lives in lower-class Negro society, however, is surrounded by people of quite different habits who make other demands and set other goals before him. His parents are very likely to separate several times during his life. Extramarital partnerships are common for both husband and wife. Fighting with fists and knives occurs within most families and is common in their cliques and their neighborhoods. Gambling and magic are accepted class-ways. Church services are held not more than twice a month, and attendance is casual. Lower-lower-class families in the urban South belong neither to a church nor to a lodge. The ministers and deacons preach the class-ways, confining their ethics to warnings against dancing, card playing, Sunday baseball, and "too much" science and education. The parents have attended only a few grades in school and the educational goal they set for their children is not much higher than their own. In general, lower-lower-class parents hope that their children will complete graded school (six grades); upper-lower-class parents hope for the completion of junior high school (nine grades). Illegitimate birth runs from one-fourth to one-third of all lower-class births; delinquency is far higher than in the lower-middle class and school retardation is almost universal. Within the lower class itself, there are status differences between upper- and lower-lower-class people upon the basis of economic behavior and church and lodge participation. In their habits of aggression, sexual behavior, recreation, and etiquette, however, all lower-class people are sufficiently alike so that their habits as a group may be compared with those of lower-middle-class people.

In considering the Negro child of either class in his concrete training environment, there are three useful questions which one may ask: (1) What do his parents want to teach him? (2) What methods do they use for teaching him? (3) What do they actually succeed in teaching him?

Like parents of all classes, lower-class people wish their children to learn the fundamental controls upon eating, disposal of excreta, and masturbation. They also enforce the universal American taboos upon open preferences within the family, sex relations with close kin, and violations of age restrictions. In addition, they try to teach the child not to lie to, or steal from, his parents, not to steal from his schoolmates or teachers, not to stay away from school when sent by the parents, not to fight white people unless attacked, and not to be arrested by the police.

But with regard to sex, education, recreation, and aggression toward other Negroes, the parental demands of the lower class are unlike those in the other classes. This is by no means to say that no attempt is made to train the child in these fields, but rather that lower-class society has a standard of its own in these matters.

In their efforts to teach, lower-class Negro parents punish their children with great energy and frequency and reward them seldom. They cannot offer the more effective status rewards to their children because both economic and educational privileges are class-bound and there are very few to which the child in the lower class has access. The chief reason for the relative lack of socialization of lower-class children seems to be that their incitement to learn, which means in part to renounce direct impulse gratification and to build up more complex habits and skills, is crippled by the scarcity of available rewards. There must be a push behind human beings to make them learn, and this push is most effective when it not only punishes undesired actions but also rewards the constant effort required to build more effective habits.

A lower-class boy in Natchez, fifteen years old, tells the interviewer that he has failed the fifth grade twice. "Everytime I gits home from school, my papa say I ain't goin' to be nothin' nohow, but he whips me jes' the same." His father not only punishes his failure to study but he also withholds the spur of ultimate reward, of higher position, that is, of "being somebody." The son points the behavioristic moral, "I tells him I ain't goin' to be bad in school no more when he's hittin' me, but that don't do no good, seems lak. I comes right back, an' do's it agin."

The source of discipline in a lower-class family changes frequently from mother to father, to aunt, to grandmother, to uncle or to an older child. But whoever the disciplinarian at any given moment may be, he is certain to believe that the way to make a child learn is to beat him. Locking the child in the house or withdrawing his play privileges may be used, but whippings are inevitable no matter what other forms of punishment the child may have to suffer. A lower-class mother in New Orleans says of her son of thirteen, "He went out when I told him not to. I tried to choke his neck off when I got him." Equally typical was the woman who said of her son, "I can't understand why he is so bad. I licks him all the time." The mother of a fifteen-year-old boy who, like all his clique members, had been arrested several times for stealing, said that the only "satisfaction" she got for his disobedience to her was "beating on him." Another boy showed the interviewer two scars on his face which his uncle had given him as a child. One of the most conscientious mothers known to the interviewers was a lower-class woman who said that she whipped her son "all the time" when he was a small child to make him obey her. Nevertheless, the boy at the age of thirteen would not attend school, lied to his mother, and stole from stores. The mother put him in a home for delinquents because, she said, he could be whipped more regularly there after each infraction of the rules.

It seems clear, however, that a child cannot be trained in this fashion to undergo the long periods of renunciation which the middle-class ideal of socialization demands of him. If a parent wishes to teach a child to save money, he must not only try to prevent him from buying candy or a toy whenever the impulse seizes him, but he must also constantly tell him what more desirable object (a train, a doll, a rifle) he *will* be able to buy in the distant future with his savings. And this day may not be postponed indefinitely; the child must occasionally be reinforced in his saving by being allowed to take part of his hoard downtown to buy a doll or rifle.

As a child grows older, the effective learning rewards are increasingly those of status, those associated with middle-class and upper-class privileges and dominance. In this class setting, reinforcements are of long range, and learning is driven by powerful anxiety. To have his teachers whip him when he fights on the streets is not an effective control upon a lower-class boy because he knows, by seeing and being a part of life in his position, that he is not going to be rewarded if he is a "good little boy," if he leaves girls alone, or if he studies his lessons. The long-range goals do not seem to be "there" in his world; he does not see other people in his class attaining them, or practicing the behavior required of him, and he feels his parents and teachers are "crazy" when they demand it of him.

Strange as it may appear on first sight, his learning reinforcements are weak also on the side of punishment. He is whipped severely but not at the right time. If punishment is to be effective in reinforcing the avoidance of an action by a young child, it must be administered immediately before or after this action. The child is thus taught exactly what acts will be painful to him, and that the pain will always be an integral part of this action sequence. But the lower-class mother is usually not able to punish the child promptly or to prevent his repeating the behavior because she is at work. The child makes the goal responses and is reinforced in the habit. If his action is reported to his parents, their tardy punishment does not break down the habit. Furthermore, the lower-class child spends most of his time out of the home—in the streets, theaters, or beer parlors—where his parents cannot observe his behavior and where he is reinforced by the approval of his clique.

On the other hand, the lower-middle-class parent insists that the child "stay off the streets" or play in front of the home where the parents can maintain constant supervision of his behavior. He may not go to the movies unattended, nor may he stay out after dark except in good hands. He has the status of a child, of a person whose free movement is controlled, until he is in late adolescence. But the lower-class child is a man sociologically at a much earlier age, that is, he has opportunity for exploration of all the possible goal responses.

What behavior do the great masses of colored lower-class children learn in this situation? What habits do their parents actually succeed in teaching them? To begin with, the parents drive in the feeding, cleanliness, and masturbation training as rigorously as do middle-class and upper-class parents. There is no evidence in the Old City research, moreover, that incest is relatively any more common in the lower class than in other classes (Negro or white). It seems certain from our records of child training that these early controls upon the child's use of his erogenous zones are equally effective in all classes, and that the rigors of this training give rise to the same kind of personality strain.

With regard to the later sexual, aggressive, and more complex training, however, both the aims and the results differ as between the lower class and the lower-middle class. Lower-class Negro children grow up to be fighters, cutters, and shooters, and they are reinforced in this behavior by their parents. They live in a part of the society which is largely outside of the protection of the white law. The parent tells the child to strike out in defense of his body and to be certain to strike first. (In lower-middle-class families, on the other hand, the parental instruction is the same as the court's: "When anybody hits or damages you, come and tell *me*.") It is worth our while to examine for a moment the instruction of our lower-class parents on aggression. Each statement given below is from a different parent.

"Sure, my children fight. I told my married daughter to take a gun to that nigger she's married to, if he bothers her again."

"I tell John to fight anybody his size or bigger. If he can't beat them, I can. A man hit him the other day, and I went out after that nigger with a broom."

"A girl hit Rose at school de othuh day. I went to de school and got Rose and dis girl togethuh, an' I tol' Rose to pick up a brick and hit dat gal if she bothered her again, an' I'd help her."

"I tells my children to fight it out."

"Gerald fights a lot. But he takes that after me. When I was goin' to school, I'd fight all the time."

"I tell Ernest to fight back, an' ef he don't, I'm gonnuh beat him myse'f."

Within the family itself, lower-class children see their parents fighting and begin to take part in these battles as they grow older. A girl of sixteen told the interviewer how she learned to curse her father. "My papa used to cuss at us all the time when he'd get mad. I didn' start cussin' him till the time he began beatin' on my mamma. All of us jumped on him, and beat him up. He was cussin' us, an' we cussed him back. An' ever since then I say anything that comes in my mind to him." In Natchez, a lower-class boy "took a gun to" his father for beating his mother. In a New Orleans family, the children used a hatchet and a gun, as well as their fists, against their father. Another lower-class adolescent, a colored Creole, said, "My father is a war-horse, an' my mamma is pure hell. She'll crawl (fight) anybody any time. You see I come by my fightin' natural. The ol' man an' ol' lady used to fight anybody who jumped on us, an' if we didn't fight, they'd whip us themselves."

If he does not fight when challenged, a lower-class child is punished both by his family and by his clique. If he is a ready fighter, on the other hand, he wins prestige and deference from his clique and approval from his parents. From the middle-class point of view, it seems strange that the pain of being hit or cut does not deter the lower-class child from overt aggression. Two facts which have previously appeared in our case histories must be kept in mind, however. First, a lower-class person becomes habituated to receiving blows and learns that they are not likely to prove fatal or even serious. This is not an anxiety-producing experience, for anxiety develops only in the face of a punishment which an individual considers overpowering and before which he feels himself helpless. This is the situation with middle-class children who are taught that overt aggression is extremely dangerous from the point of view of both physical survival and social acceptance. They are therefore intimidated with regard to making and receiving any physical attack. Their anxiety on this score is generalized, furthermore, to a great variety of "dangers" which never occur and which really do not exist as physical threats at all. But the lower-class child learns, by receiving blows and cuts, that they do not kill and that his part of the society will not "declass" him for fighting back.

In the second place, the pain of physical conflict is a very weak deterrent for the lower-class child because it occurs in a sequence of actions which also lead to the basic goal responses of rage and of hitting. To express violent anger is a tremendously gratifying and cathartic experience. In its end-form of hitting, aggressive behavior is a basic goal response and one which middle-class and upper-class people learn to inhibit only at the expense of great strain and anxiety. The necessity of continually repressing the aggressive impulses is a conflict which lower-class children escape. In order to give a blow, they learn quite early to be willing to take one. The really effective reinforcement soon comes to be that of hitting or cutting the person who attacks or frustrates you. This basic, though primitive, reaction, which is deeply rooted in the impulsive nature of all men, is strengthened in lower-class people by the social approval of their family and cliques. For this reason, the lower-class person, unlike the lower-middle-class individual, does not have to endure in his class world the feelings of incoherent rage and helplessness which result from the chronic suppression of aggressive impulses.

With regard to the sexual goal responses, the lower-class child finds his class-ways equally permissive. It is true that his parents warn him against sexual relations before adolescence, but at the same time they present him with an example which is just the opposite of their precepts. He observes that their own extramarital behavior is not punished and he learns at an early age, therefore, that there are no serious penalties in his class for sexual exploration. He discovers at a later age, furthermore, that his white employer will not discharge him if he is sexually promiscuous with Negroes.

No matter what the sociologists may say on the matter, parents know that the sexual impulses are deep-laid and persistent. Middle-class and upper-class parents throw the whole weight of their power against sexual exploration by their children. In the lower class, on the other hand, the average mother will live with several men during a child's life. The father, mother, and grandmother will almost certainly have extramarital affairs. The mother is usually at work, furthermore, and cannot prevent the sexual play of her children, nor their excursions to cabarets, deserted lots, and dark lanes. Most of our lower-class adolescents were able to "stay out" at night until eleven or twelve o'clock, and many of the girls frequently stayed at cabarets until three or four o'clock in the morning. Almost invariably, a lower-class girl is taught that a man is not to be regarded as a provider and status anchor, but as an object for exploitation. "I tells my girls," a lower-class mother in New Orleans reports, "don't hear what no man say, but see how much he got."

Since lower-class parents know that the road to sexual gratification will be an open one for their children, they instruct them early in matters of pregnancy and sexual diseases. The middle-class interviewers learned, to their astonishment, that most of our lower-class children had been provided by their parents with "books" on sexual matters. Unlike the dangerously uninformed and intimidated lower-middle-class children, they had an exact and detailed knowledge on these points. Their mothers informed them early and warned the girls specifically against the methods of sexual approach by men. But precept, as they often complained to the interviewers, could not take the place of supervision.

Nor could this factual instruction of children on sexual behavior counteract the daily example of parents and clique members. If there are no rewards and punishments in terms of status for inhibiting sexual impulses, people will certainly seek sexual responses. In the lower class, status is not lost by sexual exploration. In the child's clique, for example, sexual gratification is general and approved. In the typical lower-class clique of one fourteen-year-old girl, there were six boys and eleven girls. In the majority of these families, the mother had taken another sex partner without losing status in her own clique. Seven of the eleven girls between the ages of thirteen and seventeen, had been pregnant or had borne babies before they had been married. This fact did not injure their position in their churches or in their cliques. A lower-class boy of fourteen in Natchez reported that in his clique of girls and boys between the ages of fourteen and sixteen, sexual intercourse was common. They discussed this relationship freely in cross-sex groups, he said, and when they gathered in the bayou, a boy and girl would slip off from the group into the woods and nobody would be " 'shamed" of this behavior. That is, nobody would be denied membership in the group or socially punished.

But if a lower-class adolescent attempts to associate intimately with lower-middle-class boys and girls, the first change in his habits which his new clique requires is in sexual behavior. In the lower-middle class, sexual exploration by the adolescent is punished by both his clique and his family. One of the girls in our study who was attempting mobility into the lower-middle class, was constantly warned by her mother to resist the sexual approaches of boys. "I want to raise her," the mother said, "so she'll be able to get a nice husband." The girl steadily refused to have sex relations with men and her level of class participation rose just as steadily. She was courted by even upper-middle-class men and became engaged to one young man of this position. She explained to the interviewer, however, that she was "only going out with him to get in society." During this process, the sanctions of the lower-middle class were internalized in the form of anxiety concerning sexual relations. The student continually stated that she was afraid to have sexual intercourse because "I don't want to have a baby, and the baby won't have a name. No, not me."

There are two crucial reasons for the effectiveness of lower-middle-class restraints upon the sexual, aggressive, and school behavior of children. The techniques of training which parents use are (1) constant, detailed supervision, and (2) threats of loss of status if the child is not a "good" boy or girl. Parents know the effectiveness of these training methods quite well; they likewise know the constant danger of the impulse demands. They therefore maintain a solid front with teachers, church leaders, and members of their own cliques, all of whom are recognized as legitimate supervisors of the child.

In the Negro lower-middle class, as contrasted with the lower class, a child is a member of a permanent family group and has strongly sanctioned obligations to all members of his immediate family. The father is almost invariably present during the child's early life and he is the ultimate authority in the family. From the age of five or six years, the child is made to attend school regularly. His report card is carefully examined by the parents; punishments and rewards are steadily maintained to insure good marks and deportment in school. The child is sent to Sunday school and later to church, and is required to say his prayers each night. His recreation and play are supervised and his clique members directly or indirectly selected for him, even into the period of adolescence. The lower-class children in his neighborhood are kept at a distance by his parents, and any lower-class clique to which the child may have become attached in the public schools is tabooed by the parents long before the child reaches adolescence.

Within the family, supervision of the child's play, work, and recreation, is chiefly in the hands of the mother, but infractions of discipline are punished by the father. Whipping is very rare; a child is usually punished by being "kept in the house," forced to miss his club meetings, or denied his weekly trip to the movies. In moments of open revolt, he is threatened with loss of economic support, a punishment which entails loss of education and other status supports. "You can't do that and live in my house." "If I tell her I won't go to school, she'll tell me to work, or starve." From his earliest years, the child is trained to be an obedient, respectable, "nice" child. As he comes into adolescence, the anxiety arising from this training is usually sufficient to maintain his lower-middle-class habits. The secret of the "goodness" of the children of this class, as compared with those of the lower class, is largely in the continual early supervision to which they have been subjected. If one attempted to state quantitatively this class difference in training, one would probably be justified in saying that the average lower-middle-class mother is actually in the company of her young child twelve hours a day, whereas the lower-class working mother who goes to work at six in the morning and stays until eight or ten at night, is with her child only one-sixth as long. The difference in training can be most clearly stated as follows: the mother in the lower-middle class is able to enforce her demands upon the child fifty times a day, let us estimate, whereas the lower-class mother is able to punish or reward her child's actions only eight or ten times a day. One of our lower-middle-class boys expressed the constant supervision which his mother exerted over his behavior by saying, "Mother is always anxious for us not to get in any trouble" (that is, to be "good" children). His mother gave a detailed account of her training demands, including the rule that the boys should not leave their neighborhood after school hours, nor leave their yard after dark. "Bend a twig while it is young," the mother stated, in explaining the "good" behavior of her son.

Overt aggression was universally punished by the parents of the Negro children interviewed in the lower-middle class. Fighting and cursing are among the few actions for which a child is whipped. A typical comment from children in this class was "My mother don't allow us to fight or curse. She got that out of us early." Children in this position are even more severely intimidated with regard to sexual behavior. Most lower-middle-class parents maintain an awful and complete silence on this subject except to make terrifying threats concerning masturbation and to punish severely and without explanation any form of sexual play. Sex is made to appear horrible and extremely dangerous; it is a form of feeling and action which is so reprehensible that even one's own parents cannot mention it.

The result of this training, as seen in our middle-class children, is to make them bear a severe burden of anxiety concerning their sexual impulses and responses. They are afraid to talk of their sexual life to parents or teachers, afraid to have intercourse, terribly ashamed and humiliated by their masturbation, afraid that having a baby will kill them, and convinced that all sexual behavior is sinful. This is the price which middle-class people must pay, in order to maintain their class position and to make a good marriage.

As yet, lower-middle-class society knows only one way to train a girl to make a "decent" marriage. In order to make her stay in school and keep her "reputation," her parents block the road which leads to sex. If it is made optional whether she is to undergo the renunciations necessary for "respectability" or to follow the sexual urges, parents know well that the constantly stimulated sexual impulses will usually win. One must therefore block this road by punishment and anxiety. Soon the child begins to be rewarded by his clique and class members for *inhibiting* sex. The girl learns to act on this basis, "If I wait, if I work and refuse to have sexual intercourse, then I can look forward to the fine day when I shall get a good husband and be married in a church."

From the standpoint of the dominant classes in our society, she would then be a good child. The serious difficulties of educators, ministers, statesmen, and social workers are not with people of her class. Her family and their class members are the very backbone of Negro society, as their white counterparts are of white society. They are the "poor but respectable" people, "the decent poor," whose motivation to work hard, to sacrifice their own gratifications for their children's training and education, and to safeguard the monogamous family, is deep and vigorous.

If one wishes to know how they became decent and moral, in this sense, how they developed these strong habits of impulse renunciation and status striving, one must turn his attention to a very commonplace but little appreciated fact. The lower-middle-class child is systematically prevented by his parents from exploring the society around him. His learning is supervised so that he will experience only certain goal responses. His resultant habits are maintained by the sanctions of the status structure in which he lives. Whereas the lower-class child is usually a "child of the streets," able to explore the life of the streets, the beer parlors, the cabarets, and the free world of sex, the lower-middle-class child's random, exploratory behavior is checked by his parents and their clique, and by his teachers. His parents even tell him what movies he may see and what magazines he may read. He must be present at mealtimes and he must be in bed by eight or nine o'clock on school days. His parents always know where he is and what he is doing until he is well into the period of adolescence.

The degree of supervision by parents increases still further and the class range of the child's play group narrows steadily, as one moves into the more privileged classes. Mothers are less frequently employed; they have fewer children at wider intervals and can therefore train them more carefully; and the child's friends are selected from a smaller circle of acquaintances. As one of our upper-middle-class boys said, "My mamma doesn't want me to go anywhere. Just to school, and play in front of the house." His mother explained her training methods in brief, "The reason we don't let him go anywhere with other boys is to keep him out of mischief. You know how children are. If you let up on them, they'll start going the wrong places and doing the wrong things." By restricting the child's associates to the children of their own friends, the parents narrow the circle of supervisory adults and thus lessen the chances of his exploring new types of behavior. Whereas in the clique of a lower-middle-class child there will very likely be one or two lower-class children with whom he may identify for a time, such children will be excluded from the upper-class cliques. The child is kept so close in many upper-class families indeed that his intimate associates may be counted on the fingers of one hand and are largely restricted to his own kin.

CHAPTER XIII

SOCIAL CLASS AND SCHOOL LEARNING

In the foregoing chapter it has been shown that the aggressive and sexual habits of a Negro child are usually class-typed. We know from the study of Old City, furthermore, that there is a high degree of equivalence between the behavior of parallel classes in the white and colored societies. This similarity in class training accounts for the fact that any of our Negro adolescents seems in most respects to act and feel "just like a white child" who has a similar type of personality and has been trained in a parallel class position. We may now propose an answer to a question which we have previously asked ourselves, namely, "What is the practical application of the class analysis?" The study of the class modes of behavior tells us (1) what behavior we may expect of a person when we know his class position, (2) what goals he is seeking, and (3) what reinforcements are effective in his learning.

The stubborn economic, political, and war-ridden habits of our society make it increasingly clear that neither government nor social reformers can change the behavior of human beings over night, even when their very biological survival seems to demand a change. In order to change an individual's familial, sexual, economic, or educational relationships, the social engineers must first know what his present class-typed habits are and how they are being reinforced. They will then be in a position to use this knowledge for the establishment of new modes of behavior in our society. But there can be no new learning with regard to war, economic relations, education, or family life, unless old habits are first broken and old rewards and punishments withdrawn.

The evidence from our life histories and from the studies of the class-typing of behavior in Old City and Southerntown, indicates that the sanctions of class position are the basic reinforcements of social behavior. These class controls upon learning may be identified more specifically by analysis of the school society of the Negro child. We know from school records that the great majority of lower-class Negro children in southern cities are retarded in graded schools. Their retardation is not the result of late entrance because most of them are sent to school at the age of five or six. Nor is there any evidence that school learning is correlated with hereditary factors, either for "racial" or for class groups. Today, geneticists agree that in the human species, where interbreeding has been taking place over long periods, hereditary segregation of physical or mental characteristics will *not* operate so as to distinguish large groups of people in any important biological equipment. The question of group differences in school learning must therefore be considered primarily in relation to (1) class training, and (2) the status controls of the school. Our problem here may be phrased more clearly, as follows: "Why do lower-class Negro children usually fail to develop and maintain habits of study in graded school, and why do children of upper-middle-class and upper-class status usually maintain such habits?"

To begin with, we remember the discovery of the behavioristic psychologists that an animal does not learn unless he is rewarded in a way which reduces his biological tensions and drives. This mechanism also seems to be the basis of habit formation in man. If there are no effective reinforcements for a child, he does not learn. Once established, moreover, these rewards or punishments must be maintained or the habit will be extinguished.

In his school behavior, the Negro child is reinforced in learning, or in fleeing from the learning situation, by the rewards and punishments which he receives from his teachers, his family, and his clique. These reinforcements upon school learning consist of (1) the favorable attention and opportunities for dominance which the child obtains, and (2) of his being denied such rewards or physically punished. A Negro teacher in New Orleans may reward a pupil if she gives him a role in a school operetta, if she makes him a proctor, if she accords him preference in classroom recitations, if she praises him or pats him on the shoulder, or if she gives him high grades. His parents may reward him by giving him a bicycle, or "fare" to the movies, or by praising him. In addition, a child is reinforced in his learning habits when he *avoids* punishment and disapproval from his teachers, his parents, and his clique. To escape punishment, and thus to reduce anxiety, is in itself a powerful reward.

Punishment and the anxiety it establishes may not alone maintain complex human learning, however. Apparently a simultaneous biological or status *reward* is also useful. If we visit the first grade of any Negro school in New Orleans or Natchez, we soon observe that certain of the children obtain the approval and caresses of their teachers more readily than others. They are usually the children whose parents have upper-middle-class or upper-class status. They begin to receive favors and status privileges from their teachers as soon as they enter school. They must work, as their parents and teachers demand, but they are also immediately rewarded. Their anxiety is thus reduced, and they are reinforced in repeating those actions which have pleased the teacher. Before long, the person of the teacher, her smile or praise, become subgoal responses in themselves. The average lower-class child, however, who on status grounds is systematically punished by his teacher, becomes a sullen, hostile child. Anger, overt or repressed, is a barrier to effective learning.

In order to comprehend fully the class reinforcements in the child's school behavior, we must likewise consider the goal responses which his teachers, parents, and clique members obtain *from the child*. Behavioristic psychologists have recently pointed out that social reinforcement of the kind which a favored child receives from his teacher is a two-sided experience.[1] In the first

[1] We are indebted to Professor Hull of Yale University and the Institute of Human Relations for this application of the principle of circular reinforcement. See statement by Clark L. Hull in *Abstract of S-R Sessions of Monday-Night Group, 1938-39* (mimeographed), Institute of Human Relations, Yale University, 1939, p. 4.

place, the acts of the teacher in praising the pupil and granting him dominant relationships to his fellow students diminish his anxiety and thus reinforce him in learning his lessons and in maintaining good "deportment." At the same time, the student's successful learning reinforces the teacher in continuing her acts of preference toward him. The teacher is herself a member of the class system. She is rewarded by the behavior of the good student, first, because his habits are evidence that she is a proficient teacher, and, secondly, because through the child she is able to gain the approval of his upper-middle-class or upper-class parents.

This type of "circular reinforcement" operates also between the successful pupil and his parents. If parents have a child who is a good student, they are reinforced in sending him to school regularly, in supporting him economically through sixteen to twenty years of school life, and in blocking contradictory types of behavior. Through their child's successful school behavior, the family's class position is maintained. If he should "turn out bad," on the other hand, it would be an indication that his parents were "common" or "ordinary" people, and his failure would be a crucial threat to the future status of his family.

Similar reinforcements are operating between the pupil and his clique. Within an upper-middle-class or upper-class clique, there are social punishments for the member who fails to achieve good marks or to become a school leader; on the other hand, a student is praised and accorded relationships of equality if he meets the clique's standards. In turn, his success and prestige increase the status of his clique in the school society and thus reinforce its other members in seeking similar goals.

The nature of these social class reinforcements will become clearer if we compare the sanctions upon school learning in the lower class with those in the higher class positions. Following their usual method of training, the lower-class parents begin whipping the child at an early age to make him study his lessons and obey his teacher. As a flight from this punishment, the small child goes to school and even opens his books at home upon the parents' demands. But he does not become a good student be-

FIGURE I

CONTROLS UPON SCHOOL BEHAVIOR

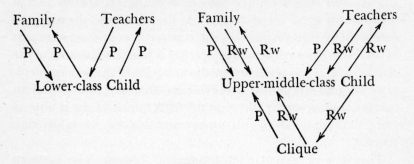

P = Punishment, Biological or Social
Rw = Reward, Biological or Social

Explanation: The school-learning habits of the upper-middle-class Negro child are reinforced not only by punishment and resultant anxiety, but by his obtaining status privileges which reduce punishment and anxiety to the level where the child can work effectively. Furthermore, the child's successful learning reinforces his teacher, clique, and family in their efforts to teach him. On the other hand, the lower-class child experiences only punishment. He is not reinforced by class or school privileges to seek the goals of high status.

cause he does not obtain in school the anxiety-reducing privileges and status goal responses. The parents attempt to "beat it into him," but he still does not learn his lessons. In the meantime, he begins to make the other goal responses of sex, fighting, gambling, and dancing which *are* allowed him by his class; he can obtain these responses, and therefore can be reinforced in seeking these goals.

One becomes better motivated to study, however, when he sometimes experiences the social rewards of study. The eliciting of such approval diminishes the student's anxiety and thus reinforces him in all those actions—"good deportment," study, attention, and renunciation of impulse gratification—which have been the instrumental steps to winning approval.

The Negro lower-class child is usually not allowed by his

Figure II

REINFORCEMENTS OF SCHOOL LEARNING

UPPER-MIDDLE-CLASS CHILD

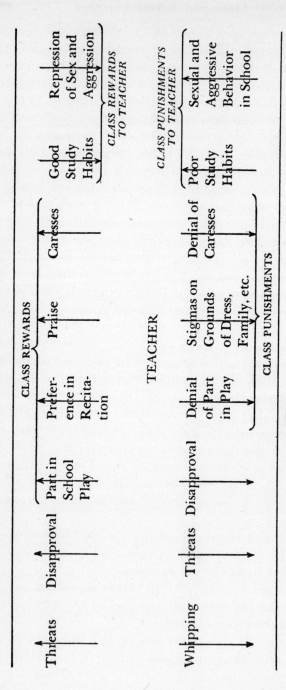

LOWER-CLASS CHILD

Explanation: The arrows lead from the rewarding or punishing agent. They point toward the person whose behavior is reinforced by the end responses. Both the lower-class and the upper-middle-class Negro child in New Orleans and Natchez are threatened with physical punishment by the teacher and subjected to disapproval which arouses a fear of punishment. But the upper-middle-class child is also reinforced in his study habits by the class privileges which he receives from the teacher; his successful learning in turn reinforces the teacher in her efforts to instruct and supervise him. The lower-class child, however, is subjected to class punishment by the teacher, involving denial of privileges, and is thus reinforced in flight toward other goal responses, such as playing hooky or aggression toward the teacher. His behavior likewise motivates the teacher in punishing him further.

teacher to make the goal responses of privilege. He sees the upper-class and upper-middle-class children being accorded preference, not only in classroom recitations but also in school entertainments and in intimate friendship relations with the teacher. He finds that he is not granted these privileges; instead, he is stigmatized by teachers and their favored students on grounds of the "ignorance" of his parents, the dialect which he speaks, the appearance of his clothes, and, very likely, the darkness of his skin. It does not take him long to discover that something is wrong and that the teacher's "pets" of high status are the only ones who can make the prestige goal responses. If there is no reward for learning, in terms of privilege and anxiety-reduction, there is no motive for work. The lower-class child soon becomes a "dummy." Frequently he is openly aggressive toward the teacher; if not, he plays hooky, and he displaces his aggression from the powerful teacher to the more vulnerable upper-class and upper-middle-class pupils. He becomes like his parents, "bad" and "ignorant."

When he reaches adolescence, moreover, the lower-class child is no longer subjected to punishment by his parents to make him study, and his anxiety concerning school learning is virtually extinguished. The child knows also that his parents cannot afford to support him after eight or ten years of schooling. He has learned that his parents' friends, their minister, their club officers, and they themselves are only semiliterate; as a result, his own educational level of aspiration is low. The child usually identifies with these symbolic adults; his anxiety is therefore extinguished *when he has attained or just surpassed their educational status.*

The relaxing of the family pressure for study habits upon the lower-class child at adolescence is evidenced in the following typical situations from our life histories:

A fifteen-year-old boy said that he usually signed his own report cards and that his mother did not yet know that he had not been promoted the previous year.

A fourteen-year-old boy remained in the basement of his school most of each day, playing with a group of boys. When his mother discovered him there one day, she did not seemed disturbed, nor did she send him back to his classroom.

Two sisters, one fifteen, the other sixteen, were allowed by their mother to withdraw from high school in order to marry.

Most of the lower-class students interviewed who were in junior high school, said that their parents did not ask to see their report cards.

A boy of fourteen said that his mother did not mind if he had one or two marks of "Unsatisfactory" on his report cards, but she did object to four or more failures.

A mother stated that she was determined her son should "finish the seventh grade," even if he was 100 years old when he came out.

In short, the goals of white-collar or professional occupation and of middle-class status which are at the end of the school route, are not made to appear valuable, near, or certain for the lower-class child. He learns from his family and teachers that the chances for a person in his lower-class position to finish high school and college, and to become socially mobile through education, are so slight in view of the economic position and classways of his family, that they scarcely exist. He finds that neither his parents nor his teachers *expect* a person in his social position to "go far" in school. The teaching and professional positions in Negro life require more training than he can hope to pay for, and more impulse renunciation than he has been taught to make. He learns that the faster and surer ways to become socially mobile are to learn to tap-dance, to box, to sing, or to play dance music.

In the upper-middle class and upper class, however, the training situations with regard to the school behavior of the child are quite different. Whereas the lower-class parent aligns himself with the child *against the teacher* on grounds of class antagonism, the parents in the higher class positions maintain a solid front with the teacher in the latter's demands upon the child. The teacher becomes an effective disciplinarian for him because her demands must be met if he is to escape punishment at his parents' hands.

The fact that the teacher's approval is a necessary step toward escaping parental punishment seems to be established by statements of the following kind, which were made by all of our middle-class and upper-class students.

"If these teachers told my mama I was acting up here, she would be keeping me at home every night for two years."

"I don't tell my parents about any trouble I have in school. My mama and papa always say the teacher's right."

A boy of thirteen told us he was kept in the house after school hours for one week because he was impudent to his teacher.

"My mama won't take up for me at school. She always thinks I'm in the wrong and the teacher is right."

Not only does the Negro parent of middle-class or upper-class position make the teacher the parent-surrogate in school, but he steadily blocks alternative goal responses in the child. In the life history material, this training appears so unlike that in the lower class that it seems worthwhile to quote from the records at some length. In this way, the reader may grasp the deep and powerful hold of the class-typing of behavior among Negroes.

"The mother said, 'I just stay on my knees and pray for Louise. I prayed for her to finish high school. I already put her in an education insurance, too. I want her to go away to the University of Chicago, so when she gets out she will be able to get some good work.' "

"The mother stated, 'When Melvin failed at junior high school, it made me feel very ashamed. I am going to send him to Tuskegee. I think he will study better if he gets away from his bunch.' "

"My mama and grandmama stay up with me at night and help me with my lessons."

"My mama is always telling me to be like my sister. She was second in her class at Normal School. She and my mama are always fussing with me to make me study. My mama says I can't quit school because she don't want no ignorant people around her. She says she'll send me to reform school first. My papa says I better not think about quitting school."

"My mama even made me go to school the morning after Mardi Gras. If it's raining hard, and if we say we sick, we still got to go. She says that even though my daddy can't work, we're going to school, if we have to go barefoot. A son of a friend of my mama's quit school and got married, and my mama is still lecturing on it." The mother herself stated, "One thing, we're trying to bring all our girls up to be nice and decent, and get 'em a good education, so they can be somebody."

"I can't quit school. My mama will whip me, an' make me go. I've never played hooky or cut classes since I've been in school."

"If I don't pass in school, I'll get whipped or something. I won't be able to ride my bicycle, or go to the show, or see my girl for a while."

"My mama won't let me quit school. She'll make me go until I do learn something."

"Because of my own educational background, and my husband's profession, I tell my children they have no excuse not to do well in school."

"Even if I have to go out and work, I won't let my children stop school."

"I tell my daughter she must finish school before marrying. I tell her men don't want ignorant wives nowadays."

"I tell Marjorie I don't want her to get good marks without working. She wouldn't learn nothing then."

At the same time that the child of higher class position is supervised by his parents so as to prevent his making the impulse goal responses, he is also reinforced by them in all those actions which lead to the gaining of prestige in school. His position also differs from that of the lower-class child in the models of identification which it offers him. He sees the deferential treatment which his parents and their clique members obtain from lower-class people, as well as from teachers. By observing the social rewards which they receive and the social punishments which they avoid as a result of their status, he is reinforced in forming those habits of school learning which lead to status in the school society. In order to understand the desire for prestige in children in these higher positions, we must visualize the social punishments and resultant anxiety which loss of status involves. It is this anxiety, systematically maintained by his relationships with parents, teachers, and cliques, which drives the child toward the status goals. Once he experiences dominance relations with his schoolmates and diminution of anxiety as a result of his successful learning, he is reinforced in all those acts which have led to the gaining of these goal responses. His striving for the prestige goals then becomes more constant.

The therapeutic results which may be obtained by removing the class punishment from the delinquent pupil are indicated by the remedial work accomplished in this study with Ellen Hill and Judy Tolliver. In their relationships with the interviewers of higher class position than their own, these students were never stigmatized on class grounds. They were allowed to express freely their class antagonisms to their teachers and they were not punished by the interviewer for expressions of such hostility. With the elimination of class punishment, the pupil was able after a time to identify with the interviewer. Reinforced by the approval and friendship of the interviewer, both of these formerly delinquent pupils changed their school behavior so markedly that they won the praise of their teachers, and escaped severe class punishments. It seems possible that nonprofessional, volunteer workers of high social status, if given preliminary training in the methods of establishing good rapport and then carefully supervised, could achieve similar results on a large scale with the great majority of retarded Negro school children.

Long and detailed research on this problem is needed. The hints which have appeared in our studies of class training and of personality development may be temporarily organized in the following way. School learning is reinforced by rewards and punishments which consist of whipping and social disapproval, on the one hand, and of escape from these punishments and the attaining of positive biological and status rewards, on the other. In effective human learning, these reinforcements are maintained within the individual by anxiety (which is the anticipation of physical or social punishment if the individual does *not* learn), and by its positive counterpart of striving. In lower-class relationships, a child is not rewarded on biological or status lines for school learning; he is only punished. His motivation to study is thus weakened, for he never *experiences* the rewarding goal responses of prestige, and thus can never be reinforced in seeking the higher status goals of education. In short, his anxiety with regard to school behavior is very low because (1) he is not subjected to the status demands for successful learning, and (2) constant, unsupported physical punishment not only loses its effect as a reinforcing agent, but actually drives the child in other directions. Instead, he chooses to make those goal responses of sex, aggression, and entertainment which are not blocked by his class position but are made easily available to him.

In contrast, the upper-middle-class or upper-class child is in a social position where his impulse gratifications are punished by his parents and clique as well as by his teachers. By constant supervision he is prevented from making these goal responses which are in conflict with study habits. At the same time, he is steadily reinforced by his family, clique, and teachers in moving toward the prestige goals. In his case, anxiety can be reduced only by good school behavior. His anxiety therefore becomes a constant and effective push toward those acts of study and of repression of impulse which are demanded by his part of the society.

APPENDIX

NOTE ON JUDY TOLLIVER

The problem is to find the sources of Judy's marked aggressiveness and his chronic fear. Until he was three years old, he experienced constant pain in connection with eating; since he was unable to eat solid foods, he was probably continually hungry. To this deprivation was added the suffering of diarrhea, which to a child could appear only as an undeserved and endless punishment. He learned to expect unpredictable interruption of his oral habits, as well as chronic pain. Anxiety became his dominant anticipatory response.

His aggressive behavior must have been learned in the experiences of neglect and scorn which he met at the hands of his family and playmates. He was constantly soiled by diarrhea and was probably rejected by his brothers and sisters on this score. Moreover, he was unable to walk until he was four. Through a much longer period than most children, therefore, he was dependent upon his mother or his brothers and sisters to bring things to him. Since his older brothers and sisters were at school, and his mother busy, he was certainly a neglected child. He could not walk to get what he wanted or needed; he had to sit in his soiled clothes, and fret. Human beings seem to respond to such basic frustration with chronic, and often irrational, aggression. When Judy's mother says that he is a bad boy now because he had "such a hard time" as a small child, she is saying that his deprivation and frustration impelled him to attack, and to take, when he became able.

Judy not only experienced pain and neglect; he also suffered ridicule and marked social rejection as a small child. His abnormally large head made him a continual target for the jeers of his siblings and playmates. Since he was physically helpless, he tried to ward off these attacks by agreeing with his tormentors, by pointing to his own head and stigmatizing himself as "Head." He probably learned then to expect constant attack from people. Now he tries to avoid social punishment by attacking first. Today he is aggressive, "impudent," "rude," but still fearful.

If Judy now thinks and acts as if he were the helpless, ridiculed child *he once was,* the berserk, irrational nature of his aggression toward siblings, teachers, and clique members may be explained. He flies into a blind, infantile tantrum at any imputation of his inferiority. With his father, however, he appears unusually intimidated. There seems to be no doubt that the father hates Judy. Although Judy denies that he hates his father, this attitude may be viewed as a protective mechanism against his fear of being punished by the father. Judy admits his great fear of the father, and says furthermore, "I gits mad jes like him." Seeing the power which the father maintains over the family by his tyrannical rage and aggression, Judy has copied his behavior; but at the same time he has learned not to be openly aggressive toward the father or other equally powerful individuals.

Judy's chronic resentment and hostility seem therefore to be displaced from his father and directed at his brothers and sisters, as well as at middle-class and upper-class Negroes, who are also in a position to subordinate him. He does not attack white adults because they are physically dangerous, but he does attack his teachers and light-colored children, who cannot punish him severely even though they are superordinate to him in class status.

Judy's fear of his father generalizes to all those actions which are tabooed by the father. The "fit" in which he saw a terrible man approach him while he was sleeping with his mother, and other dreams he has told, are evidence that some of Judy's irrational fears stem from the violent imposition of the incest taboo by the father. Judy is afraid of the dark because his father has punished him for being out after dark. The father and mother themselves remain indoors after dark, and close up the house.

Judy's resistance to any type of subordination, even that of pupil by teacher, incapacitates him for social mobility even into upper-lower class. He is not able to subject himself to the necessary learning situations. As he points out, he will be a man before he completes graded school. In order to overcome the social and economic barriers to upward mobility which are inherent in his family's lower-lower-class status, he would need the disciplined aggression and strong impulse renunciation of a Chester Olivier, as well as the stimulus and supervision of a parent like Chester's mother. The training and goals of lower-lower class have been too great a mobility handicap for even Judy's more effective siblings. None of the older children has yet been able to complete high school; Lillie, who is a senior, is unable to meet the sexual demands of higher status, and is now living with a man. The sexual and aggressive permissiveness of lower-lower-class society is so congenial to Judy's personality that he feels no urge to flee upward. His wild aggression and his inability to accept learning controls dispose him to the lower-lower-class way of life, where there are no complex, organized relationships and few systematic demands for impulse denial.

INDEX

INDEX

Adams, W. A., vii

Adolescence, and caste controls, 250-51; and lower-class relaxation of pressure for education, 285-86; and sociological adulthood, 269

Age-grading, 165-66

Aggression, xxvii-xxviii; as expression of personality, 23-43, 48-50, 62-63, 80-83, 119-20, 157-59, 186-88, 191-95, 293-94; in response to caste-punishments, 41-43, 66, 121-25, 169-71, 202-03, 237-55; in response to class-punishments, 178-79, 199, 285; Negroes compared with whites, 244

American Youth Commission, vii-ix

Anxiety, 7, 263-64, 271, 281; caste-anxiety, 17, 41-42, 122-23, 125, 155, 170-72, 201-04, 237-43, 247-50, 252; class-anxiety, 17, 39, 56, 70, 95-96, 99, 107, 110-12, 120-21, 142-45, 156, 159-61, 164, 166-69, 172-82, 198, 200, 264, 275-76, 282-85, 289, 290, 294; due to primary socialization, 8, 9, 11, 23, 26-27, 28-33, 38, 40, 42, 114-21, 146-47, 151-53, 161-62, 187, 191-95, 204, 263-64, 268, 271, 276, 293-94

Bourke-White, M., 249

Bowers, A. M., 29

Bronner, A. F., 29

Caldwell, E., 249

Case for the reader, xxvii, 207-33

Caste, color (see also Creoles, colored), xxiii-xxviii, 4, 12-13, 17-20, 41-43, 52, 65-67, 87, 93, 102, 121-25, 127-28, 134-36, 142, 153-55, 169-72, 201-04, 229-32, 237-55

Class analysis, utility of, 259, 279

Class terms used by informants, 22, 168, 259-61

Classes, social (see also Lower classes, Middle classes, Upper class), xxvi-xxviii, 12-17, 20, 256-62; identified on basis of social participation, 13-14, 259-60; importance of family and clique in, 12-16, 261-62; number and ranking of, 15-16, 135, 260-61; traits of (class-ways), xxvii, 4, 16-17, 19, 44-45, 82, 98, 256-58, 259, 260, 262, 265-78, 279-90; references to white class structure, 15, 261, 279, of lower class, 65, 134-35, 155, 240-41, of middle class, 66-67, 139, 265, of upper class, 66-67, 87, 184, 265

Cleanliness training, 10, 11, 29, 89, 113, 147, 161-62, 188, 263, 266, 269, 293

Cliques, social, 13-14, 16, 54-55, 75, 76, 102-03, 107-09, 125-26, 130-31, 137-39, 166-69, 197-98, 259, 261-62, 264, 275, 278, 282

Creoles, colored, xxvi, 100, 127, 128-55, 176-77, 253-54

Culture (see also Caste, color; and Classes, social, traits of), xi-xii, 3-4, 8, 11, 12

Davis, A., xii, xv, xix, xxvi, xxvii, 16, 107, 258, 259

Davis, E., xxvii

Deference, lower to upper caste, 203-04, 237, 251; lower to upper class, 288

Dillard University, xvi

Dollard, J., xii-xiii, xvi, xix, xxvi, 16

"Dozens, the," 82-83, 212-13, 225-26

Drives, 5-9, 10, 151-53, 243-44, 250-51

Economic and social indices for Negro population (see also Caste, color; and Classes, social, traits of), of New Orleans, xxiv-xxv, 246-47; of Natchez, xxv-xxvi, 246-47; of the South, 18

Educational standards and attainments, of lower class, 47, 88, 200, 252-53, 257, 266, 280, 282-86, 290; of middle class, 130-31, 137-38, 140-41, 168, 252-53, 265, 275, 280, 282-85, 286-89, 290; of upper class, 126, 256-57, 280, 282, 285, 286-89, 290

Family, importance of in social class (see also the life histories, 23-233), 2-16, 128, 172-76, 259, 261-62; lower-class, extended, 45, 48, 60, 73, 74, 85, 95-96, 132, 267; middle-class patriarchal, 130, 131-33, 146, 173-74, 274-76; training in caste behavior, 16-17, 250-52; training in class behavior, 16-17, 263-78

"Fight gangs," 25, 37-39, 42, 76-79, 81-83, 93, 102, 118, 125, 199

Frazier, E. F., vii

Freud, S., 4, 7, 8-10

Gardner, B., xii, xvi, xxvi, xxvii, 16, 107, 258, 259, 261

Gardner, M. (Mrs. B.), xii, xvi, xxvi, xxvii

Goals, basic biological and social (see also Drives), 3, 243-44

Hair form and skin color as class marks, 41-42, 44, 56-57, 67, 111, 128, 129, 134, 136-37, 153-55, 176-77, 196-97, 226-28, 253-55
Healy, W., 29
Hull, C. L., 4, 281

Infantile behavior, 27-28, 31-33, 62-63
Institute of Human Relations, xiii, xvi-xvii, 281
Institutions and social class lines, 15, 53, 75-76
Interviewing techniques (*see also* Therapy, xx, xxiii; establishing rapport, 23-24, 69-72, 99-100, 179-80

Johnson, C. S., vii
Junker, B. H., vii

Learning, social (*see also* Socialization), 4-5, 7-11; and caste controls, 16-17, 243-55, 256; and class controls, 16-17, 156, 256-58, 259, 262, 263-78, 279-90; mechanisms of, 4-10, 263-64, 280
Life histories, v, xxiv, 23-233
Lower classes, 2), 23-96; compared with middle (upper, 35, 102-03, 125, 132-33, 1 9, 146, 172-75, 196-97, 200-01, 240-/, 252-55, 256-58, 264-77, 280, 2 2-86, 290; lower-lower class, 22, /3, 58, 62, 68-96, 207-33, 261, 266, 94; upper-lower class, 22, 23-43, 44 7, 76, 261, 264, 266
Lynchings 93, 171, 247-49

Marriage and forms of paternity in lower lass, 95-96; mixed-class marriages 14, 35-37, 56, 252
Method (*see also* Interviewing technique), xxvii-xxviii, 13-14, 258, 259-60
Middl classes, 98, 99-182; compared wit lower or upper, 35, 50, 74, 79-80, 92-93, 240-41, 252-55, 264-78, 280, 282-85; lower-middle class, 35, 101-05, 130, 156-82, 197, 260, 264-65, 269-70, 274-77; middle-middle class, 101, 127-55, 260; upper-middle class, 168, 176-77, 185-204, 260, 264, 278, 281, 282-85, 286-90
Mobility, social, 12, 14-15, 20; downward, 14, 22, 23-43, 68-96, 98, 103-05, 143-45, 156-82; declassed, 20, 52, 94-96; upward, 14-15, 16, 98, 99-126, 185-204, 252-53, 262, 274, 286, 294; strivings for, 56-59, 87-89, 143-45, 166-69, 180-82, 196-99
Mowrer, O. H., 264

Negro-white class equivalences, 279
Negroes, erroneous beliefs about, 237-38, 244-45

Oedipus complex, xx, 189-90, 195

"Passing," 20, 67, 135, 155
Personality (*see also* Learning, social; and the life histories, 23-233), vii, xi-xii, xxiii, xxvii-xxviii, 3-11, 16-17, 23-34, 59-65, 89-92, 112-21, 145-53, 156-62, 185-96, 207, 208-13, 293-94; caste determinations of, 17, 237-55; class determinations of, 16-17, 256-90; conflicts, 9, 110-11, 200-01, 252-53
Punishment (*see also* Sanctions and controls), 7, 9, 10, 11, 263-64, 267-69, 275-76, 293-94; caste punishments, xxviii, 12-13, 17-20, 41-43, 93-94, 121-25, 153-55, 169-71, 201-03, 237-55; class punishments, xxviii, 12-13, 16-17, 39, 44, 58, 82, 86-87, 106-07, 110-12, 136-37, 156-57, 161, 167-69, 172-82, 196, 199, 226-29, 262, 265, 280-90; in socialization and family discipline, xxviii, 28-38, 60-62, 74-75, 89-92, 113-15, 119, 139-40, 147-49, 151-53, 161-62, 186-87, 191-93, 195

Rainey, H. P., vii-viii
Reid, I. DeA., vii
Reinforcement, 12, 16, 62-63, 148, 156, 192, 194-95, 207, 263-64, 268-69, 280-90
Reward, 6-7, 8, 9, 16, 38, 71, 147, 251-52, 263-64, 267, 268-69, 277, 280-90
Rural-urban differences in caste taboos, 247-48

Sample, nature of, xxiii-xxviii, 17, 258
Sanctions and controls (*see also* Punishment; and Reward), xi, xxvii; on caste behavior, 17, 19-20, 243-55; on class behavior, 16-17, 256-59, 263-78, 280-90
Sex training, early, 10, 29-32, 61-62, 113-14, 147-48, 151-53, 162, 188-89, 195, 264, 265, 266, 269-70, 272-74, 276-77; and class mores, 50-52, 63-64, 83-85, 116-17, 151-53, 272-74, 276-77; class-deviant behavior, 25-26, 34, 39-41, 63-64
Socialization (*see also* Learning, social), xx, xxiii, xxvii, 7-11, 28-34, 60-63, 89, 112-15, 146-48, 161-62, 188-90, 213-15, 267, 268
Social participation, 12, 13, 14, 19-20, 22, 125-26, 166-69, 259-60, 265, 278
Social stratification (*see also* Caste, color; and Classes, social), class and caste as forms of, 12-20; hierarchies, evidence for by caste, 19, by class, 14-15, 16, 135, 259-61; variable degrees of, 15-16, 134-36
"Student," use of term, 23

Subclass distinctions, 15, 260-61
Sutherland, R. L., viii

Therapy through removal of class punishments, 159-61, 176-80, 232-33, 289-90

Unconscious, 9
Upper class, 176-77, 184, 197-98, 281, 282, 286-90; compared with lower or middle class, 107-08, 119-121, 125, 240-41, 252-55, 256-58, 278, 280

Warner, W. L., vii, xii, xvi, xxvi, 259
Weaning and food training, 10, 28-29, 31-33, 35, 60-61, 89, 112, 146-47, 161, 188, 263, 266, 293

Photograph on jacket by Post, Farm Security Administration

Drawing on cover adapted from photograph by Lee, Farm Security
Administration

THE AMERICAN COUNCIL ON EDUCATION

George F. Zook, *President*

The American Council on Education is a *council* of national educational associations; organizations having related interests; approved universities and colleges, technological schools, and private secondary schools; state departments of education; and city school systems. It is a center of cooperation and coordination whose influence has been apparent in the shaping of American educational policies as well as in the formulation of American educational practices during the past twenty years. Many leaders in American education and public life serve on the commissions and committees through which the Council operates.

Established by the Council in 1935, the American Youth Commission consists of the persons whose names appear on a front page of this publication. It operates through a staff under the supervision and control of a director responsible to the Commission.